FORMULA ONE
DRIVER BY DRIVER

ALAN HENRY

The Crowood Press

First published in 1992 by
The Crowood Press Ltd
Ramsbury, Marlborough
Wiltshire SN8 2HR

British Library Cataloguing in Publication Data

A catalogue record for this book is available from the British Library.

ISBN 1 85223 706 6

Acknowledgements
The author would like to thank the following enthusiasts for their
help, advice and information:

Denis Jenkinson, Adriano Cimarosti, Francisco Santos, Duncan
Rabagliati, Doug Nye, Innes Ireland, Tony Brooks, Nigel Roebuck,
Sheridan Thynne, Jabby Crombac, Wim Oude Weernink, Eoin
Young, Howden Ganley, Franco Lini, Andrew Ferguson, Jo Ramirez,
Mercedes-Benz AG, David Tremayne, Tim Parnell, Brian Hart and
Peter Warr.

Typeset by Inforum, Rowlands Castle, Hants
Printed and bound in Great Britain by BPCC Hazells Ltd
Member of BPCC Ltd

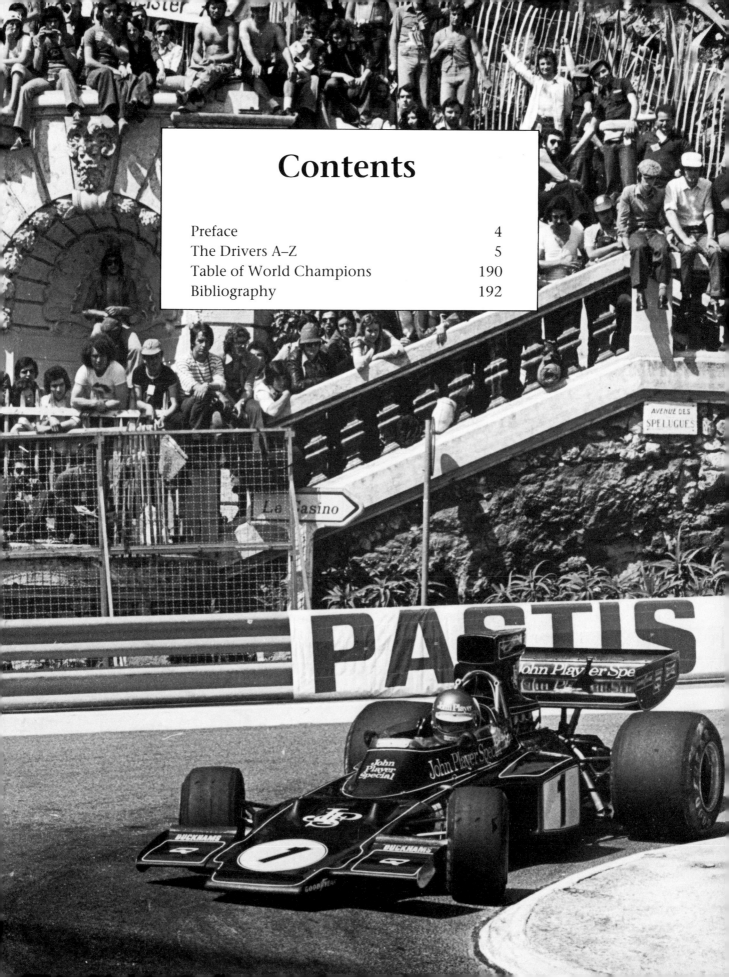

Contents

Preface

Although the history of Grand Prix motor racing extends back to the early years of the century, it was only in 1950 that the sport's governing body, then the Commission Sportive International (CSI), presided over the inauguration of an official World Championship. Whereas prior to this turning point in the sport's history there were a handful of internationally recognized events which stood out as being particularly prestigious jewels on the international calendar, the introduction of a Championship series imposed a consistent, identifiable form on a season's topline motor racing.

Between the covers of this book you will find profiles on all the 504 drivers who took the start of a World Championship Grand Prix between 1950 and the end of the 1991 season. In this context the words 'Grand Prix' should be emphasized as the eleven Indianapolis 500 events which were on the World Championship schedule between 1950 and 1960 are not included. They were not Formula 1 races and virtually no cross-over in terms of participation took place between European competitors and their US counterparts. It was an anomalous, irrelevant situation which has been responsible for scrambling the motor racing records books ever since.

This book also does not cover those drivers who participated solely in the varied schedule of non-Championship F1 races which proliferated during the 1950s and 1960s before dwindling away steadily by the early 1980s.

The terms of reference are therefore solely confined to those drivers who have taken the start in a World Championship Formula 1 Grand Prix. Those who have simply practised and failed to qualify for a start also fail to qualify for this book. By the same token, the figures given for the number of races contested by a driver do not include events for which he was entered, but failed to qualify.

Quite obviously, a large number of drivers have taken part in many races over a long period and have therefore driven for a wide variety of teams. Where necessary their entry is supplemented with 'career span' details specifically identifying their spells driving for individual teams. Where a driver has only participated in a very small number of events, often for the same team, this reference has been omitted and is instead mentioned in the main text.

Formula 1 motor racing is one of the most compelling of 20th-century sports. Over the period covered by this book it has gathered together drivers from a wide variety of backgrounds and nationalities – a veritable microcosm of international society. What other sport saw a Siamese prince and a Spanish nobleman race against the son of an Argentinian mechanic, or brought together a Scottish farmer, a one-time paratroop officer and a Texan oil millionaire on the same starting grid?

As far as illustrations are concerned, there are obviously many key personalities, photographs of whom are absolutely essential. As far as the lesser drivers are concerned, however, the world of the interesting also-rans whose off-track stories and business backgrounds provide such fascinating fine detail to the overall story, the choice has been unashamedly subjective. It will become obvious which drivers really held my fascination and interest; I hope it will do the same for the reader.

Alan Henry
Tillingham
Essex
February, 1992

KEY TO NATIONALITIES

A	Austria	DK	Denmark	MA	Morocco	RSM	San Marino
AUS	Australia	E	Spain	MC	Monaco	RSR	Rhodesia
B	Belgium	F	France	MEX	Mexico	S	Sweden
BR	Brazil	GB	Great Britain	NL	Netherlands	SF	Finland
CDN	Canada	H	Hungary	NZ	New Zealand	T	Thailand
CH	Switzerland	I	Italy	P	Portugal	USA	United States of America
CO	Colombia	IRL	Republic of Ireland	RA	Argentina	YV	Venezuela
D	Germany	J	Japan	RCH	Chile	ZA	Republic of South Africa

ABECASSIS, George (GB)

b. 21 March 1913
d. 18 December 1991
2 Grands Prix
Career span: 1951–2 (HWM)

There were only a couple of Swiss Grand Prix outings for this essentially amateur driver who co-founded the HWM team, but who gained most recognition for his driving of Aston Martin sports cars. He married Angela Brown, daughter of Aston boss Sir David, before retiring from racing in the mid-1950s.

ACHESON, Kenneth (GB)

b. 27 November 1957, Belfast
3 Grands Prix

Outstanding product of the British domestic Formula Ford scene who drove three races in 1983–5 for the RAM March team. He was second at Le Mans in 1989 with a Sauber Mercedes.

ADOLFF, Kurt (D)

b. 5 November 1921
1 Grand Prix

A wealthy German privateer who raced the ex-Ecurie Espadon Ferrari 166 in the 1952 German Grand Prix at Nurburgring plus several non-championship events.

AHRENS, Kurt (D)

b. 19 April 1940, Braunschweig
4 Grands Prix

The son of a top German speedway champion with the same name who retired in 1963 after a successful switch to cars, Ahrens developed into one of his country's best single-seater drivers in the 1960s. He graduated through F/Junior into F2 and became an effective Brabham privateer, running three German GPs in the F2 class. He drove the third works F1 Brabham-Repco in a rain-soaked 1968 race at Nurburgring and was also a highly accomplished member of the works Porsche sports car team. He retired in 1971 to work with his father in the scrap metal business.

ALBORETO, Michele (I)

b. 23 December 1956, Milan
153 Grands Prix; 5 wins
Career span: 1981–3 (Tyrrell); 1984–8 (Ferrari); 1989 (Tyrrell and Larrousse); 1990 to date (Arrows/Footwork)

In a business which cruelly tends to erase memories of anything prior to last weekend's results, Michele Alboreto cut rather a forlorn figure towards the end of the 1980s. His mop of curly hair became flecked with grey, and his bubbling character became somewhat subdued. Watching this pleasant fellow struggling with a succession of uncompetitive machines, one had to remind oneself that this was the man who carried the battle against Alain Prost for the 1985 World Championship through to September with a run of skilful performances at the wheel of a Ferrari.

When Enzo Ferrari originally announced his decision to sign up Michele for the 1984 Grand Prix season, he likened him to the legendary Alberto Ascari. He was the first Italian driver to join the most famous team in motor racing for more than a decade and spent five seasons driving for the Scuderia. Yet Alboreto's silky-smooth driving style was never rewarded with the success it so manifestly deserved and, having fallen foul of the complex political forces at Maranello, he was bundled out of the team at the end of 1988.

His F1 career started when Ken Tyrrell offered him the number two spot alongside Eddie Cheever in his team at the start of the 1981 European season. Ken's attention had been drawn to Michele by an Italian businessman who was keen to sponsor him in the San Marino, Belgian and

Happy times ahead? Michele Alboreto (left) poses with his new team-mate René Arnoux prior to the start of their 1984 Ferrari season together.

Alboreto

A close call for Alboreto. This shot of Michele's Ferrari 156/85 was taken during the 1985 GP of Europe at Brands Hatch, the race in which the Italian was finally overwhelmed by the McLaren-mounted Alain Prost in his battle for the Championship.

Monaco Grands Prix. Ken shrewdly agreed, reserving the option to sign Michele on a three-year contract if he considered him to have any long-term potential.

Michele qualified eighteenth for his first race and Ken took up the option. Alboreto quickly earned himself a reputation as a talented and consistent performer, although he had to wait until the 1982 Brazilian GP before scoring his first championship points with a sixth place finish, promoted to fourth after Piquet and Rosberg were disqualified.

Although Tyrrell was slow to equip itself with turbo engines, Alboreto sustained the team's reputation with two timely victories at Las Vegas (1982) and Detroit (1983), the latter being the last non-turbo F1 victory until turbos were finally phased out at the end of 1988.

Then it was off to Ferrari for 1984, every Italian racing driver's dream. A single, commanding victory in the Belgian GP at Zolder confirmed Michele's potential, but 1984 was the year of the McLaren-TAG and he had a dismal time thereafter.

Things were better in 1985. He won both the Canadian and German GPs, lost his chance at Monaco through a puncture, and led the drivers' World Championship points table for much of the summer before Prost hauled past him. In the remaining three years of his Ferrari contract no more victories came his way and, when Berger joined the team in 1987, Michele began to find himself increasingly out of step with the Maranello management.

The romance had gone out of the relationship. In 1989 he returned briefly to Tyrrell, fell out with Ken over clashing sponsorship deals, and switched to Larrousse Lola. Michele's career had sunk to its lowest ebb. In 1990 he joined the Footwork Arrows team and in 1991 went through a dismal time wrestling with the hopeless Porsche V12 engine. The loyalty of Footwork boss Waturu Ohashi kept him on the payroll for 1992, when the team would use Mugen-prepared Honda V10 engines. For the likeable Alboreto this would definitely be the final throw of the dice.

6

ALESI, Jean (F)

b. 11 June 1964, Avignon
39 Grands Prix
Career span: 1989–90 (Tyrrell); 1991 to date (Ferrari)

Jean Alesi's initially spectacular F1 progress at the wheel of a lightweight, agile Tyrrell-Cosworth in 1989 and 1990 sent several top teams scurrying for their cheque books as they sought to get his signature on a contract for 1991. But although this cheerful little Frenchman had finished fourth on his Grand Prix début at Paul Ricard in 1989 and followed this up with splendid second places at Phoenix and Monaco the following year, this proved far from a passport to instant success when he switched to the Ferrari team.

Alesi sprang to prominence in 1987 as winner of the French F3 title, after which he switched to a March fielded by the Marlboro-backed ORECA Formula 3000 team the following year. This proved less than totally successful and in 1989, determined to win the championship, Alesi moved to England to join Eddie Jordan Racing. At the wheel of their Reynard-Mugen he won at Pau, Birming-

ham and Spa to put the title easily beyond the reach of his rivals.

The dream-like F1 début with Tyrrell was followed by a more sobering first season with Ferrari in 1991. Inevitably his progress as Alain Prost's team-mate would put him under the microscope and Alesi had a difficult time. Yet while he did not display the out-and-out speed predicted by some of his over-optimistic fans, he demonstrated strategic flair on several occasions with regard to tyre compound choices in potentially difficult conditions.

There is little doubt that Alesi has what it takes to get the job done in F1. Unfortunately, that is more than could be said for the Ferrari team as far as 1991 was concerned.

ALLIOT, Philippe (F)

b. 27 July 1954, Voves
93 Grands Prix
Career span: 1984–5 (RAM); 1987–9 (Larrousse Lola); 1990 (Ligier)

A genial, somewhat over-enthusiastic F1 exponent, Alliot

Jean Alesi. Thumbs up for Ferrari, but the Frenchman's first try with the famous Italian marque produced only a moderately promising 1991 season.

drove Guy Ligier to distraction during his last F1 season when he set an unofficial record for crashing cars, damaging more than a dozen chassis during the course of the year. This brought to an end Alliot's Grand Prix ambitions which had started at the Nogaro driving school in 1975 and included considerable success in F3 as well as a third place at Le Mans at the wheel of a Porsche 956. After two years in F1 with the miserably uncompetitive Hart-engined RAMs, Alliot dropped back into Formula 3000, but gained restoration with the Ligier team mid-way through 1986 in the wake of Jacques Laffite's serious accident at Brands Hatch. For the next three seasons he drove for Gerard Larrousse's team, then returned to Ligier for a spectacular finale, before taking up more tranquil employment as a member of the Peugeot sports car racing team.

ALLISON, Cliff (GB)

b. 8 February 1932, Brough, Cumbria
16 Grands Prix
Career span: 1958 (Lotus); 1959–60 (Ferrari); 1961 (Lotus)

Had the 1958 Belgian Grand Prix lasted another lap, this garage owner from Cumbria would have earned Team Lotus its first Grand Epreuve victory. Brooks' winning Vanwall finished with its gearbox on the point of seizing, Hawthorn's second place Ferrari blew its engine as it came down to take the chequered flag and Lewis-Evans's third place Vanwall broke a steering arm on the run down to the line. Allison finished fourth!

The way we were. Cumberland farmer and garage owner, Cliff Allison, wears a smart V-neck pullover, white shirt and a tie for this test outing in an F1 Ferrari Dino 246 at Modena in 1959. From left to right behind, engineer Carlo Chiti, team manager Romolo Tavoni and Enzo Ferrari himself do not quite know what to make of it all!

AMON, Chris (NZ)

b. 20 July 1943, Bulls, North Island
96 Grands Prix
Career span: 1963 (Lola and Lotus); 1964–5 (Lotus); 1966 (Cooper); 1967–9 (Ferrari); 1970 (March); 1971–2 (Matra); 1973 (Tecno); 1974 (Amon and BRM); 1975–6 (Ensign)

When it came to taking strategic career decisions, this mild-mannered son of a prosperous New Zealand sheep farmer could be relied upon, time and again, to pluck the joker from the bottom of the pack. Yet despite nearing his Grand Prix century fruitlessly as he vainly pursued his first victory, Amon's sheer artistry at the wheel places him amongst the Grand Prix greats.

Mauro Forghieri, for almost two decades the chief designer at Ferrari, reckons that Chris was in the same class as Jim Clark, an opinon based on three years' work with the New Zealander who drove for Maranello between 1967 and 1969. Driven to frustration by the unreliability of the Ferrari V12 engines, he switched to the fledgeling March team – where he seemed set to benefit from a Cosworth V8 engine – only for the Italian team to come good in 1970 with its powerful flat-12 engine.

Ngaio Amon, Chris's father, bought him an old 1½-litre Cooper-Climax in 1960 in which he finished second on his maiden outing. The following year he won two races in a by then veteran Maserati 250F, and in 1963 drove a 2½-litre Cooper-Climax in the Tasman Championship. It was at the latter race that he was spotted by Reg Parnell and plucked from this domestic backwater into the cockpit of a Lola-Climax F1 car at the age of nineteen.

After a patchy European apprenticeship at the wheel of a variety of uncompetitive cars, he was signed by Ferrari in 1967 and embarked on a glittering top-line career which never quite yielded the results it manifestly deserved. Despite starting from the front row on nineteen occasions, the best result Chris could ever muster in a World Championship Grand Prix was a hat trick of second places, two of which were literally feet away from that first victory. It was poor recompense for such obvious talent.

At Brands Hatch in 1968 he briefly squeezed ahead of Jo Siffert's winning Rob Walker Lotus 49B, but remained a couple of seconds adrift at the chequered flag. Two years later at Spa, Pedro Rodriguez's BRM P153 displayed a rare burst of mechanical reliability to head Amon's March home by a similar margin. During his Ferrari career there were also many occasions when he was dominating races only to fall victim to mechanical problems. After switching to the French Matra team at the end of 1970 he would dominate the 1972 French Grand Prix at Clermont-Ferrand, leaving his rivals for dead as he stormed away from the field. Then a puncture intervened, he pitted for fresh tyres . . . and finished third.

Grand Prix driving in the classic manner. Chris Amon holds his 1968 Ferrari 312 in a beautiful power slide during the non-Championship Oulton Park Gold Cup race.

When Matra withdrew from F1 at the end of 1972 there was another catastrophic career wrong-slot: he signed for the Italian Tecno team, but their cars were hopeless. It seemed as though this was as bad as things could get, but Chris then embarked on a hopelessly underfinanced project to build his own Cosworth-powered F1 challenger. This staggered to a halt after a handful of races in 1974, and he then boosted his flagging morale with some promising runs in an underpowered BRM.

In 1975, having been out of work since the start of the year, he was invited to drive for Morris Nunn's tiny Ensign team, a task he assumed with considerable gallantry through to the summer of 1976. His last attempt to qualify for a Grand Prix came at Mosport Park in 1976, when his uncompetitive Wolf-Williams spun and was T-boned by another car. Chris was badly bruised, but otherwise unhurt.

In 1977 he retired to the family farm with his wife Tish where they live happily to this day with their daughter Georgina and twin sons. He watches Grand Prix with interest on television, but never returned to the pit lanes to watch. Amon's was a huge talent wasted.

A member of the Ferrari F1 squad in 1959 to 1960, he finished second to McLaren's Cooper in Buenos Aires before being badly injured while practising at Monaco when he was flung from his Dino 246. That ended his Ferrari career, but he recovered and returned to F1 at the start of 1961, only to crash badly in a UDT/Laystall Lotus 18 during practice at Spa, breaking both his legs. Cliff never raced again.

ANDERSON, Bob (GB)

b. 19 May 1931, Hendon, North London
d. 14 August 1967, Silverstone
25 Grands Prix
Career span: 1963 (Lola); 1964–7 (Brabham)

An accomplished motorcycle racer who made the switch to car racing in 1961 in F/Junior, Anderson acquired an ex-Bowmaker Lola and striked off as an F1 private entrant at the start of 1963. He switched to a Brabham for 1964 and scored his best Championship result with third place behind Bandini and Ginther in the Austrian GP at Zeltweg. A loner, he bravely struggled on against the tide, equipping his Brabham with an outdated four-cylinder 2.7-litre Climax engine at the onset of the 3-litre F1 in 1966. Testing in the rain at Silverstone in preparation for the 1967 Canadian GP, Anderson aquaplaned into a marshals' post. He sustained serious thoracic injuries and died shortly after being admitted to Northampton hospital.

ANDERSSON, Conny (S)

b. 28 December 1939
1 Grand Prix

A highly respected Swedish F3 charger whose F1 career amounted to a single abortive outing in the Stanley BRM P207 in the 1976 Dutch GP at Zandvoort.

ARNOUX, René (F)

b. 4 July 1948, Grenoble
149 Grands Prix; 7 wins
Career span: 1978 (Martini and Surtees); 1979–82 (Renault); 1983–5 (Ferrari); 1986–8 (Ligier)

Arnoux started life as a garage mechanic in the French skiing resort where he was born, but his enthusiasm for motor racing and high performance cars eventually led him to a position with Conrero, the Alfa Romeo tuning specialist based in Turin. On the advice of Jean-Pierre Beltoise, who had recently won the Monaco Grand Prix, René's own competition career started at the Winfield racing school at Magny-Cours where he won the prestigious Volant Shell competition and moved into Formula Renault for 1973.

René Arnoux displayed all the enthusiasm of youth as a Renault driver in the early 1980s, but his subsequent career with Ferrari and Ligier never quite sustained his early promise.

He struggled into F2 with the Martini team in 1976, just losing the European Championship to Jean-Pierre Jabouille, but won the title in the following season. In 1978 he graduated to F1 with Tico Martini's Cosworth-engined F1 car and gained promotion to the Renault ranks the following year.

By 1980 René had become a Grand Prix winner with victories in both Brazil and South Africa, but when Jabouille was replaced by Alain Prost in 1981 René began to find himself outpaced. Nevertheless, in 1982 he won the French Grand Prix against team orders, then triumphed in the Italian Grand Prix at Monza the day before it was announced that he would be joining Ferrari.

Arnoux was initially eclipsed by Patrick Tambay in the Maranello ranks, but he eventually won the 1983 Canadian, German and Dutch races in confident style, the latter race from tenth place on the grid.

René retained his seat with Ferrari alongside the incoming Michele Alboreto although some observers felt that he, rather than Tambay, deserved to be dropped from the line-up. Thereafter Arnoux's level of achievement became worryingly inconsistent and, after only one race of the 1985 season, he was released from his contract.

Formula 1 had not seen the last of this quiet and uncomplicated country boy, however. In 1986 he returned to the F1 fray with Ligier for whom he drove for the next four seasons before fading away from F1 at the end of 1989.

ANDRETTI, Mario (USA)

b. 28 February 1940, Montana, Italy
128 Grands Prix; 12 wins; World Champion 1978
Career span: 1968–9 (Lotus); 1970 (March); 1971–2 (Ferrari);
1974–6 (Parnelli); 1976–80 (Lotus), 1981 (Alfa Romeo); 1982
(Williams and Ferrari)

Mario Andretti's life story has the essence of the great American dream about it. Born near Trieste in the early months of World War II, Mario's family spent the first seven years of his life in a displaced persons' camp before emigrating to the United States in 1955.

His own passion for racing was fuelled by childhood memories of the Mille Miglia road race; he remembers cycling from the family's subsequent home near Lucca to stand and watch in awe as the Stirling Moss/Denis Jenkinson Mercedes 300SR yowled through on its way to victory in 1955. Within a matter of weeks, the Andretti family was *en route* to its new life on the other side of the Atlantic.

Mario and his brother Aldo carried that enthusiasm across the water where they scratched and clawed their way into the motor racing game. Mario first ran at Indianapolis in 1965, winning his first – and so far only – 500 four years later. By then he had also had a taste of F1. A few months after Jim Clark's death he started his first Grand Prix from pole position at Watkins Glen. For 1969 he did as many F1 races for Lotus as his Indy car schedule allowed, but switched to driving an uncompetitive March in 1970 for STP boss Andy Granatelli, the man for whom he had won at Indy the previous year.

This relationship yielded next to nothing, but a switch to Ferrari earned him his first Grand Prix victory at Kyalami the following year. He drove for Maranello on an 'as and when' basis throughout 1971 and 1972, but Indy car commitments kept him away in America until the end of 1974 when he rejoined the F1 circus in the striking Maurice Philippe-designed Parnelli VPJ4. He raced this through to the start of 1976 before the team packed up, then switching to a below-par Team Lotus mid-season. He administered them a welcome pick-me-up by winning the Japanese GP at Fuji on the day James Hunt won the World Championship, and forged a bond with Colin Chapman which at times seemed close to the rapport the team owner had enjoyed with Jim Clark.

In 1977 he won four races in the epochal Lotus 78 'wing car' and took six races to clinch the World Championship with the equally radical Lotus 79 the following year. Andretti might not have been the fastest man in the F1 business, but the painstaking manner in which he worked with Chapman on honing the technical package raised the Team Lotus game on to another level. It was therefore sad to see Mario struggling through 1979 and 1980 as the Lotus design concept was picked up by others and refined to levels which Chapman's men seemed unable to match.

King of the Road. Mario Andretti brought to international racing an unmatched blend of longevity, versatility and charisma.

In 1981 Mario made a catastrophic switch to Alfa Romeo, scoring his only points with a fourth place in the opening race of the year at Long Beach. He quit full-time F1 at the end of the season, but guested for Williams at Long Beach in 1982 and was lured back to make an emotional appearance for Ferrari at Monza where he started his 126C2 turbo from pole position and finished third in the Italian Grand Prix. Retirement with a suspension breakage at Las Vegas finally wound down the curtain on his illustrious F1 career.

Bursting with star quality, Mario continues racing to this day on the Indy car scene, partnering his son Michael in the Newman/Haas Lola line-up. His one remaining ambition is to see Michael follow him into F1 – his son took the first step in 1991 with a couple of McLaren-Honda test outings.

ASCARI, Alberto (I)

b. 13 July 1918, Milan
d. 26 May 1955, Monza
32 Grands Prix; 13 wins; World Champion 1952 and 1953
Career span: 1950–3 (Ferrari); 1954 (Maserati, Ferrari, Lancia);
1955 (Lancia)

One of Milan's favourite sons, Alberto Ascari was born into a motor racing family and is regarded by many as a greater driver than even the legendary Juan Manuel Fangio, the Argentinian star who was his great contemporary in the early 1950s. Some people regard it as a bizarre coincidence that his father Antonio, the great Alfa Romeo star of the 1920s, was also killed on the twenty-sixth day of the month (July) when he crashed in the French Grand Prix at Montlhery – indeed, an idiosyncratic sub-culture subsequently developed attempting to attach a deeper significance to these two unrelated facts.

Alberto's career started on motorcycles before World War II, when he was a works rider with the Bianchi team, and he gained the distinction of being one of the first two drivers to race a Ferrari-made car. After Enzo Ferrari left Alfa Romeo in 1939, he commissioned engineer Alberto Massimino to design a couple of 1½-litre, eight-cylinder sports cars which were driven in the truncated 1940 Mille Miglia by Ascari and the Marchese Lotario Rangoni Machiavelli di Modena, a well-heeled local aristocrat who was sadly destined to die in a wartime bomber crash.

Ascari also finished ninth in the 1940 Tripoli Grand Prix in a Maserati 6CM, but by now Italy was embroiled in World War II and Alberto would not race again until 1947.

During the war, Ascari managed to build up a thriving

Alberto Ascari at the wheel of the gorgeous Lancia D50 prior to winning the 1955 non-title Pau Grand Prix.

A grim-faced Ascari (left) walks back to the Monza pits after the last corner tangle which cost him a possible victory in the 1953 Italian Grand Prix. Onofre Marimon (second from right) tries to look casual about his involvement in this incident.

road transport business in partnership with his friend Luigi Villoresi (qv) hauling fuel to Mussolini's armies in North Africa, an enterprise which exempted him from military service. He returned to racing at the wheel of a Cisitalia and scored his first victory on four wheels on 28 September 1947 at Modena in a sports Maserati.

By the end of the war Ascari was married with a son and had seriously toyed with the idea of abandoning racing altogether, but Villoresi persuaded him otherwise. Together they raced under the Scuderia Ambrosiana banner through 1948 in a pair of F1 Maserati 4CLTs, Alberto winning the San Remo Grand Prix, and finishing runner-up in the British Grand Prix at Silverstone.

In 1949 he and Villoresi joined the Ferrari works team and Alberto's racing career really began to take off. He led his old friend Villoresi to a 1–2 in the Swiss Grand Prix at Berne's fabulous Bremgarten circuit, thereby achieving Ferrari's first post-war international success at the wheel of the supercharged 1½-litre Tipo 125. It was a victory made easier, perhaps, by the temporary absence from the scene of Alfa Romeo who were to return in 1950 and dominate the first official World Championship contest.

Ascari rounded off the 1949 season by leading the Italian Grand Prix from start to finish in the latest two-stage supercharged tipo 125, but the following year saw Maranello wrestling with the introduction of their naturally aspirated Aurelio Lampredi V12s and success was patchy. However, Ascari signalled what was to come by driving the 4½-litre Ferrari 375 to victory in the non-title Penya Rhin Grand Prix on Barcelona's Pedralbes circuit, an event which rounded off the 1950 European season.

Alberto was essentially a team man and it was this sense of overall loyalty which prevented him from becoming the first man to win a World Championship Grand Prix for Ferrari. After Froilan Gonzalez had generously relinquished his 375 to Ascari in the French Grand Prix at Reims in 1951, thereby enabling him to finish second behind Fangio's Alfa Romeo, he declined to exercise the *droit de seigneur* which went with his team leadership status and did not take over Gonzalez's car in the British Grand Prix a fortnight later. So it was the bulky Argentinian, rather than Ascari, who went on to score that historic maiden victory.

At the end of 1951 the sport's governing body, concerned about the shortage of cars to the current 1½-litre supercharged/4½-litre non-supercharged regulations, decreed that the 1952 and 1953 World Championships would be held under 2-litre F2 regulations. It was then that Ascari really got into his stride. Armed with the Ferrari 500 he won the European Grand Prix at Spa, plus the French, British, German and Italian races to take his first title crown. He sustained the momentum through into 1953 with wins in the Dutch, Belgian, British and Swiss races to retain his title.

In 1954 he signed for Lancia to drive the new V8-engined D50 under the new 2½-litre F1 regulations, but the car was late in development and Alberto spent most of the season twiddling his thumbs on the sidelines. Gianni Lancia generously released him to drive a Ferrari 625 in the Italian Grand Prix at Monza where he gave Fangio's Mercedes a nasty fright until the Italian car's engine blew up.

At the end of the season Ascari gave the Lancia D50 a sensational début at Barcelona, qualifying commandingly on pole position and leading easily before retiring with clutch trouble. At the start of the 1955 season, Ascari drove the Lancia to victories in the non-title Turin and Naples Grands Prix, and then crashed spectacularly into the Monte Carlo harbour whilst poised to take the lead of the prestigious Monaco race.

He survived this unexpected ducking, but was shaken and had a broken nose. A week later he unexpectedly turned up at Monza on the Thursday. Lancia had given him permission to drive a Ferrari sports car with Eugenio Castellotti in the following Sunday's Supercortemaggiore 1,000km race at the Milan circuit. He had not intended to drive at the mid-week test, but borrowed Castellotti's helmet and went out for a few laps. On the third lap he crashed inexplicably at the fast Vialone right-hander, was thrown out on to the track and suffered fatal injuries.

It was left for Fangio to bestow the ultimate accolade. 'I have lost my greatest opponent,' he said quietly.

ARUNDELL, Peter (GB)

b. 8 November 1933, Ilford, Essex
11 Grands Prix
Career span: 1964, 1966 (Lotus)

Probably the best number two driver Team Lotus ever employed, Peter Arundell was inwardly convinced that he had the legs of Jimmy Clark. It might have been an over-optimistic assessment, but such hopes represented the power house of his ambition. Certainly, he looked an absolutely outstanding performer during the first half of the 1964 season in which he replaced Trevor Taylor, another talented F/Junior graduate, as number two to the great Scottish star, but his career was ruined by a huge shunt in the Reims F2 race and he was never the same driver again.

Arundell won the 1962 British F/Junior Championship with a level of domination that prompted respected German journalist Richard von Frankenberg to have a brainstorm and accuse Colin Chapman of running an illegal engine in Peter's works Lotus 22. He challenged Colin to bring the car to Monza, have the engine capacity checked and see if Arundell could reproduce the speed he had demonstrated whilst winning the Monza Lottery. Arundell achieved this easily, winning US$3,000 for his smiling boss.

In 1963 he did a handful of non-Championship F1 races before being promoted to the Grand Prix team the following year. Third places at Monaco and Zandvoort were pretty good starts, but the shunt at Reims extinguished his spark. Chapman loyally reinstated Peter to the F1 team in 1966 after a painful struggle back to physical fitness, but the magic was gone.

Arundell's front-line F1 career was over at the age of thirty-two, although there are many who believe that in 1966, the first year of the new 3-litre F1, the cars he was provided with gave him significantly less than a fair chance to prove whether or not any latent talent still lingered.

His most dispiriting moment of the 1966 season came in the United States Grand Prix at Watkins Glen when he inadvertently chopped across the bows of John Surtees's Cooper-Maserati, spinning wildly. Both cars made precautionary pit stops during which Surtees gave Arundell a very candid piece of his mind. It did nothing for his already-flagging morale.

ASCARI, Alberto

See pages 12–13.

ASHDOWN, Peter (GB)

b. 16 October 1934
1 Grand Prix

A leading light on the British F/Junior scene, Ashdown ran a Cooper-Climax F2 in the 1959 British Grand Prix at Aintree. He lives in Danbury, Essex, where his wife deals in *haute couture*.

ASHLEY, Ian (GB)

b. 26 October 1947
4 Grands Prix

A quick but erratic F3 tyro from the mid-1960s who had a handful of spectacular F1 outings in tail-end machinery, culminating in a huge shunt during practice for the 1977 Canadian GP. Subsequently he made a career piloting corporate jets in the USA.

ASHMORE, Gerry (GB)

b. 25 July 1936
3 Grands Prix

Ashmore was the son of privateer garage owner Joe Ashmore who, with his brother Fred, raced private Maseratis in partnership with Reg Parnell in the immediate post-war years. Along with his brother Chris, he contested several non-title F1 races in the early 1960s, running in the 1961 British, German and Italian Grands Prix in a private Lotus 18. He now lives in West Bromwich.

ASTON, Bill (GB)

b. 29 March 1900, Stafford
d. 4 March 1974
1 Grand Prix

A company director and former test pilot from Buckingham who raced an Aston Butterworth F2 special in the 1952 German Grand Prix. He set up 500cc world records in 1951 with an aerodynamic Cooper-JAP.

ATTWOOD, Richard (GB)

b. 4 April 1940, Wolverhampton
17 Grands Prix
Career span: 1965 (Parnell-Lotus); 1967 (Cooper); 1968 (BRM); 1969 (Lotus)

Attwood was the son of a successful motor trader and sprang to international prominence by winning the 1963 Monaco F/Junior race in a Midland Racing Partnership Lola. He had something of an 'in and out' F1 career during the 1960s, the high spot of which was a magnificent second place for BRM in the 1967 Monaco GP. He was also fourth at Monaco in a Lotus 49 two years later, deputizing for an injured Jochen Rindt. He won Le Mans in 1970 with Hans Herrmann in a Porsche 917 and retired the following year.

BAGHETTI, Giancarlo (I)

b. 25 December 1934, Milan
21 Grands Prix; 1 win
Career span: 1961–2 (Ferrari); 1963 (ATS); 1964 (BRM); 1965 (Brabham); 1966 (Ferrari); 1967 (Lotus)

The eldest son of a wealthy Milanese industrialist, Baghetti earned himself a distinguished entry in the pages of the motor racing history books in 1961 when he became the first – and so far the only – driver to win a World Championship Grand Prix at his first attempt.

At the wheel of a Ferrari 156 entered by the Federazione Italiana Scuderie Automobilistiche (not to be confused with FISA which much later became the initials of the sport's international governing body), Baghetti found his early specification 65-degree-engined car the lone survivor of four Ferrari entries in the closing stages of the French Grand Prix at Reims. In a wheel-to-wheel battle with Dan Gurney's four-cylinder works Porsche, the young Italian kept his head to hold off the vastly more experienced American by a couple of lengths at the chequered flag.

It was a splendid highlight to a season which had also seen Baghetti win the non-Championship Naples and Syracuse Grands Prix for the Scuderia, but no more success was destined to come the way of this pleasant young man who had only started his competition career six years earlier with a couple of production Alfa Romeos.

In 1962 Ferrari's fortunes plummeted, tempting Baghetti to make a disastrous career choice for the following year. Along with Phil Hill he signed to drive for ATS, a team headed up by a group of Ferrari renegades including engineer Carlo Chiti, but it effectively sank the career of both its drivers. Baghetti sought restoration behind the wheel of a Centro-Sud BRM in 1964, but these machines were now long in the tooth and suffered from ragged preparation.

From then on Baghetti 'guested' from time to time in a variety of F1 machines, his last such outing being in a third works Lotus 49 in the 1967 Italian Grand Prix. The following year he quit professional motorsport and today is involved in magazine publishing and photography, specializing in cars and female models – often together!

BAILEY, Julian (GB)

b. 9 October 1961
7 Grands Prix

Julian Bailey gambled a lot of money to buy his drive, but his F1 career was washed away thanks to an uncompetitive car.

Julian Bailey caught Ken Tyrrell's eye when he won a Formula 3000 international at Brands Hatch in late 1987 and was recruited to drive for the Surrey-based F1 team the following year, mortgaging himself up to the hilt to pay for the privilege. Unfortunately, the Tyrrell 017 was a truly awful car and Julian's promise was squandered. He tried again at the start of 1991, raising the finance to buy his drive in the second Lotus 102B alongside Mike Hakkinen for the first four races of the season. He finished sixth in the San Marino GP at Imola, but did not retain his seat after Monaco.

BALDI, Mauro (I)

b. 31 January 1954, Reggio Emilia
36 Grands Prix
Career span: 1982 (Arrows); 1983 (Alfa Romeo); 1984–5 (Spirit)

Baldi began motor racing in 1975 with a few Renault 5 Cup events, and by 1980 he was a front runner in F3, winning the Monaco GP supporting classic at the wheel of a Martini and following that up with the European Championship in 1981, achieved by dint of a record eight victories. He had two decent seasons in F1 with Arrows and Alfa Romeo, his best being a fifth at Zandvoort for the latter team. He was edged out of Alfa when Benetton took over the sponsorship programme in 1984, and switched to the tiny Spirit team which gradually faded away at the start of the following year. Subsequently he has made a good living from sports car racing with Lancia, Sauber-Mercedes and Peugeot. His most memorable F1 moment came at the 1984 European GP at the new Nurburgring; Championship contender Niki Lauda spun his McLaren as he lapped Baldi's Spirit and the Austrian sought him out afterwards. After being torn off a strip by the then twice World Champion, Baldi rounded on his accuser and told him that the incident had been his fault and that he should get stuffed!

BALSA, Marcel (F)

b. 1 January 1909, St Frion
d. 11 August 1984
1 Grand Prix

A French veteran who drove in the 1952 German Grand Prix in a BMW-engined special.

BANDINI, Lorenzo (I)

b. 21 December 1936, Barce, Cyrenaica, North Africa
d. 10 May 1967, Monaco
42 Grands Prix; 1 win
Career span: 1961 (Cooper-Maserati); 1962 (Ferrari); 1963 (BRM and Ferrari); 1964–7 (Ferrari)

Without doubt Italy's best Formula 1 driver of his decade, the even-tempered Bandini spent much of his Ferrari career dutifully playing second fiddle to the brilliant John Surtees. It was a role which he fulfilled happily and without tension, for Lorenzo was an easygoing and non-political individual with an uncomplicated disposition.

Lorenzo's father died when he was only fifteen, and he left the family home in Florence to seek employment in the Milan garage of a Signor Freddi, whose daughter Margherita he later married. Freddi loaned him a Lancia Appia in which he won his class in the 1958 Mille Miglia, then a milder, rally-type event after the death of the no-holds-barred road race the previous year.

In 1959 he graduated through Formula Junior, driving both Volpini and Stanguellini machinery, before moving into F1 for the first time in 1960 with an old Cooper-Maserati fielded by Guglielmo Dei's Scuderia Centro Sud. He was recruited by Ferrari for F1 in 1962, but then dropped in favour of Willy Mairesse for 1963, returning to Centro Sud to campaign their works-maintained BRMs.

Lorenzo Bandini at speed in the 3-litre Ferrari 312 V12 during the 1966 French Grand Prix at Reims.

After Mairesse was badly injured in the German Grand Prix, Bandini was re-adopted by Ferrari mid-way through a season which had also seen him share the winning 250LM at Le Mans with Ludovico Scarfiotti.

In 1964 he won the first Austrian Grand Prix, held on the bumpy Zeltweg military aerodrome circuit, almost a stone's throw from the site of the magnificent Österreichring which was opened five years later. He would continue as Surtees's loyal lieutenant through to the end of the 1½-litre F1, but suddenly found himself propelled into the Ferrari team leadership after 'Big' John split with Maranello early in 1966.

Bandini concentrates hard to keep his Ferrari V6 ahead of Phil Hill's Cooper in the 1964 Monaco race.

In 1967 he led the opening stages of the Monaco Grand Prix only to be displaced by Denny Hulme's winning Brabham-Repco. Mounting a counter-attack late in the race, Lorenzo clipped the chicane and rolled his Ferrari 312, suffering appalling burns as the car erupted in flames. He died from these burns, and from serious internal injuries, three days later shortly before his wife suffered a miscarriage in the same hospital. This handsome Italian driver is remembered fondly by all who knew him and his accident marked a significant turning point in attitudes towards improving motor racing safety.

BARBER, John (GB)

1 Grand Prix

This enterprising Billingsgate fish merchant made his racing name with a 1,000cc Cooper twin. He sallied forth to Buenos Aires in 1953 to contest the Argentine GP in a Cooper-Bristol Mk2.

BARBER, Skip (USA)

b. 16 November 1936, Pennsylvania
5 Grands Prix

Wealthy American privateer who drove his own private March 711 in a handful of races in 1971–72.

BARILLA, Paolo (I)

b. 20 April 1961
9 Grands Prix

The Italian pasta magnate friend of Giancarlo Minardi, Barilla drove alongside Pierluigi Martini from the start of the 1990 season, but was not quick enough to qualify regularly and found himself replaced by Gianni Morbidelli before the end of the year.

BARTH, Edgar (D)

b. 26 November 1917, Herold-Ergeberge
d. 20 May 1965, Ludwigsburg
4 Grands Prix

Barth was a BMW sports car driver who moved to West Germany in the mid-1950s from the Communist-controlled eastern bloc. He won the 1959, 1963 and 1964 European Mountain Championship titles for Porsche and had four outings in the German Grand Prix, the last with a Cooper-Climax in 1964 barely nine months before he succumbed to cancer. His son Jurgen also became Porsche works sports car driver.

BASSI, Giorgio (I)

1 Grand Prix

Drove Scuderia Centro Sud BRM in 1965 Italian Grand Prix at Monza.

BAUER, Erwin (D)

b. 17 July 1912
d. 2 June 1958
1 Grand Prix

A German amateur who drove a Veritas RS in the 1953 German GP at Nurburgring.

BAYOL, Elie (F)

b. 28 February 1914
7 Grands Prix
Career span: 1952–5 (Osca); 1954–6 (Gordini)

A Gordini stalwart whose best placing for the marque was a fifth place in the 1965 Argentine Grand Prix at Buenos Aires.

BEAUMAN, Don (GB)

b. 26 July 1928
d. 9 July 1955, Wicklow
1 Grand Prix

Beauman was a close friend of Mike Hawthorn who competed in the 1954 British Grand Prix at Silverstone with a Connaught A-type owned by Sir Jeremy Boles, having cut his teeth in 1953 on Hawthorn's 1½-litre Riley. He was killed just after setting the fastest lap in the Leinster Trophy when at wheel of this Connaught.

BECHEM, Gunther (D)

b. 21 December 1921
1 Grand Prix

A German amateur who drove one of Alex von Falkenhausen's AFM-BMWs in his home Grand Prix at Nurburgring in 1953.

Behra

BEHRA, Jean (F)

b. 16 February 1921, Nice
d. 1 August 1959, Avus, Berlin
52 Grands Prix
Career span: 1952–4 (Gordini); 1955–7/8 (Maserati); 1958
(BRM); 1959 (Ferrari)

Jean Behra captured the imagination of his French compatriots for his giant-killing performances behind the wheel of an underpowered four-cylinder Gordini in the early 1950s. He was a man who approached his motor racing with unquenchable and genuine passion, whose commitment to his chosen career was total, and whose achievements in terms of hard results never accurately reflected his guts and inspiration behind the wheel.

Behra came to motor racing in 1950 after winning four French championships on two wheels riding Moto Guzzi machines. His initial outings on four wheels came in a Maserati 4CLT and a 4½-litre Talbot Lago, but it was not long before Amedee Gordini shrewdly picked him to join Maurice Trintignant, André Simon and Robert Manzon in his works team the following year. The Simca-engined Gordinis were frail to a fault, however, and, although Behra flung himself into battle after battle in heroic style, they were seldom rewarded with race finishes, let alone victories.

Nevertheless, Behra became enshrined as a French national hero in the summer of 1952 when his Gordini emerged triumphant in the non-championship Reims Grand Prix on a day when Alberto Ascari's pace-setting Ferrari wilted with mechanical trouble. At the time there was a lot of speculation that Gordini had in fact been running a 2½-litre engine on this occasion, but such gossip was not permitted to intrude upon the joy of that sun-soaked afternoon.

There was another such victory awaiting Behra in the 1954 Pau Grand Prix, where he beat Trintignant's Ferrari, and that same year he hung on brilliantly in the slipstream of the vastly more powerful streamlined Mercedes W196s during the Berlin Grand Prix at Avus until his Gordini's over-taxed engine finally exploded.

This performance brought him to the notice of the gargantuan Mercedes team manager Alfred Neubauer who briefly toyed with the idea of signing Behra to drive one of the Silver Arrows in 1955. By that stage, however, Jean had already signed to drive for the Maserati team and was about to enter the most satisfying phase of his career as a Formula 1 driver.

At Maserati, Behra partnered Sergio Mantovani, Roberto Mieres and Luigi Musso. Armed with the elegant 250F, he won the non-championship races at Pau and Bordeaux and scored his best result in a Championship Grand Prix at Monaco, sharing third place with Perdisa. At Aintree he was the only rival to get in amongst the all-conquering Mercedes, but lasted only ten laps, while his season came to a

Jean Behra captured the imagination of his French compatriots with his indomitable determination and love of the sport.

near-disastrous end with a huge accident in the Dundrod Tourist Trophy. He survived to recover but had a false, plastic ear to replace the one severed in this brutal crash . . .

In 1956 Behra stayed with Maserati, accepting with characteristic dignity the reduced role as number two driver alongside Stirling Moss who had moved in as team leader following Mercedes's withdrawal from racing. Nevertheless, Behra finished second in the Argentine Grand Prix and third in Monaco, France, Britain and Germany. The following year he found himself paired with the great Juan Manuel Fangio now that Moss had gone off to join Vanwall. Behra was running away with the British Grand Prix at Aintree, arguably his finest drive of all, when his Maserati's clutch exploded and victory was delivered into the lap of the Vanwall team.

He also won non-championship races at Pau and Modena in a 250F and, arguably his greatest victory, in the Moroccan Grand Prix at Casablanca which, although not counting for the championship, attracted a world-class field. He also won the non-title Caen Grand Prix and Silverstone International Trophy, guesting for BRM whom he joined the following year, scoring third in Holland and fourth in Portugal. That first Grand Prix victory continued to elude him, but 1959 promised better things as he was signed to partner Tony Brooks and Cliff Allison in a Ferrari team decimated by the loss of Mike Hawthorn, Peter Collins and Luigi Musso.

Behra believed himself to be the team leader, but Brooks's winning pedigree asserted itself, a situation hardly helped by the Commendatore's continuing unwillingness to nominate a number one driver, an irksome habit which inevitably caused intra-team friction.

On the twenty-ninth lap of the French Grand Prix at Reims, Behra's Dino 246 rolled into the pits with a melted piston. In his highly-charged emotional state, this was no time to start a debate with the French driver, but team manager Romolo Tavoni accused him of over-revving the engine. Behra lost his temper and thumped Tavoni, for which malfeasance he was immediately fired.

A little less than a month later, driving his Porsche RSK in the sports car race the day prior to the German Grand Prix at Avus, Behra lost control on the rain-slicked banking, suffering fatal injuries as he was flung out against a flagpole. The whole of France mourned this gallant little driver, but there was not so much as a wreath at his funeral from the still bitter Ferrari team.

BELL, Derek (GB)

b. 31 October 1941
9 Grands Prix
Career span: 1968–9 (Ferrari); 1970 (Brabham and Surtees);
1971 (Surtees); 1972 (Tecno); 1974 (Surtees)

This immensely popular and companionable 1-litre F3 graduate became an F2 privateer and beat a path into the Ferrari F1 team in 1968 only to catch it at the wrong moment. His sole Championship point was scored with a sixth place at Watkins Glen in 1970 with a Surtees TS7. He then dallied with the abortive Tecno F1 project and briefly again with Surtees before concentrating on sports cars. The most experienced of all Porsche 956/962 drivers, he won Le Mans five times and the World Sports Car Championship twice. Now living in the United States.

Superstar in the making. The late Stefan Bellof locking his Tyrrell-Ford over for the Loews hairpin at Monaco in practice for the 1984 Grand Prix in which he finished a fine third.

BELLOF, Stefan (D)

b. 20 November 1957, Giessen
d. 1 September 1985, Spa-Francorchamps
20 Grands Prix
Career span: 1984–5 (Tyrrell)

Bellof was a spectacular, Rindt-like talent who exploded to prominence with a brace of F2 wins early in 1983 at the wheel of a Maurer-BMW. He joined Tyrrell the following year and scored a superb third place at Monaco in the pouring rain, headed only by Prost's McLaren and Senna's Toleman in the shortened race. Recognized as a star in the making, he was killed at Spa when he tried to force his Porsche 962 inside Jacky Ickx's similar works machine going into Eau Rouge, and slammed head-on into the barrier.

BELSO, Tom (DK)

b. 27 August 1942
2 Grands Prix

This ever-smiling Danish saloon car ace drove for Williams in the 1974 South African and Swedish Grands Prix.

BELTOISE, Jean-Pierre (F)

b. 26 April 1937, Paris
86 Grands Prix; 1 win
Career span: 1966–72 (Matra); 1972–4 (BRM)

This son of a Paris butcher won no fewer than eleven national titles in three years on motorcycles before making the switch to four wheels with a 1.1-litre René Bonnet sports car in 1963. His career almost finished with a huge shunt in the Reims 12-hour race from which he emerged with burns and a badly broken left arm – thereafter this would always offer only restricted movement. He put his name on the map in 1965, however, by giving Matra a splendid victory in the F3 international at Reims after which he moved into F2 with the French national marque.

Beltoise won the F2 section of the 1966 German Grand Prix and rounded off his F3 career the following winter by winning all four races in the Argentine Temporada series. By the end of 1967 another good F2 year had firmly established his credentials as a future F1 candidate and Matra duly rewarded his persistent efforts, entrusting him with their own V12-engined F1 machine which would be fielded under the Matra Sport banner while Jackie Stewart's Ford-powered sister car was run by Tyrrell as Matra International.

The highlight of Beltoise's first F1 season was a splendid second place to Stewart in the rain-soaked Dutch GP at Zandvoort after which he was taken aboard into the Tyrrell camp as Stewart's number two for 1969. He was a splendid second to the Scot at Clermont-Ferrand and ran with the leading bunch to finish third at Monza, almost thwarting Stewart's Championship-clinching efforts as he made his own last corner bid for victory in the Italian GP.

The Matra factory had missed the 1969 season to work on the V12 engine development, and Beltoise led the team when they returned to the fray in 1970. The French V12 was a hard-working, high-revving tool and Beltoise used it with gusto, making up for what he lacked in sheer natural talent with lashings of bravado and derring-do. He was third at Spa and Monza, but victory continued to elude him, as it would again in 1971 when he stayed loyal to the French marque.

In 1972 he was lured away to BRM by the attraction of team leadership and it was for the once-proud British team, by now in a steady decline, that he finally notched up his one and only Grand Prix victory. Driving with terrific audacity in monsoon conditions, he thrust his BRM P160 into the lead of the Monaco Grand Prix going into the first corner, and never looked back. It was an inspired performance in which 'JPB' eclipsed even the acknowledged wet weather ace of that era, Jacky Ickx. The Belgian's Ferrari was left trailing by more than half a minute at the chequered flag, and the Belgian driver was the first to congratulate his adversary.

Beltoise never won another Grand Prix. Neither did BRM, although Beltoise took the ungainly P180 to a lucky victory in the end-of-season non-title race at Brands Hatch and stormed to a strong second at Kyalami in 1974 with the P201. At the end of that season Beltoise reached the end of the F1 road, but there was plenty of touring car racing still to be done before he finally called it a day.

This twinkling little Frenchman still sometimes appears at his home Grand Prix and remains married to Jacqueline, sister of the glamorous François Cevert who was killed while practising for the 1973 United States GP. Beltoise may not have been amongst the very first rank when it came to Grand Prix driving, but he was a dogged, determined performer and worthwhile team player whose versatility extended to some fine performances in the Matra sports car team.

BERG, Allen (CDN)

b. 1 August 1961, Alberta
9 Grands Prix

This compact Canadian entered karting and ice racing events, before taking up open-wheelers, winning the 1983 North American F/Pacific title. He was runner up in the 1984 British F3 series in 1984 and squeezed into F1 with a horrifyingly uncompetitive Osella-Alfa, qualifying for eight races in 1986. Lack of sponsorship ended his F1 career and by 1991 he was driving a private BMW saloon in the German Touring Car Championship.

Jean-Pierre Beltoise was generally regarded as a good, strong number two driver, but his splendid victory in the rain-soaked 1972 Monaco Grand Prix was the high water mark of his career. Here his BRM P160 splashes out of Casino Square ahead of Jacky Ickx's Ferrari.

BERGER, Gerhard (A)

b. 27 August 1959, Worgl, near Innsbruck
112 Grands Prix; 6 wins
Career span: 1984 (ATS); 1985 (Arrows); 1986 (Benetton);
1987–9 (Ferrari); 1990 to date (McLaren)

There is an outward effervescence about Gerhard Berger when he is away from the intense business of the pit lane, and this sometimes disguises the sheer steel and determination which suffuses his character. Blooded in the high-pressure political environment of the Ferrari team for three years, he faced the unenviable task of succeeding Alain Prost alongside Ayrton Senna at the wheel of the second McLaren-Honda at the start of 1990.

It took the lanky Austrian the best part of two seasons to come to terms with the challenge, but in the latter stages of 1991 he finally seemed to have got on top of his new position and, in qualifying at least, proved more than capable of holding his own with Senna. It was as if Gerhard had finally got the last pieces of a complex jigsaw in place, a puzzle which it had seemed certain he would complete much earlier in his career, judging by his startling initial progress in the sport's premier league.

With F3 and touring car experience under his belt, this son of an Austrian road haulage contractor breezed into F1 at the wheel of an ATS-BMW towards the end of 1984. He failed to finish on his home ground at Österreichring, but stormed home to finish strongly at Monza a few weeks later in the Italian GP. Sadly he had not originally been entered as a regular championship contestant and so was not awarded the point normally accruing to sixth place.

Barely twenty-five years old, Berger's racing horizons

seemed to be widening dramatically, but his career very nearly ended in the winter of 1984/1985 with a serious accident near his home in the Tirol. He fractured a vertebra in his neck and spent most of the off-season

BERGER, Georges (B)

b. 14 September 1918
d. 23 August 1967
2 Grands Prix

Another Gordini 'renta-driver' who competed in the 1953 Belgian and 1954 French Grands Prix.

BERNARD, Eric (F)

b. 28 April 1964, Istres
31 Grands Prix

A graduate of the Elf-Winfield F2 team in 1987, Bernard was the most impressive newcomer to F3000 in 1988 and made his F1 début for the Larrousse team guesting in the 1989 French GP. Taken on full time by Larrousse the following year, he took an outstanding fourth place in the

British GP at Silverstone and stayed with the Paul Ricard-based team as they struggled through 1991 on a shoestring budget. He suffered leg fractures in a practice shunt for the Japanese GP and found himself on the sidelines again at the start of the 1992 season.

BEUTTLER, Mike (GB)

b. 13 April 1940, Cairo
d. 29 December 1988, San Francisco
28 Grands Prix
Career span: 1971–3 (March)

A talented F3 graduate from the late 1960s who made it into F2 and F1 with the March team thanks to financial support from a group of stockbroker friends. This confirmed bachlor retired from racing at the end of the 1973 season.

The two faces of Gerhard Berger. *Left:* the intense, committed professional, and *above:* the light-hearted, fun-loving sportsman.

recuperating. He recovered in time to join Thierry Boutsen in the Arrow-BMW line-up for 1985, highlighting his season with a fifth place in South Africa and sixth in Australia.

For 1986 he switched to the emergent Benetton-BMW team and really began to mature, displaying considerable flair and expertise. After leading his home Grand Prix commandingly at the Österreichring, only to be thwarted by battery problems, his great day finally came when he won in Mexico City. In searing heat, he judged the situation superbly, profiting from a non-stop run on his Pirelli rubber when his Goodyear-shod rivals were obliged to stop for fresh tyres on two and even three occasions.

By this time, Berger's signature was already dry on a Ferrari contract for the following season and, after a shaky start to 1987, he picked up the pace and soon asserted his quality as a front runner. He won the Japanese GP to return the 'Prancing Horse' to the winners' circle for the first time in over two years. A fortnight later he followed that up with a flag-to-flag victory in Adelaide, raising hopes for a serious championship challenge the following year.

However, this turned out to be a forlorn hope. The McLaren-Hondas steamrollered the opposition, but Berger picked up a somewhat lucky win at Monza when both Senna and Prost faltered. He had a rotten year in 1989 (now partnered by Nigel Mansell) and was lucky to escape with superficial injuries from a spectacular, fiery accident during the San Marino GP at Imola.

At the end of 1989 he was offered the plum job at McLaren alongside Senna. However, much of the 1990 season was spent settling into the team which took a disappointingly long time making his lanky frame fully comfortable in the MP4/5B cockpit. It was an unhappy period and his morale began to suffer, but he got back in control of his career towards the end of 1991 and the old Berger grin began to reappear once more. Being paired with a genius like Senna was never going to be easy, but Berger made the best of it.

Mike Beuttler showed promise in F2 and F3 which was never sustained when he graduated to F1.

BIANCHI, Lucien (B)

b. 10 November 1934, Milan
d. 30 March 1969, Le Mans
17 Grands Prix
Career span: 1960 (Cooper); 1961–2 (Lotus); 1963 (Lola); 1965 (BRM); 1968 (Cooper)

The son of an Alfa Romeo mechanic, Bianchi moved to Belgium as a youngster when his father started working for Johnny Claes, and Lucien got involved in motorsport through events such as the Tour de France. He had an intermittent F1 career until 1968 when he joined the Cooper-BRM line-up for his first full season, also winning Le Mans that year (with Pedro Rodriguez in a JW/Gulf Ford GT40) but losing the London–Sydney marathon when his Citroën was in collision with a non-competing car. He was killed when his Alfa Romeo T33 spun into a telegraph pole nearing the end of the Mulsanne straight during Le Mans testing the following year.

BIANCO, Gino (BR)

4 Grands Prix

A Brazilian driver who handled a Maserati A6GCM for compatriot Heitel Cantoni's Escuderia Bandeirantes during the 1952 season.

BINDER, Hans (A)

b. 12 June 1948
13 Grands Prix
Career span: 1976 (Ensign and Wolf); 1977 (Surtees)

This moderately promising Austrian journeyman raised the sponsorship necessary to buy a place in the Surtees team for much of the 1977 season, his best placing being eighth in the Dutch GP at Zandvoort.

BIONDETTI, Clemente (I)

b. 18 June 1898, Budduro, Sardini
d. 24 February 1955
1 Grand Prix

Four times Mille Miglia winner (1938, 1947, 1948 and 1949), this distinguished Italian ace was well past his best when he drove a Jaguar-engined Ferrari 166 special in the 1950 Italian Grand Prix at Monza. His last competitive outing was the 1954 Tour of Italy before he succumbed to cancer.

'BIRA, B' (T)

b. 15 July 1914, Siam (now Thailand)
d. 23 December 1988
18 Grands Prix
Career span: 1950 (Maserati); 1951 (Osca); 1952 (Gordini);
1953 (Connaught and Maserati); 1954 (Maserati)

'B Bira' was the pseudonym used by Prince Birabongse Bhanutej Bhanubandh, a member of the Siamese royal family whose grandfather, King Mongkut, became the inspiration for the late 1950s musical, *The King and I* starring Yul Brynner. Bira came to England at the age of thirteen to be educated at Eton and Cambridge, and began racing when he was twenty-one under the patronage of his cousin, Prince Chula Chakrabongse.

In 1936, when only twenty-two years old, Chula's White Mouse Stable purchased an ERA for Bira to drive and he quickly became its most successful exponent, winning three races during the course of that season including the Coup de Prince Ranier at Monte Carlo. He proved consistently successful throughout the years remaining prior to World War II, and although he raced a 2.9-litre Maserati in 1936, he concentrated almost exclusively on racing various ERAs after abandoning a financially over-ambitious project to rebuild the 1,500cc Delage the team had purchased from Dick Seaman at the end of the 1936 season.

During the war Bira and Chula (by now married to a couple of English society women, Ceryl Heycock and Lisba Hunter) remained in Britain, taking a house at Rock, near Wadebridge in Cornwall. In the immediate post-war period the White Mouse Stable was revived, but was dissolved at the end of the 1948 season, although Bira continued driving in a Maserati 4CLT entered by Enrique Plate's stable. He briefly joined the HWM team, Gordini and Osca, but by 1953 he was driving his own 2-litre F2 Maserati A6G which was painted in the distinctive blue and yellow livery of Thailand's international racing colours.

He became one of the very first private entrants to order a Maserati 250F, but while his new car was being completed he raced his 1954 machine with a new 2½-litre

The immaculate, compact Prince 'Bira' was a well-heeled privateer whose ability peaked during the pre-war years.

engine installed. With this machine he won the 1954 Grand Prix de Frontières at Chimay in southern Belgium, continuing to take his best result in a Championship race, a fourth place in the French Grand Prix at Reims with the new 250F. This matched an identical placing at Berne four years earlier in the 4CLT, and he also finished fifth at Monaco in 1950 with the same car.

He raced through to the end of 1954, when he married for the second time, and scored his final victory with the 250F in the 1955 early season non-championship New Zealand Grand Prix before retiring from the cockpit altogether a few months later. He sold his 250F to Bristol garage owner Horace Gould and returned to live in Thailand, although he maintained a European base in the form of a superb three-master schooner berthed at Cannes, close to his other home, Villa les Faunes, at Mandelieu.

A versatile and cultured man, Bira was also an accomplished sculptor; motor racing fans can see an example of his work in the form of the bronze bas-relief on the fountain erected to the memory of Pat Fairfield in a corner of the Silverstone paddock. He later maintained a European base in Geneva and became heavily involved in Thailand's international sporting interests on a wide basis. He died in 1988, after collapsing on a London Underground station from a heart attack.

BIRGER, Pablo (RA)

b. 6 January 1924
d. 9 March 1966
2 Grands Prix

Argentinian privateer who rented a Gordini for his home Grand Prix at Buenos Aires, and for the same event two years later.

BLANCHARD, Harry (USA)

d. 31 January 1960
1 Grand Prix

Blanchard finished seventh in the 1959 US GP at Sebring with a Porsche RSK F2 special.

BLEEKEMOLEN, Michael (NL)

b. 2 October 1949
1 Grand Prix

A Dutch Super Vee graduate who briefly flirted with Gunther Schmid's ATS team during the second half of 1978 to little effect.

BLOKDYK, Trevor (ZA)

b. 30 November 1935
1 Grand Prix

A South African privateer who raced an elderly Cooper-Maserati in his home Grand Prix at East London in 1963, and who later recovered from multiple injuries to race a limited programme of European F3 in 1968.

BLUNDELL, Mark (GB)

b. 8 April 1966, Barnet
14 Grands Prix

An outstanding new F1 talent, Blundell had an impressive first season at the wheel of a Brabham-Yamaha in 1991. He started with motorcross in 1980 and pursued a career on two wheels until switching to cars in 1984 with dramatic and immediate success in Formula Ford and FF2000.

Mark Blundell won his spurs as the Williams team's official test driver and, after an unsuccessful maiden F1 season with Brabham in 1991, became McLaren test driver at the start of 1992. Definitely one of the most outstanding young British drivers of the decade.

He moved to F3000 in 1987 and impressed spectating F1 team managers with a strong drive to second place in the Belgian GP supporting race at Spa. In 1988 he finished sixth in the International F3000 Championship and expanded his racing involvement to drive for Nissan in Group C as well as being recruited as test driver for the Williams-Renault team in 1990.

His best placing in 1991 was a strong sixth place at Spa, but financial pressures on Brabham meant that he was replaced in 1992 by two sponsored drivers. Nevertheless, he kept his hand in as chief test driver for the McLaren-Honda team and seems certain to have a considerable future in Grand Prix racing.

BOESEL, Raul (BR)

b. 4 December 1957, Curitiba
23 Grands Prix

Boesel originally intended to follow his brothers into the equestrian world and was an outstanding show jumper before motor racing intervened, and he arrived in Britain in 1980 to contest Formula Ford. He contested the British F3 series in 1981 before moving into F2 with RAM March at the start of 1982 with little success. An even worse time was in store for him at Ligier in 1983, after which he carved out a US racing career in Indy cars.

BONDURANT, Bob (USA)

b. 27 April 1933, Evanston, Illinois
9 Grands Prix

Bondurant was one of the key drivers involved in the Shelby American Cobra sports car project which won the Manufacturers' World Championship in 1965, and was a regular sports car competitor through the 1960s. He ran a 2-litre BRM under the Team Chamaco Collect banner in 1966, the first year of the new 3-litre F1, taking a steady fourth place at Monaco thanks to the high retirement rate amongst the competition.

BONNETTO, Felice (RA)

b. 9 June 1903, Brescia
d. 21 November 1953 during Carrera Panamaericana
16 Grands Prix
Career span: 1950 (Maserati); 1951 (Alfa Romeo); 1952–3 (Maserati)

Bonetto was a pre-war Alfa Romeo sports car driver who did not make the big time until the immediate post-war period when he got a break with the Cisitalia company. He briefly drove for Ferrari before being recruited as number three in the Alfa works team for 1951. The next two

Raul Boesel was a cheerful and popular Brazilian who forsook F1 after a disappointing career to concentrate on Indy car racing.

seasons saw him compete at the wheel of a Maserati, doing a full F1 programme in 1953 before his fatal accident at the end of the year.

BONNIER, Jo (S)

b. 31 January 1930, Stockholm
d. 11 June 1972, Le Mans
102 Grands Prix; 1 win
Career span: 1957–8 (Maserati); 1959–60 (BRM); 1961–2 (Porsche); 1963–4 (Cooper); 1964–5 (Brabham); 1966–8 (Cooper); 1969 (Lotus); 1970–1 (McLaren)

Scion of the powerful Stockholm-based publishing group, Bonniers Aktiebolag, Bonnier's great claim to fame was giving BRM its maiden Grand Prix victory at Zandvoort in 1959. Often aloof and distant, in fact the immaculate, bearded Swede was a great socialite and one of the first F1 drivers to make his base in Switzerland for tax purposes. One of the driving forces behind the Grand Prix Drivers' Association, he raced in F1 long past his peak to the point where he was little more than a nuisance in high-speed company. He was killed at Le Mans when his private Lola-Cosworth T280 sports car collided with a Ferrari Daytona driven by Swiss amateur, Florian Vetsch, and he was catapulted into trees.

BONOMI, Roberto (RA)

b. 30 September 1919, Buenos Aires
1 Grand Prix

Bonomi drove a Centro-Sud Cooper-Maserati in the 1960 Argentine Grand Prix, finishing eleventh, four laps behind Bruce McLaren's winning Cooper. He was Argentine sports-car champion in 1952–3 and a member of the Argentine team to Europe in 1953–4.

BORGUDD, Slim (s)

b. 25 November 1946
10 Grands Prix

The one-time drummer with the Swedish pop group Abba, Borgudd sampled F1 with ATS and Tyrrell to little effect in 1981–1982. He subsequently made the grade as World Truck Racing Champion.

The bearded Jo Bonnier (seen here in Rob Walker's Brabham-Climax) won the BRM marque its first Grand Prix victory in 1959, and also drove for Porsche in one of whose cars he is seen at Monaco in 1961 (*below*).

BOTHA, Luki (ZA)

1 Grand Prix

A privateer who drove a 2.7-litre four-cylinder Climax-engined Brabham in the 1967 South African GP at Kyalami.

BOUTSEN, Thierry (B)

b. 13 July 1957, Brussels
136 Grands Prix; 3 wins
Career span: 1983–6 (Arrows); 1987–8 (Benetton); 1989–90 (Williams); 1991 to date (Ligier)

This cool and stylish Belgian driver was inspired by the example of his compatriot Jacky Ickx in the early 1970s and has worked hard to develop a similarly polished style behind the wheel. However, although Thierry enrolled in a racing school as soon as he was old enough to get a driving licence, his path to F1 was strewn with pitfalls and disappointments.

He fought his way through Formula Ford into F3 and eventually took over the works Martini in 1981 which had been vacated by the F1-bound Alain Prost at the end of the previous season. He finished second behind Michele Alboreto in the 1980 European F3 championship and then became somewhat bogged down in Formula 2, first with a private March and then with the Spirit team.

Thierry was understandably disappointed when his team-mate Stefan Johansson was chosen to drive the team's Honda-engined Formula 1 car in 1983, but Thierry raised sufficient sponsorship backing to land a seat in the second Arrows car. He drove for the Milton Keynes-based team for three-and-a-half seasons, developing a reputation as an unflappable, smooth and very reliable performer. That he was also extremely quick was not fully demonstrated until he joined Benetton in 1987.

In 1988 he finished third six times in a season dominated by the McLaren-Hondas. He was then invited to

Underrated by many, Thierry Boutsen (right) celebrates his victory in the rain-deluged 1989 Canadian GP by soaking his Williams-Renault team-mate Riccardo Patrese in champagne.

take Nigel Mansell's position as team leader in the Williams squad, winning both the 1989 Canadian and Australian Grands Prix in conditions of torrential rain.

In 1990 he added the Hungarian GP to his tally of successes, but there was a feeling within the Williams ranks that he did not quite have the sharp edge of aggression which makes a champion. In turn, he felt unwanted and unappreciated; a correct assessment, as things transpired, as Williams dropped him from their line-up to make room for the returning Nigel Mansell at the end of 1990.

BRABHAM, David (GB)

b. 5 September 1965
6 Grands Prix

Youngest son of Sir Jack, David Brabham got his F1 break with the team carrying the family name, replacing Gregor Foitek after the first two races of the 1990 season. He only qualified the uncompetitive Judd-engined car six times out of fourteen races and was replaced by the end of the season.

David Brabham, Jack's youngest son, briefly drove for the team carrying his family's name early in 1990.

BRABHAM, Jack

See pages 30–1.

BRACK, Bill (CDN)

b. 16 December 1935
3 Grands Prix

A capable Canadian semi-professional who drove in three of his home Grands Prix in a hired works BRM (1968, 1969 and 1972).

BRAMBILLA, Vittorio (I)

b. 11 November 1937, Monza
74 Grands Prix; 1 win
Career span: 1974–5 (March); 1976–8 (Surtees); 1979–80 (Alfa Romeo)

A frantic, often erratic racer, Vittorio and his elder brother Tino – a former MV Agusta works motorcycle racer – were dubbed the 'Monza Gorillas' by their rivals in the early 1970s, this cachet being applied with a mixture of affectionate respect and mild apprehension. Tino missed the F1 boat, despite practising in an F1 Ferrari at Monza in 1969, but his younger brother successfully shed much of his 'wild man' image and matured into a respectable F1 performer.

Vittorio's great day came at Österreichring in 1975 when he surfed to victory in the rain-shortened Austrian Grand Prix in a works March 751 in a season which had also seen him start from pole position in the Swedish Grand Prix. He will be remembered for spinning off and deranging the nose of the March after he took the chequered flag in Austria, completing the slowing down lap with the front of the car askew, and waving madly to the crowd with unbridled delight.

A three-year stint with Team Surtees produced a succession of stirring performances, but all too frequently he over-drove his machinery and paid the price with accidents and mechanical retirements. He suffered serious concussion in the multiple pile-up at Monza which cost the life of Ronnie Peterson in 1978, but recovered to drive briefly for the Alfa works team in 1979 and 1980 after which he drifted into retirement.

BRANCA, Antonio (CH)

b. 15 September 1916
d. 10 May 1985
3 Grands Prix

A Swiss amateur whom, legend has it, had his motor racing financed by an admiring Belgian countess!

BRABHAM, Jack (AUS)

b. 12 April 1926, Hurstville, near Sydney
126 Grands Prix; 14 wins; World Champion 1959, 1960 and 1966
Career span: 1955–61 (Cooper); 1962–70 (Brabham)

One of motor racing's great practical heroes, Jack Brabham applied a down-to-earth attitude to his motor racing and was rewarded not only with three Championship titles, but gained the third while at the wheel of a car bearing his own name. It was a unique achievement, made all the more satisfying by the fact that Jack was forty when he took his last title in 1966 and was regarded as over the hill by many motor racing commentators.

In fact, Brabham drove on competitively until the end of the 1970 season when, at the age of forty-four, he finally hung up his helmet and began to concentrate on his many other business interests. The grandson of a cockney who emigrated to Australia in 1885, Jack was born in Hurstville, about ten miles south of Sydney, the only son of a greengrocer. Early experience gained while working on his father's trucks and cars at a local garage imbued him with a keen sense of mechanical resourcefulness which would pay dividends in the years that followed.

Brabham joined the Royal Australian Air Force at the age of eighteen, dearly wanting to fly, but by then it was 1944 and such was the progress of World War II that there was more demand for flight mechanics than aircrew. He worked on Bristol Beaufighters before being demobbed in 1947, after which he succumbed to the lure of motor racing.

After proving a highly competitive runner on the Australian national scene, Brabham aspired to a professional racing career. He was well ahead of his time when he attracted Redex sponsorship for his Cooper-Bristol in 1954, but the Australian motorsporting authorities were very haughty about that idea and made him remove the identification. In 1955 he made tracks for England where he became involved with John and Charles Cooper, making his Grand Prix début in the 1955 British GP at Aintree in a centre-seat Cooper sports car.

Thereafter he rode the crest of the wave as Cooper rewrote the parameters of F1 car performance with their agile central-engined machines. It may have been Stirling Moss who won the marque its first Grand Prix with Rob Walker's machine in Buenos Aires in 1958, but once Jack got into his stride during the summer of 1959 there was no stopping him.

With the Vanwall and Maserati out of the fray, Ferrari still wrestling with its outdated Dino 246 and Lotus yet to come to full flower, Cooper enjoyed a two-year window of success in which Brabham won seven races and two Championships. It was a question of perfect timing: the right machine – and the right man – for the right moment.

Jack had long-term plans to set up in production race car manufacturing in his own right, a project which relied on the collaboration of his old Australian friend, Ron Tauranac, and it was perhaps inevitable that this should be carried to its logical conclusion with the construction of his own F1 machine. He left Cooper at the end of 1961, by which time their star was fading, and gave the first Brabham F1 car its race début in the 1962 German Grand Prix.

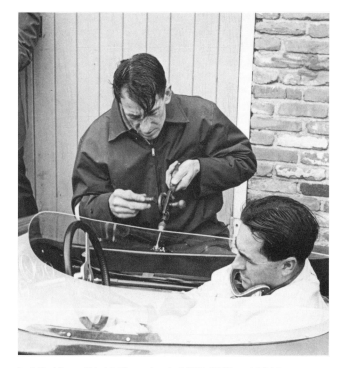

Jack Brabham, World Champion in 1959, 1960 and 1966, checks the instruments of one of his own Brabham F1 cars while designer Ron Tauaranc drills a hole to secure a rear view mirror in the cockpit surround.

For the 1963 season, Jack signed the lanky American Dan Gurney as his second driver and the Climax-engined Brabhams quickly established a reputation as highly competitive machines, albeit not strong on reliability. Not until the 1964 French Grand Prix at Rouen did Gurney score the marque's first victory, and while he followed that up with a second win at Mexico City, there would be no further successes for the team until the advent of the 3-litre F1 in 1966.

Having originally received some assistance from Repco (the Australian manufacturer of replacement car components) in locating the premises in Surbiton where he would build his production racers, Brabham beat a path to their door for 1966. Repco had developed a 2½-litre V8 on the General Motors Oldsmobile F85 block, to replace the ageing 2.7-litre Climax four-cylinder engines which were the mainstay of the Australasian Tasman series. He succeeded in persuading them to build a 3-litre engine for F1 purposes and the rest is history.

Brabham scored his first victory with a car bearing his own name in the 1966 French Grand Prix at Reims. He followed this up with wins in the British, Dutch and German races, celebrating his fortieth birthday at Zandvoort by walking out on to the grid with a false beard and a walking stick. This was Jack's way of responding to the critics who regarded him as over the hill.

The Brabham-Repco momentum continued into 1967 when Jack's team-mate Denny Hulme won the title, although by the end of the season the writing was on the wall for the Australian V8. The new Cosworth DFV V8 engine had made its début in the epochal Lotus 49 and everything else was suddenly consigned to the role of also-ran.

Jack's disappointment was to be compounded by the failure of the four-cam Repco-type 860 V8 which gave nothing but trouble throughout 1968 and prevented the team from retaining the services of Jocken Rindt. Reluctantly, Jack severed the Repco link the following year to follow the Cosworth path, but there was one more win waiting for him – in South Africa at the start of 1970 – before he decided to call it a day.

Jack Brabham will be recalled by all who worked with him as a man who never wasted words; monosyllabic replies were the most even his closest friends could expect in the F1 pit lane. But he was shrewd to the point of sheer cunning, a great mechanical improvisor and an all-rounder prepared to turn his hand to any chore if the necessity arose. Team-mates Dan Gurney and Denny Hulme recall that he played his cards close to his chest even with them, and they never quite knew what technical tweaks he had up his sleeve to turn to his own advantage. His chief mechanic in 1969–70 was young Ron Dennis, today managing director of the ultra-successful McLaren International Team. He was the quintessential owner, driver-cum-mechanic – as well as triple World Champion. The family name is perpetuated on the international racing scene by his three sons Geoff, Gary and David, their old man being recognized for a lifetime of endeavour with a knighthood in the 1985 New Year's Honours List.

BRANDON, Eric (GB)

b. 18 July 1920, London
d. 8 August 1982
5 Grands Prix

One of the pioneering Cooper F3 stars of the early 1950s, this electrical goods wholesaler was a close friend of John Cooper and drove a handful of Grand Epreuves in a Cooper-Brisol F2 in 1953 and 1954.

BRIDGER, Tommy (GB)

b. 24 June 1934
1 Grand Prix

A British minor-league privateer who contested the 1958 Moroccan Grand Prix in an F2 Cooper-Climax where he crashed and sustained slight injuries.

BRISE, Tony (GB)

b. 28 March 1952
d. 29 November 1975, near Arkley
10 Grands Prix

A brilliant young English rising star, the son of John Brise,

Tony Brise was one of Britain's great F1 hopes of the 1970s, but perished in the air crash which claimed Graham Hill and his team.

a well-known 500cc Formula 3 racer of the mid-1950s, Tony dominated the British F3 and F/Atlantic scene before moving into F1 with Frank Williams for the 1975 Spanish GP at Barcelona. He then switched to Graham Hill's Embassy-backed team, effectively being adopted as the former World Champion's protégé on his retirement from driving that summer. He was killed along with his team boss and four colleagues when Hill's Piper Aztec crashed on Arkley golf course in dense fog whilst attempting to land at Elstree.

BRISTOW, Chris (GB)

b. 2 December 1937, London
d. 19 June 1960
4 Grands Prix

This dazzlingly talented south Londoner was recruited to drive for the BRP Cooper team in 1960, and was rated by Stirling Moss as a great future talent. He was killed in a grisly accident at the tricky downhill Burnenville right-hander as he diced with Willy Mairesse's Ferrari Dino 246 for third place in the Belgian Grand Prix.

BROEKER, Peter (CDN)

b. 15 May 1929
1 Grand Prix

This ambitious and enterprizing Canadian privateer drove a Stebro-Ford special to seventh place in the 1963 US Grand Prix at Watkins Glen.

BROWN, Alan (GB)

b. 20 November 1919, Malton, Yorkshire
8 Grands Prix
Career span: 1952–3

One of the stars of the immediate post-war 500cc firmament, this truck sales representative employed by Dennis Motors at Guildford made his name by winning the 1951 Luxembourg GP in a Cooper 500 F3. He finished fifth in a Cooper-Bristol in the following year's Swiss Grand Prix, was later entrusted with tests of the first Vanwall at Odiham airfield before handling it on its maiden race.

BROWN, Warwick (AUS)

b. 24 December 1949
1 Grand Prix

This Australian Formula 5000 ace drove one of the Wolf-Williams FW05s in the 1976 US Grand Prix at Watkins Glen.

BROOKS, Tony (GB)

b. 25 February 1932, Dunkinfield, Cheshire
38 Grands Prix; 6 wins
Career span: 1956 (BRM); 1957–8 (Vanwall); 1959 (Ferrari); 1960 (Yeoman Credit); 1961 (BRM)

Many people have described Charles Anthony Standish Brooks as the most underrated Grand Prix driver of the post-war era. In truth, it would be more accurate to describe him as the most undersold. He is imbued with such modesty and a sense of rectitude that, in retirement, it is almost difficult to believe that this was the man who mastered Spa, Nurburgring and Monza with such magical assurance at the wheel of the elegant 2½-litre Vanwall during the golden summer of 1958.

The son of a dental surgeon, Brooks also qualified in dentistry; even when flying down to Sicily to contest the 1955 Syracuse Grand Prix for Connaught he was glued to his books, studying for his finals. He did so on the return trip as well, although the intervening few days had seen him enter the motor racing history books as the driver who earned Britain its first Continental victory since Sir Henry Segrave won the San Sebastian Grand Prix in his Sunbeam thirty-one years earlier.

Brooks's successful foray to Syracuse, where he beat off a Maserati challenge headed by Luigi Musso, was also the Englishman's first trip abroad. He had started racing at the wheel of a Healey Silverstone only three years before, moving on to a Frazer-Nash and then to an F2 Connaught entered by John Riseley-Pritchard. A fourth place at Cyrstal Palace attracted Connaught's attention and he was also signed on to drive in the Aston Martin sports car team at the start of the 1955 season.

In 1956 he was offered a place in the BRM team, but only contested the British Grand Prix at Silverstone where he came close to disaster. After a pit stop to tend a malfunctioning throttle, it stuck open at Abbey Curve on his return to the race. The car turned over, tossing its driver out, before bursting into flames. 'It was the best thing that could have happened to that particular motor car,' he remarked later, reflecting on an accident that had left him with a badly broken jaw.

For 1957 Brooks signed to drive alongside Stirling Moss and Stuart Lewis-Evans in the Vanwall line-up, but an unfortunate crash at Le Mans, where he rolled his works Aston Martin, meant that he was well below par when it came to the British Grand Prix at Aintree. Nevertheless, he played a crucial role in Stirling Moss's historic victory, the team's number one driver taking over Tony's still-healthy car after his own retired.

In 1958 Brooks's meticulous style and gentle mechanical touch earned him superb victories in the Belgian, German and Italian Grands Prix, all classic races on prob-

Tony Brooks's talent and flair behind the wheel of a Grand Prix car was of the highest order, and he was capable of matching Stirling Moss's performances during their heyday together with Vanwall.

ably the three most challenging tracks in the world. Although Moss was the official Vanwall team leader there was no doubt that Brooks was virtually his equal, as well as being an ideal team man with an obliging and even temperament.

Vanwall's withdrawal at the end of the 1958 season saw Brooks accept an offer to join Ferrari, although he made it quite clear to the Commendatore that he would only sign up as long as he was not required to race at Le Mans. A deeply religious man, Brooks was of the firm view that taking ridiculous risks came philosophically close to trying to commit suicide, and to him that was unacceptable.

It was this rigid self-discipline which wiped out his chance of winning the 1959 World Championship. Having taken his Dino 246 to masterly wins at Reims and Avus – and missing out on potential victories at Spa and Aintree when Ferrari stayed away – he went into the US Grand Prix at Sebring with an outside chance of taking the title.

Unfortunately, on the opening lap his team-mate Wolfgang von Trips ran into the back of Tony's Dino 246 and the Englishman pulled in to check for damage. It might well have cost him the World Championship, but to do anything else would have been out of step with Brooks's personal creed. In the event, he finished third with

Brabham pushing his out-of-fuel Cooper home fourth to take the first of his three titles.

By this time Brooks's thoughts had turned towards retirement and the establishment of his garage business in Byfleet, close to the old Brooklands banking. Despite fully realizing that Ferrari would be highly competitive with its new V6 engine for the 1½-litre F1, due to start in 1961, he wanted to be in England with his wife Pina, whom he had met in Italy, in order to supervise his fledgeling business.

For 1960 he signed to drive a rear-engined Vanwall-powered Lotus. The car never materialized and, by the time this became clear, all the decent drives were gone. He was doomed to drive an uncompetitive Cooper-Climax for the Yeoman Credit team 'about which the less said the better'. An equally disappointing year with BRM followed in 1961 and, after finishing the season with a third place behind the Innes Ireland and Dan Gurney at Watkins Glen, he walked away from the sport to which he had given so much.

Today Tony Brooks lives in pleasant surroundings at St George's Hill, Weybridge, close to his garage which is now a successful Ford dealership. He is a man who coupled star quality behind the wheel of a Grand Prix car with a genuine lack of conceit that earned many friends and admirers all over the world.

BRUDES, Adolf (D)

b. 15 October 1899
2. 5 November 1986
1 Grand Prix

Another German 'one-off' merchant who drove the 1952 German GP in a Veritas RS-BMW.

BRUNDLE, Martin (GB)

b. 1 June 1959, Kings Lynn
83 Grands Prix
Career span: 1984–6 (Tyrrell); 1987 (Zakspeed); 1989 (Brabham); 1991 (Brabham)

Few drivers have taken the gamble of stepping down from F1 in an attempt to consolidate their reputation, but that is precisely what Martin Brundle did – twice. At the end of 1987, frustrated at his lack of success with Zakspeed, he reasoned that a spell with the highly competitive TWR Jaguar team would better serve his long-term career interests.

Twelve months later, as World Sports Car Champion, Brundle was restored to the Grand Prix élite as a member of the seemingly revitalized Brabham team. However, at the end of 1989 he chose to have another spell with Jaguar, winning the 1990 Le Mans 24-hours before returning to Brabham again in 1991. This strategy finally paid off at the start of 1992 when Brundle landed a seat with the Benetton-Ford team, one of whose directors by now was his old Jaguar sports car chief Tom Walkinshaw.

For some years Brundle has generally been regarded as significantly better than most of the machinery that has been at his disposal. His father, John, was a keen rally driver and a successful motor trader, so Martin was born into a world of fast cars and cut his teeth in saloon cars before switching to F3 in 1982. The following season saw him fighting tooth and nail for the British F3 title against no less a celebrity than Ayrton Senna who finally pipped him in the very last race.

Brundle was signed by Ken Tyrrell for the 1984 season and he started well with a fifth at Rio in his maiden race. Later came a set-back at Dallas where he crashed in practice, breaking both ankles and being forced to sit out the rest of the season.

He stayed with Tyrrell through to the end of 1986, made the disastrous switch to Zakspeed before adopting that 'in out' strategy which served him so well. He knew that the 1992 season with Benetton was his big break – and his last chance.

BUCCI, Clemar (RA)

b. 4 September 1920
4 Grands Prix

This dour, pipe smoking Argentinian took the South American land speed record with a Porsche-designed Cisitalia F1 prototype, later taking in four World Championship Grand Prix in a Gordini during the summer of 1964.

BUCKNUM, Ronnie (USA)

b. 5 April 1936, California
d. 14 April 1992
11 Grands Prix
Career span: 1964–6 (Honda)

Bucknum's is possibly the strangest story in contemporary F1 racing history. A West Coast SCCA club driver, he was plucked from obscurity to début Honda's new F1 car in the 1964 German Grand Prix, following the somewhat convoluted logic that since the Japanese company did not have any F1 experience it made sense to have a driver of corresponding status. He scored his only World Championship points at Mexico City in 1965 when he finished fifth, eclipsed by team-mate Richie Ginther's outstanding victory. He died from the effects of diabetes in April 1992 at the early age of 56.

BUEB, Ivor (GB)

b. 6 June 1923, Dulwich; South London
d. 1 August 1959, Clermont-Ferrand
5 Grands Prix

This fun-loving extrovert Cheltenham garage owner is best known for sharing a winning Jaguar D-type with Mike Hawthorn in the tragic 1955 Le Mans, a success he repeated with Ron Flockhart for Ecurie Écosse two years later. He started seriously in a F3 500cc Cooper in 1953, graduating to occasional starts in Grands Prix with a Connaught and private Maserati. He died from fatal injuries sustained when he crashed his British Racing Partnership Cooper-Borgward F2 car at Clermont-Ferrand.

BUENO, Luis (BR)

1 Grand Prix

Formula Ford racing contemporary of Emerson Fittipaldi who drove an F1 Surtees in the 1973 Brazilian Grand Prix.

BURGESS, Ian (GB)

b. 6 July 1930, London
16 Grands Prix
Career span: 1958–60 (Cooper); 1961 (Lotus); 1962 (Cooper); 1963 (Scirocco)

An enterprising one-time office manager at the Cooper factory, Burgess wheeled and dealed his way through F1 as a privateer through to 1963 when he became involved with the Hugh Powell and Tony Settember Scirocco organization.

BUSINELLO, Roberto (I)

b. 4 October 1927, Pistoïa
2 Grands Prix

A veteran Italian semi-professional and Autodelta Alfa GTA driver who drove in the 1961 Italian GP in a four-cylinder Alfa Romeo-engined de Tomaso special, and the 1965 race in a Centro-Sud BRM.

BYRNE, Tommy (IRL)

b. 6 May 1958
2 Grands Prix

This chirpy Irish lad showed lashings of promise in F3, winning the 1982 British Championship, but many believe he should have resisted the temptation to leap into F1 with the uncompetitive Theodore team. Either way, he never had a second chance and today pursues his career in minor league single-seater racing in the USA.

CABIANCA, Giulio (I)

b. 19 February 1923, Verona
d. 15 June 1961, Modena Aerautodrome
3 Grands Prix
Career span: 1958–9 (Maserati); 1960 (Cooper-Ferarri)

This Italian privateer's death hit the headlines more dramatically than any of his racing exploits. Cabianca was fatally injured when the throttle stuck open on his Scuderia Eugenio Castellotti Intercontinental formula Cooper-Ferrari and he shot through the gates of the Modena Aerautodrome, colliding with a passing taxi and killing three other people in addition to the luckless driver. His best performances came in Osca sports car in the Mille Miglia and Targa Florio.

CABRAL, Mario (P)

b. 15 January 1934
4 Grands Prix

The Portuguese semi-professional who ran Cooper-Maserati in the Portuguese Grand Prix 1959–1960, and private Cooper-Climax in the 1963 German Grand Prix. He drove a reworked Derrington-Francis ATS on its last outing in the 1964 Italian Grand Prix at Monza.

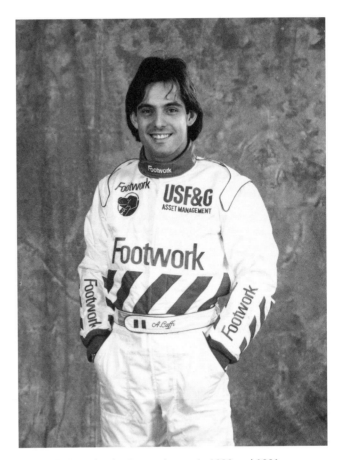

Alex Caffi drove for the Footwork team in 1990 and 1991, but the association yielded no worthwhile results for the pleasant young Italian.

CAFFI, Alex (I)

b. 18 March 1964, Rovato
56 Grands Prix
Career span: 1986–7 (Osella); 1988–9 (Dallara); 1990–1 (Footwork/Arrows)

A highly successful F3 exponent, Caffi turned a few heads with his dogged performances at the wheel of an Osella before switching to Dallara, taking a strong fourth place at Monaco in 1989. His switch to the Footwork/Arrows équipe at the start of 1990 brought nothing but disappointment and the team's disastrous Porsche V12 programme the following year virtually torpedoed Caffi's long-term F1 prospects. At the start of 1992, he was nominated as one of the drivers for the Andrea-Moda team, but withdrew from this deal after only a couple of events, when it became clear that the cars were not race ready.

Adrian Campos, seen here at Rio, was sufficiently well sponsored to get a Minardi drive, but not quick enough to keep it.

CAMPBELL-JONES, John (GB)

b. 21 January 1930
2 Grands Prix

Campbell-Jones was a London-based wheeler dealer who was a regular contender on the British domestic F1 scene in the early 1960s. He drove at the 1962 Belgian and 1963 British GPs in an Emeryson Lotus and a Parnell Racing Lola respectively.

CAMPOS, Adrian (E)

b. 17 June 1960
17 Grands Prix

This cheerful Spaniard raised sponsorship to buy a place in the Minardi team alongside Nannini at the start of 1987, his tenure lasting through to the middle of 1988 when he was replaced by Pierluigi Martini.

CANNON, John (CDN)

b. 23 June 1937, London
1 Grand Prix

This British-born, Canadian resident was a Can-Am sports car star who first made his name driving for the team part-owned by actor Dan Blocker – 'Hoss' Cartwright in the mid-1960s television cowboy series, *Bonanza* – and later won the 1970 US F5000 title in a McLaren M101B. He drove a BRM in the 1971 US Grand Prix at Watkins Glen.

CANTONI, Heitel (BR)

3 Grands Prix

Patron of the Brazilian Escuderia Bandeirantes outfit, Cantoni took part in the 1952 British, German and Italian Grands Prix in a Maserati A6GCM.

CAPELLI, Ivan (I)

b. 24 May 1963, Milan
78 Grands Prix
1985 (Tyrrell); 1986 (AGS); 1987–91 (Leyton House)

When Ivan Capelli took his Leyton House-Judd to second place behind Alain Prost's McLaren-Honda in the 1988 Portuguese GP at Estoril, it was a performance which marked out the Italian as one of the brightest stars of his generation. Disappointingly, over the next three seasons with the same team he had only a handful of opportunities to remind observers he was capable of such a performance. Even so, it did not prevent him being recruited into the works Ferrari team for the start of the 1992 season!

The bespectacled Capelli first came to prominence when he won the 1984 European F3 championship and the prestigious Monaco F3 race supporting the Grand Prix. He won the European Championship for the newly instigated Formula 3000 the following year. By then the forever-shrewd Ken Tyrrell had already given him his F1 break, with

Ivan Capelli scored only a handful of good results during five years with the Leyton House team (1987–91) but he still managed to land a Ferrari drive for 1992.

Ivan driving for him in the 1985 European and Australian GPs. He crashed in the former event, but performed with perfect discipline to finish fourth in Adelaide.

After a couple of inconclusive races with AGS in 1986, he signed for the Leyton House-March team and scored another point with a fine sixth place at Monaco. Then, in 1988 he relished that joyous moment at Estoril and briefly snatched the lead in Japan. However, he then had to wait until the 1990 French GP for the next chance to demonstrate his true form when, with the complex aerodynamics of the Leyton House chassis working well on the billiard-table smoothness of the Paul Ricard circuit, he led commandingly and was only just pipped by Prost for victory a few laps before the finish.

CARINI, Piero (I)

b. 6 March 1921, Gênes
d. 30 May 1957, St Étienne, France
3 Grands Prix

Carini was a successful Italian sports car ace who had a handful of outings in Ferrari single-seaters. He was killed in freak accident at the 1957 St Étienne sports car race when his Ferrari Testa Rossa went out of control and collided head-on with a similar car driven by the Portuguese amateur, G Barreto.

CASTELLOTTI, Eugenio (I)

b. 10 October 1930, Milan
d. 14 March 1957, Modena
14 Grands Prix
Career span: 1955 (Lancia and Ferrari); 1956–7 (Ferrari)

Eugenio Castellotti was an archetypal Italian racing driver. Fearsome and motivated, erratic yet arrogant, he flared briefly across the F1 horizon over a couple of seasons before his light was extinguished prematurely in a banal testing accident at Modena Aerautodrome. He was one of a generation of Grand Prix competitors who were pressured by, and fell victim to, the personal political strategy adopted by Enzo Ferrari in order to keep all his drivers on their toes.

An eager customer for a 2-litre Ferrari which he drove to an inauspicious fiftieth place on the 1951 Mille Miglia, Castellotti came from a family of landed aristocrats. He was dashingly good looking, fiercely competitive and, so legend has it, vain to the point of wearing built-up heels in his shoes.

In 1952 he ran second in the Mille Miglia before retiring, and was offered a drive in the Lancia sports car team for the 1953 Carrera Panamericana road race where he finished third behind Fangio and Taruffi. But when Lancia's splendid D50 F1 car arrived on the scene at the start

Castellotti

Eugenio Castellotti working hard with the Lancia D50 during the 1955 Pau Grand Prix.

of the 1955 season, he was recruited to drive as third team member alongside Ascari and Villoresi.

He finished a fine second at Monaco on the day that Ascari speared off into the harbour, and it was his sports Ferrari that the great Alberto was trying at Monza the following week when he was killed. In the wake of this shattering body blow to Lancia F1 fortunes, Castellotti proved to be a tower of strength and motivation, begging Gianni Lancia to make available a single D50 for the next race on the calendar, the Belgian Grand Prix at Spa.

Clearly in a highly emotional state of mind, Castellotti was out to win this one 'for 'Ascari's memory' and there were more than a few worried faces as the volatile Italian set out to practise on this spectacularly quick circuit. However, Eugenio did a fine job for the Turin marque, planting the D50 on pole position and hanging on well to third place in the early stages of the race before his engine expired.

When the assets of the Lancia team were handed over to Ferrari in mid-1955, Castellotti went with the package, the result being that at times it seemed as though the Commendatore had more drivers than he needed. He finished fifth at Zandvoort and third at Monza to finish the season in third place in the overall Championship table.

In 1956 he was fourth at Monaco and a close second to team-mate Peter Collins in the French Grand Prix at Reims, but by now the presence of Collins, Mike Hawthorn and Luigi Musso in the team was stepping up the pressure. At Monza he and Musso disgraced themselves by putting on a blindly nationalistic battle in the early stages of the race in which lack of imagination and adrenalin played a significant part. He finally spun violently into a barrier when one of his overstressed tyres predictably threw a tread. He finished the afternoon in eighth place, having taken over the repaired car abandoned by Fangio when it suffered a broken steering arm.

Only one more F1 race awaited Castellotti, the 1957 Argentine Grand Prix at Buenos Aires. There he suffered a hub breakage and lost a wheel whilst, as usual, going hell for leather trying to mix with the Maseratis.

In the early months of 1957 Castellotti featured extensively in the gossip columns due to his widely publicized affair with singer Delia Scala. Whilst on holiday with her in Florence, he received a message to return to Modena to test the latest Ferrari 801 – and to do something about the unofficial lap record which had just been set by Jean Behra in the latest Maserati 250F.

Irked at having his holiday interrupted, Castellotti hastened back to Modena in a rather absent and annoyed mood. On the third lap of the test session he crashed into the small grandstand near the chicane at the end of the pits straight and was killed instantly.

CECOTTO, Johnny (YV)

b. 25 January 1956, Caracas
18 Grands Prix

The son of Italian parents, Cecotto's garage owning father, a former Venezuelan champion, bought him a 750cc Honda-4 on which he contested his first races. He was then offered the use of a 750cc ex-works Kawasaki and his form on this machine led to an offer from the Venezu-elan Yamaha importers who launched him on the way to World Championship glory. He won the 350cc title in 1975 and the 750cc category crown in 1978. He switched to cars with an F2 Minardi in 1981, moving to March the following year to take a close second place in the European Championship behind Corrado Fabi. He moved into F1 with an uncompetitive Theodore in 1983, then to Toleman alongside Ayrton Senna the following year only to break his legs in a major accident during British GP practice at Brands Hatch. He switched to touring cars with BMW thereafter and is based at Treviso in Italy with his wife Martina and son Johnny-Amadeus.

CEVERT, François (F)

b. 24 February 1944, Paris
d. 6 October 1973, Watkins Glen
47 Grands Prix; 1 win
Career span: 1970–3 (Tyrrell)

The glamorous son of a Paris jeweller, this dazzling Frenchman made his name at the wheel of an F3 Matra before graduating into F2 in 1969 with a Tecno.

The charismatic François Cevert at the wheel of his Tyrrell 006 at Watkins Glen in 1973, the weekend on which he was killed.

Picked by Ken Tyrrell as successor to Johnny Servoz-Gavin after his abrupt mid-season retirement in 1970, Cevert spent the next three seasons as a loyal and devoted pupil of Jackie Stewart, maturing from strong number two to front-line contender.

He won the 1971 United States Grand Prix at Watkins Glen thanks to a combination of good luck and flawless driving, but by 1973 his talent was close to its peak and Stewart acknowledged that he was actually quicker than he in some of the mid-season races – notably the German GP at Nurburgring where Jackie scored the last win of his career.

Cervert was being groomed to take over the Tyrrell team leadership in 1974 on Stewart's retirement, but hopes for a seamless transition were dashed when François was killed in a very violent accident during practice for the US Grand Prix at Watkins Glen. The team withdrew from what should have been Jackie's final race, but the long-term consequences of Cevert's death denied Tyrrell's organization the chance of sustaining its competitive momentum into the mid-1970s.

CHABOUD, Eugene (F)

b. 12 April 1907, Lyons
d. 28 December 1983, Montfermeil
3 Grands Prix

This French veteran won the 1946 Belgian GP with a Delahaye and had a handful of Talbot-Lago outings in Championship events, his best placing being fifth at Reims in 1950.

CHAMBERLAIN, Jay (USA)

1 Grand Prix

This early Lotus sports car privateer met Colin Chapman at Sebring in 1956 and later became the US Lotus franchisee in the USA before the relationship collapsed amongst legal recriminations. Badly injured in the 1957 Reims 12-hour sports car race, he later ran a four-cylinder Climax-engined Lotus 18 in the 1962 British Grand Prix under the Ecurie Excelsior banner.

CHARLTON, Dave (ZA)

b. 27 October 1936, Yorkshire
11 Grands Prix

A cat-loving South African who took over John Love's mantle as the South African domestic F1 man to beat in early 1970s, Charlton ran Lotus 49, Lotus 72 and McLaren M23 equipment. He did the 1971 British Grand Prix with a works Lotus 72 which blew its engine virtually on the starting grid, and then bought one of the works cars himself which he brought back for a brief, but unsuccessful two-race European tour the following summer.

CHEEVER, Eddie (USA)

b. 10 January 1958, Phoenix, Arizona
132 Grands Prix
Career span: 1979 (Hesketh); 1980 (Osella); 1981 (Tyrrell); 1982 (Ligier); 1983 (Renault); 1984–5 (Alfa Romeo); 1986 (Lola); 1987–9 (Arrows)

Enormously popular and likeable, yet often highly strung and somewhat paranoid, this American driver grew up in Italy where he cut his competitive teeth in kart racing during his early teens. It seemed that Eddie might be a true motor racing prodigy – indeed, there were rumours that he was actually under seventeen when he made his F3 début – but he never quite scaled the heights of achievement promised by those early exploits.

Cheever made his F1 début for Hesketh in a one-off outing in South Africa at the start of 1978, but it was not until 1980 that he became a full-time member of the Grand Prix fraternity when his F2 entrant Enzo Osella graduated to the big time. He spent 1981 with Tyrrell, finishing fifth in the German GP, then switched to Ligier the following year to finish second in Detroit.

In 1983 he got his biggest break as a member of the Renault team, alongside Alain Prost, notching up an excellent second in Canada and third in France. At that time some people were rather ambivalent about Prost's potential, so in retrospect Cheever shaped up rather better than was perhaps appreciated at the time. Two disastrous years followed at Alfa Romeo and he was out of F1 in 1986 – apart from a guest outing for the Haas-Lola team at Detroit – before returning for a three-year stint with Arrows.

At the end of 1989 Cheever realized that his F1 career was stuck in a rut. Rather than wait for the inevitable decline to set in, he turned his back on the F1 Championship and began to build himself a career in US Indy racing. In 1992, Cheever qualified second on the grid for the Indianapolis 500, and finished fourth on only his third attempt at this US classic event.

CHIMERI, Ettore (YV)

d. 27 February 1960, Cuba
1 Grand Prix

This Venezuelan amateur drove an elderly and worn Maserati 250F in the 1960 Argentinian Grand Prix and was killed three weeks later while practising for the second round of the World Sports Car Championship in Cuba.

CHIRON, Louis (MC)

b. 1 August 1899, Monaco
d. 22 June 1979
15 Grands Prix
Career span: 1950 (Maserati); 1951 (Maserati and Talbot); 1953 (Osca); 1955 (Lancia)

Although Tazio Nuvolari claimed the distinction of being the oldest Grand Prix winner, triumphing in the 1939 Yugoslav Grand Prix at Belgrade at the age of forty-six, it is the debonair Chiron who holds the record of being the oldest driver ever to contest a World Championship Grand Epreuve. He was a few weeks short of his fifty-sixth birthday when he drove a Lancia D50 into sixth place in the 1955 Monaco Grand Prix, twenty-four years after winning the classic race at the wheel of a Bugatti.

Chiron's great days came prior to World War II. Born in Monaco just before the turn of the century, he was to benefit from dual nationality as his father was a Frenchman who became *maître d'hotel* at the very swanky Hotel de Paris in the principality. During World War I Louis served briefly as a chauffeur for the marshals Foch and Petain and, by 1923, had saved sufficient cash to purchase a 1½-litre Bugatti, the marque with which his name was to become synonymous.

An attractive man and something of a socialite, his affair with Alice 'Baby' Hoffman, the wife of Swiss industrialist Freddy Hoffman, scion of the Hoffman-LaRoche pharmaceutical empire was the talk of the Grand Prix pit lanes in the early 1930s. As a result, the Hoffmans' marriage broke up, but Chiron turned out to be so tardy in committing himself to his new amour that she eventually found solace in the arms of Rudi Caracciola, becoming the famous German driver's second wife.

Clearly, this did not bother Caracciola as, during World War II, Chiron spent some time living with Rudi and 'Baby' in Lugano before marrying a Swiss girl. Despite being almost fifty years old when racing began seriously after the war, Louis returned to the F1 cockpit in a Lago Talbot, winning the 1947 and 1949 French Grands Prix and finishing second at Monaco in 1948.

By the time the official World Championship began, Chiron was well past his best, but picked up a few decent top six results with Maserati in 1950 and 1951. Thereafter, he gradually wound down his racing involvement, taking part in a couple of races with an Osca in 1953 before making that impressive final effort for Lancia in front of his home crowd two years later.

For many years afterwards, Chiron was Clerk of the Course for the Monaco Grand Prix, only relinquishing this task to another ex-Grand Prix ace, Paul Frère, in the late 1960s. But he continued to appear, immaculately dressed and looking very dignified, right up until the 1979 Monaco race, a few weeks before his death, which severed yet another link back to the pioneering days of motor sport.

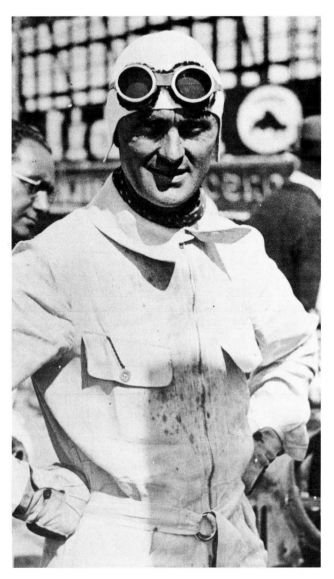

Louis Chiron was a star of the 1930s who kept his F1 career flickering into the 1950s.

CLAES, Johnny (B)

b. 11 August 1916
d. 3 February 1956
23 Grands Prix

A gregarious Anglophile who was a keen amateur racer and saxophone player with his own band, Johnny Claes and his Clay Pigeons. He raced Talbots, Maseratis and Connaughts before dying of cancer early in 1956. The best result of his career was seventh place in the 1951 Belgian GP at Spa-Francorchamps in a Talbot-Lago T26-DA, three laps behind Farina's winning Ferrari.

CLARK, Jim (GB)

b. 14 March 1936, Kilmany, Fife
d. 7 April 1968, Hockenheim
72 Grands Prix; 25 wins; World Champion 1963 and 1965
Career span: 1960–8 (Lotus)

Jim Clark was the last of the great sporting Grand Prix heroes, and his death, at the wheel of a Lotus 48 during a minor league Formula 2 race at Hockenheim, marked a watershed in the history of the sport. This mild-mannered Scottish border farmer had started racing for fun in the late 1950s, rose to be acknowledged as one of the most naturally gifted drivers of all time, and yet the taste of fame never robbed Jim Clark of his reserved, almost shy public face.

Clark's competition career began in 1956 at the wheel of a Sunbeam Talbot 90 saloon in which he contested various club rallies and driving tests through the Berwickshire countryside close to his family's farm, Edington Mains, at Chirnside, near Duns. His friend and mentor, Ian Scott-Watson, subsequently furnished him with a Porsche 356 for club racing events and, by 1958, he had graduated to a Jaguar D-type entered by Border Reivers, a private team of local Scottish enthusiasts.

At the end of 1958, Ian Scott-Watson ordered one of the sensational new Lotus Elite sports cars from Colin Chapman's fledgeling company and Clark was entered to give it its race début in the prestigious Boxing Day meeting at Brands Hatch. To the amazement of Chapman, himself an

(*Above*) Jim Clark as many people recall this genius: serene, confident and relaxed.

(*Top right*) The master at work: Clark's facial expression reflects the precarious handling of the Lotus 43-BRM H-16 during the 1966 Oulton Park Gold Cup.

(*Left*) Portrait of an artist: Jim Clark looks preoccupied as he awaits the start.

accomplished driver who was also driving an Elite in this event, the young Scot fought his way to the front of the pack. Only a tangle with a backmarker thwarted Clark's chances of victory and Chapman ducked through to win. But the Lotus boss had made a strong mental note that Jim Clark's was a name to watch.

In 1960 Clark was invited to join the Team Lotus Formula Junior team and quickly mastered this nursery of F1 talent. He had originally intended to drive for the Aston Martin F1 team, but this effort ran out of steam before Jim took a turn behind the wheel, and Chapman invited him to make his Grand Prix début with a works Lotus 18 in the 1960 Dutch Grand Prix where he ran fourth before his gearbox seized.

From then on, Clark would drive exclusively for Lotus throughout his career. At the end of the 1961 it was fellow Scot, Innes Ireland, who scored Team Lotus's maiden Grand Prix victory in the US race at Watkins Glen, but Chapman could see that Clark had much greater long-term potential and fired the hapless Ireland a few weeks later. This caused great personal resentment with Innes who, much to his regret, never made his peace with Clark in the six-and-a-half remaining years Jimmy lived.

By 1962, armed with the superb Climax V8-engined Lotus 24, Clark took the Grand Prix scene by storm. He came within an ace of winning the World Championship that year, only an engine oil leak in the South African Grand Prix handing the title to BRM-mounted rival Graham Hill. Although he only won the Championship in 1963 and 1965, the fact is that he dominated the final four seasons of the 1½-litre F1 in a manner only equalled by Alain Prost and Ayrton Senna in the late 1980s.

Clark and Chapman enjoyed a personal affinity which bordered on telepathy. They were like brothers. The onset of the new 3-litre F1 left Lotus scratching for a new source of engine supply in 1966, but Jim still managed to scrape a victory in the US Grand Prix in the makeweight Lotus 43 with its complex BRM H-16 engine. In 1967, the Cosworth DFV-propelled Lotus 49 exploded on to the scene at Zandvoort and Clark won four races that summer, although the title went to Denny Hulme.

Jim opened 1968 with a record twenty-fifth career victory in the South African Grand Prix at Kyalami, thereby beating Fangio's twenty-four wins. Three months later, he was dead. The motor racing world was rocked to the core. Clark had been regarded as inviolate; if it could happen to Jimmy, then nobody was safe. Thousands of respectful fans besieged the church in Chirnside for his funeral and, to this day, enthusiasts from all over the world regularly make a pilgrimage to that tiny Scottish village and pay silent tribute to the driver still regarded as 'the best' by those he mesmerized with his magic at the wheel.

COLLINS, Peter (GB)

b. 8 November 1931, Mustow Green, near Kidderminster
d. 3 August 1958, Nurburgring
32 Grands Prix; 3 wins
Career span: 1952–3 (HWM); 1954 (Vanwall); 1955 (Maserati);
1956–8 (Ferrari)

This genial young Englishman with the film-star good
looks was poised on the verge of becoming the United
Kingdom's first World Champion when he relinquished
his Lancia-Ferrari to team leader Juan Manuel Fangio during the course of the 1956 Italian Grand Prix at Monza.
Having already won the French and Belgian Grands Prix
that summer he had established himself as a world class
racing driver of formidable ability, but privately believed
there was still plenty of time for him to realize his great
ambition.

Born the son of a successful Kidderminster motor
trader, Peter Collins cut his racing teeth in the rough and
tumble of 500cc Formula 3 as a contemporary of Stirling
Moss in the immediate post-war years. He partnered Stirling in the precariously financed HWM team in 1951, and

Three views of the gifted Peter Collins, so nearly Britain's first
World Champion in 1956. *Above:* with Fangio and Hawthorn
on the rostrum after the Argentinian ace had beaten the two
Englishmen in the 1957 German Grand Prix. *Below:* battling
the 1956 Lancia Ferrari round a Monaco hairpin. *Right:*
hurtling down the hill at Rouen in 1957 with the Ferrari 801,
final metamorphosis of the Lancia D50.

dallied with BRM and Vanwall before joining the Ferrari team at the start of the 1956 season.

His victories at Spa and Reims put him in a commanding position to challenge for the Championship, but after Fangio's Ferrari suffered a steering arm breakage at Monza, Collins willingly yielded his own car, something which Italy's Luigi Musso had singularly failed to do a few laps earlier as team orders theoretically dictated.

Peter was not strictly required to follow this course of action, but he spontaneously obliged. It was a gesture which guaranteed him enormous affection amongst the passionate Italian motor racing fans, as well as considerable respect from Enzo Ferrari, not a man to become overly sentimental about his drivers.

In 1957 he was joined at Ferrari by Mike Hawthorn and the two men quickly forged a close personal bond, getting up to all sorts of outrageous off-track pranks and deriving a great deal of sheer fun from their motor racing. They nicknamed each other 'Mon Ami Mate' after a character in a contemporary newspaper cartoon strip.

Although Collins won non-championship events at Syracuse and Naples, there were no Grand Prix victories destined to come Ferrari's way in 1957. Nevertheless, Peter finished a strong third in the German Grand Prix behind Fangio and Hawthorn after the two Englishmen had battled vainly to keep the veteran Argentinian at bay on the day of his finest personal victory.

In 1957 Peter married an American girl, Louise King, and together they made a golden couple, living an enviable life-style based on a yacht in Monaco harbour. Despite a shaky start to the season, Collins took the new Dino 246 to third place at Monaco and then built up the momentum of his World Championship challenge with a commanding triumph in the British Grand Prix at Silverstone.

Two weeks later, the Ferrari Dinos were really up against it battling with the Vanwalls at Nurburgring, and it was on the famous German track, battling to keep pace with Tony Brooks's leading green machine, that Collins lost control on the climbing right-hander at Pflanzgarten. In Hawthorn's full view, he spun off the road and disappeared over a bank in a cloud of dust.

Hawthorn, worried sick, drove on like an automaton, fearing the worst. He was right to do so. Peter had been thrown out and suffered grievous head injuries. Despite being flown by helicopter to hospital in Cologne, he died shortly afterwards.

COLLOMB, Bernard (F)

b. 7 October 1930
4 Grands Prix

A garage owner from Nice, Collomb ran in four Grands Prix between 1961 and 1963, initially using a Cooper-Climax and later a similarly powered Lotus 24.

COMAS, Erik (F)

b. 28 September 1963, Romans
13 Grands Prix

Winner of the 1988 French F3 Championship, this former kartist was runner-up in the 1989 International F3000 Championship with a DAMS team Lola before clinching the title in a similar car the following year. He made his F1 début for Ligier in 1991 as team-mate to Thierry Boutsen.

COMOTTI, Gianfranco (I)

b. 24 July 1906
d. 10 May 1963
2 Grands Prix

A regular competitor in the Scuderia Ferrari days with Alfa Romeo in the early 1930s, he fleetingly appeared in F1 driving a Ferrari.

CONSTANTINE, George (USA)

b. 22 February 1918
1 Grand Prix

This American amateur competed in the 1959 US Grand Prix at Sebring at the wheel of a Cooper-Climax. Described as a 'Civil Defence Director' from Southbridge, Massachussetts, he had previously won the Watkins Glen GP with a Jaguar D-type.

CORDTS, John (CDN)

1 Grand Prix

A privateer who drove his own Brabham-Climax in the 1969 Canadian Grand Prix at Mosport Park.

COURAGE, Piers (GB)

b. 27 May 1942
d. 21 June 1970, Zandvoort
28 Grands Prix
Career span: 1967–8 (BRM); 1969 (Brabham); 1970 (de Tomaso)

Born into the famous brewing dynasty, this Eton-educated son of an Essex farmer was maturing into one of the most assured performers of his era when he was killed at the wheel of the Frank Williams team de Tomaso in the Dutch Grand Prix. It was a devastating blow, for Piers had played a crucial part in putting the Williams team on the map as a serious F1 proposition, and the after-effects of his death were felt by Frank for many years.

Courage was a product of the 1-litre F3 rough and tumble of the mid-1960s and there were times when it definitely seemed as though his ambition outstripped his judgement. Taken into the BRM team prematurely in 1967, his penchant for accidents almost stopped his career before it had seriously started. Only a successful run in the 1968 Tasman Championship, where he took his privately operated McLaren M4A F2 car to a brilliant win in the final rain-soaked event at Longford, Tasmania, restored his professional credibility.

He joined the works-supported Parnell Racing BRM team for 1968, scoring his first Championship point in the rain at the French Grand Prix in Rouen. At the same time he was campaigning an F2 Brabham for Williams on the European Championship circuit, and when Frank decided to move up into F1 the following year, Courage was delighted to stay with him as the driver.

The immaculate dark blue Williams Brabham BT26 made a terrific impact throughout 1969, proving that a well-run private operation could seriously shake a stick at the factory teams. Piers drove superbly to finish second at both Monaco and Watkins Glen, but his performance at

Cheery Piers Courage put 100 per cent effort into driving for Frank Williams, but sadly was to be killed in the 1970 Dutch Grand Prix.

Monza, where he stayed with the leading bunch for much of the race, was judged even more impressive. Only when fuel starvation problems intervened did he drop away to finish fifth.

Buoyed up with optimism, Frank Williams decided to expand his F1 operation for 1970. He entered into an arrangement with Alessandro de Tomaso whereby the Italian-based constructor would build and supply a completely new chassis which the Williams team would run for Piers. It was beginning to show considerable promise, running midfield at Zandvoort, when Piers inexplicably crashed. The car erupted in flames and he never stood a chance.

Courage was married to Lady Sarah Curzon, daughter of motor racing pioneer Earl Howe who had died in 1964 when she was barely out of her teens, and left two sons. Lady Sarah subsequently remarried to wildlife conservationist and professional gambler John Aspinall.

CRAFT, Chris (GB)

b. 17 November 1939
1 Grand Prix

An accomplished British national saloon car racer, Craft drove an ex-works Brabham BT33 in the 1971 US Grand Prix under Alain de Cadenet's Ecurie Evergreen banner.

CRAWFORD, Jim (GB)

b. 13 February 1948
2 Grands Prix

This mid-1970s F/Atlantic front runner had a couple of GP rides for Team Lotus during the absolute nadir of the type 72's fortunes in mid-1975. He is now an experienced hand at Indianapolis.

CREUS, Antonio (RA)

1 Grand Prix

A privateer who drove an elderly Maserati in the 1960 Argentine Grand Prix, retiring with heat exhaustion.

CROOK, Anthony (GB)

b. 16 February 1920, Manchester
2 Grands Prix

The owner of Bristol Cars and a keen semi-professional racer, Crook took part in the 1952 and 1953 British Grands Prix in a Frazer Nash 421–BMW and a Cooper-Bristol respectively.

CROSSLEY, Geoffrey (GB)

b. 11 May 1921
2 Grands Prix

He drove an Alta in the 1950 Belgian and British Grands Prix.

DAIGH, Chuck (US)

b. 29 November 1933
3 Grands Prix

This excellent engineer/driver was a close confederate of Lance Reventlow in the Scarab F1 venture and managed to qualify one of the cars for the 1960 Belgian and US Grands Prix, actually getting it to the finish in the latter event. He punctuated this troubled programme with a run in a Cooper-Climax in the British GP.

DALMAS, Yannick (F)

b. 28 July 1961, Toulon
22 Grands Prix
Career span: 1987–9 (Larrousse-Lola); 1990–1 (AGS)

Another graduate of the French F3 Championship, Dalmas won the Monaco GP F3 classic in 1986 and seemed destined for considerable F1 success, finishing

Yannick Dalmas showed initial flair in F1, but illness took the edge off his ability.

fifth at Adelaide in 1987. His confidence was shaken by a succession of bad accidents the following year and he never seemed quite the same driver after suffering a bout of Legionnaire's disease towards the end of 1988. He rejoined Larrousse at the start of 1989, but soon switched to AGS with whom he got nowhere. He switched to the Peugeot sports car team for 1991.

DALLY, Derek (IRL)

DALY, Derek (IRL)

b. 11 March 1953, Dublin
49 Grands Prix
Career span: 1978 (Hesketh and Ensign); 1979 (Ensign); 1980
(Tyrrell); 1981 (March); 1982 (Williams)

Daly was brought up in the cut and thrust of British national FF and F3 competition, having worked in Australian tin mines to bankroll his early racing. He made his F1 début with Hesketh and Ensign in the 1978–9 season before getting his big break with Tyrrell the following year, finishing fourth in the Argentine and British GPs. He lost momentum in 1981 with a switch to the uncompetitive RAM team, but was drafted back into front line F1 the

Lively and confident, Derek Daly had a stint as a works Williams driver at the wheel of the Cosworth-engined FW08 during the 1982 season.

following year with Williams after Carlos Reutemann's retirement. A good racer with the gift of the gab and a convivial personality, and let down only by his lack of speed in qualifying, Daly was eclipsed by team-mate Keke Rosberg and thereafter continued his career in Indy cars and endurance events, notably with Jaguar.

DANNER, Christian (D)

b. 4 April 1958
36 Grands Prix

From the ranks of a BMW-blessed crop of the mid-1980s, Danner was an extremely successful touring car exponent who transferred that talent to Formula 3000, winning the 1985 European Championship, and graduated to F1 with Zakspeed at the end of that year. He drove for Arrows in 1986 after Marc Surer was badly injured in a rally accident, finishing sixth in Austria, then switched to Zakspeed with Martin Brundle in 1987. His best result was a fourth place at Phoenix in 1989 at the wheel of former ATS boss Gunther Schmid's Rial, a few races before falling out with the individualistic team owner.

The cheerful Christian Danner never enjoyed decently competitive machinery during his intermittent F1 career.

DAPONTE, Jorge (RA)

b. 5 June 1923
d. March 1963
2 Grands Prix

Drove a private Maserati in the 1954 Argentine and Italian Grands Prix.

DA SILVA RAMOS, Hernando (F/BR)

b. 7 December 1925, Paris
7 Grands Prix
Career span: 1955–6 (Gordini)

The son of a wealthy businessman who raced a Bugatti in the 1930s, da Silva Ramos held dual French and Brazilian nationality and made his race début in 1947 at a series of races for MG TCs in Rio de Janeiro. He was a steady Gordini driver for three seasons through to his retirement in 1957. Now living near Biarritz.

DAVIS, Colin (GB)

b. 29 July 1932, London
2 Grands Prix

Colin Davis was the advertising executive son of the legendary SCH 'Sammy' Davis, one of the 'Bentley Boys', who later became the most famous of sports editors for the prestigious *Autocar* magazine. He competed in the 1959 French and Italian Grands Prix in a Scuderia Centro-Sud Cooper-Maserati and subsequently won the 1964 Targa Florio, sharing a Porsche 904 with Antonio Pucci.

DE ADAMICH, Andrea (I)

b. 3 October 1941, Trieste
30 Grands Prix
Career span: 1968 (Ferrari); 1970 (McLaren); 1971 (March);
1972 (Surtees); 1973 (Brabham)

Tall and friendly, the bestpectacled de Adamich began racing whilst still a law student, making his name driving for the works-backed Autodelta Alfa Romeo team in the European Touring Car Championship which he won in 1966 with a GTA coupé. He attracted Ferrari's attention with some promising runs in an Alfa T33 sports car, and was recruited to the F1 team for the non-championship 1967 Spanish GP at Jarama.

The following year he was scheduled to drive full-time alongside Amon and Ickx, but crashed during practice for the Brands Hatch Race of Champions and suffered neck injuries. He returned to win the Argentine Temporada series the following winter with the powerful F2 Ferrari Dino 166.

DE ANGELIS, Elio (I)

b. 26 March 1958, Rome
d. 15 May 1986, Marseilles
108 Grands Prix; 2 wins
Career span: 1979 (Shadow); 1980–85 (Lotus); 1986 (Brabham)

Civilized, cultured and impeccably mannered, Elio de Angelis drove racing cars with the same natural fluidity, feel and precision as he played classical music on the piano. He was twenty years old when he made his F1 début at the wheel of a Shadow DN9B in the 1979 Argentine GP at Buenos Aires, but by that stage the team was in a decline and the promising Italian new boy switched to Lotus at the start of the following year.

In 1980 his best result was a storming second place behind René Arnoux's Renault in the Brazilian GP at Interlagos, and when his team-mate Mario Andretti moved to Alfa Romeo in 1981, Elio found himself partnered with Nigel Mansell. A tense rivalry built up between the two men who, though poles apart in terms of personality, were each determined to lay claim to number one status.

In 1982 de Angelis made his mark in the history books when he won Lotus's first GP victory since the glorious days of Mario Andretti and the ground-effect type 79 four years earlier. After a nail-biting last lap, he held off Keke Rosberg's Williams to win the Austrian GP by a wheel. It was the last Lotus win to be witnessed by Colin Chapman who died suddenly from a heart attack the following December, leaving Elio with the feeling that he had lost a father figure.

In 1983 Lotus was in a transitional phase, switching to Renault turbo power with more than a few glitches along the way. But in 1984 de Angelis had a simply superb year with the Gerard Ducarouge-designed Lotus 94T. Battling against the McLaren-TAGs of Prost and Lauda, Elio's consistency paid off to the point where he sustained an outside challenge for the Championship through to the late summer before a spate of mechanical failures blighted his progress.

In 1985 Mansell was replaced by Ayrton Senna, a man who clearly had world championship potential. Although

Elio de Angelis was a stylish gentleman, both in and out of the cockpit. *Right:* in action with the Lotus 81 leading Ricardo Zunino's Brabham during the 1981 Belgian Grand Prix at Zolder.

Ayrton was content with joint number one status for his first season at Lotus, he quickly asserted himself as the more convincing performer. However, Elio won the San Marino GP, a lucky victory inherited when Prost's

The 1970 season saw him struggling with the Milan company's underpowered V8 engine installed in a McLaren chassis, and a similar arrangement followed for 1971 when he was in partnership with March. In 1972 he turned to Team Surtees, running a third works TS9B in which he scored the best results of his F1 career to date with fourth place in Spain. Switching to Brabham he duplicated that result in the 1973 Belgian GP before suffering a badly broken leg in the multiple pile-up at Woodcote corner which brought that year's British Grand Prix at Silverstone to a premature halt.

That was the end of de Adamich's professional career, but he remains around the Grand Prix scene as a popular and respected television commentator.

DE BEAUFORT, Carel Godin (NL)

b. 10 April 1934, Maarsbergen
d. 3 August 1964, Nurburgring
28 Grands Prix
Career span: 1957–8 (Porsche); 1959 (Porsche and Maserati); 1960 (Cooper F2); 1961–4 (Porsche)

McLaren was excluded for failing the post-race weight check. Then Senna won in both Portugal and Belgium, making it clear to Elio that if he wanted to stay on in 1986 it would have to be in a subordinate role.

De Angelis accepted what amounted to an invitation to seek his fortune elsewhere, He joined compatriot Riccardo Patrese in Bernie Ecclestone's Brabham-BMW line-up, struggling with the complex 'low-line' type BT55. The week after the Monaco GP he journeyed along the Mediterranean coast to Paul Ricard for a routine test session.

Going into the 180mph (290kph) flat-out kink beyond the pits, the car suffered a component breakage and crashed heavily. Grand Prix racing's last gentleman player died of his injuries a few hours later in a Marseilles hospital.

This tall, broad-shouldered Dutch Count started erratically in F2 but later gained much respect for the way he drove his elderly four-cylinder Porsche, the only contemporary F1 car in which he could insert his large frame. Trying desperately to qualify for the 1964 German Grand Prix, he crashed heavily at the Bergwerk corner, dying in hospital three days later from his injuries. It was a sad end to the career of this genial amateur who, although regarded as something of a dilettante in his early years, had matured into a competent and responsible competitor by the time of his death.

DE CESARIS, Andrea (I)

b. 31 May 1959, Rome
165 Grands Prix
Career span: 1980 (Alfa Romeo); 1981 (McLaren); 1982–3 (Alfa Romeo); 1984–5 (Ligier); 1986 (Minardi); 1987 (Brabham); 1988 (Rial); 1989–90 (Dallara); 1991 (Jordan)

This Italian driver's career has been characterized by more than a degree of unpredictability, stemming in part from the disconcerting nervous facial twitch which has always

51

worried his rivals. Some days de Cesaris will drive with a disciplined assurance and flair; on others he displays an erratic over-aggression which makes him a hazard to his fellow competitors.

He has been sustained in the business largely through contacts with Marlboro, the multi-national tobacco giant which has been F1 racing's biggest sponsor over the last two decades. Andrea's Grand Prix début came at Montreal in 1980 at the wheel of an Alfa Romeo, after which he was recruited into the McLaren International line-up for 1981.

Unfortunately, Andrea's impetuosity triggered a considerable number of silly accidents and there was no way in which he was going to be retained for 1982 with Niki Lauda on offer. He switched back to Alfa Romeo for two years, scoring his best results with second places in the 1983 German and South African races. Then it was off to Ligier for 1984 and 1985, followed by Minardi, Brabham and Rial in unproductively quick succession.

After two years of driving the Scuderia Italia Dallaras, Andrea switched to Jordan for the start of the 1991 season and almost bagged a second place to Senna's McLaren in the Belgian GP at Spa. But the end of the season saw him

Sponsorship support kept the genial de Cesaris in F1 even when his perceived form made his place hard to justify.

out of work again – and no nearer winning his first Grand Prix.

DE FILLIPIS, Maria Teresa (I)

b. 11 November 1926
3 Grands Prix
Career span: 1958 (Maserati); 1959 (Porsche)

This attractive woman from Rome raced six-cylinder Maserati sports cars before trying a 250F in the 1958 Belgian, Portuguese and Italian Grands Prix. She retired after failing to qualify at Monaco with an F2 Porsche the following year.

DE GRAFFENRIED, Emmanuel (CH)

b. 18 May 1914, Lausanne
22 Grands Prix
Career span: 1950 (Maserati and Alfa Romeo); 1951–6 (Maserati)

The dapper, trim profile of 'Toulo' de Graffenried continues to be a familiar sight in the European Grand Prix paddocks more than forty years since he won the second post-war British Grand Prix at Silverstone in 1949.

In the early 1930s he raced his own private 1½-litre Maserati in national events at Berne's Bremgarten circuit, striking out to take in overseas events in partnership with an old school friend, John de Puy. In the immediate post-war years he teamed up alongside Bira in Enrico Plate's team of Maserati 4CLTs during which he won his memorable victory at Silverstone. He stayed with Maserati right through to the end of his F1 career, interrupted only by three outings in an Alfa 158 during the summer of 1951, including his home race at Berne.

In 1953 he scored his best placing in a World Championship Grand Prix with fourth place at Spa, now driving an F2 Maserati for the Plate team. His final F1 outing came with a Maserati 250F at Monza in 1956 after which his career petered out, but not before coming out of semi-retirement in order to double for Kirk Douglas in action scenes during the making of the film *The Racers*.

In retirement, Baron de Graffenried continued his successful Lausanne-based garage which had sold Alfa Romeos since 1950 as well as selling Rolls-Royces and, between 1959 and 1967, was also a Ferrari dealership. In the early 1970s he started attending races as an ambassador for the Lausanne-based Philip Morris tobacco concern who have become the biggest commercial sponsor in Grand Prix racing over the last two decades through their Marlboro brand.

De Graffenried was a major force in the 'retrospective' staged at the 1974 French Grand Prix at Dijon-Prenois, which brought together many racing stars of the past for a memorable reunion.

International bobsleighing ace, jockey, racing driver, all-round sportsman and lothario, the Marquis de Portago at the wheel of a Lancia-Ferrari in the pits at Silverstone during practice for the 1956 British Grand Prix.

DE PORTAGO, Alfonso (E)

b. 11 October 1928, London
d. 12 May 1957, Mille Miglia
5 Grands Prix
Career span: 1956–7 (Ferrari)

His full name was Don Alfonso Cabeza de Vaca y Leighton, 17th Marquis de Portago, and he was the son of a Spanish nobleman by his marriage to Olga Leighton, a one-time Irish nurse who was the widow and heir of Frank J Mackey, founder of the Household Finance company. Raised in Biarritz while his father fought for Franco in the Spanish Civil War, 'Fon' developed into a fine all-round sportsman, riding twice in the Grand National and once qualifying for the Spanish Olympic bobsleigh team. He was a tremendously attractive, *dégagé* cosmopolitan who shared the second-place Lancia-Ferrari in the 1956 British Grand Prix. Sadly, he is more widely remembered for his death in the accident which resulted in the Mille Miglia being banned after nine spectators were scythed down by his wayward Ferrari.

DE TERRA, Max (CH)

b. 6 October 1918
d. January 1983
2 Grands Prix

A Swiss amateur who did his home Grand Prix in 1952 and 1953 in a Simca-Gordini and a Ferrari 166C respectively.

DE TOMASO, Alessandro (RA)

b. 10 July 1928
2 Grands Prix

An Argentinian entrepreneur best known for his own sports car company which he established at Modena and later sold to Ford. He subsequently took a controlling interest in Maserati.

DE TOURNACO, Charles (B)

b. 7 June 1927
d. 18 September 1953, Modena Aerautodrome
2 Grands Prix

This wealthy Belgian amateur racer was killed when he rolled his F2 Ferrari 500 whilst testing at Modena.

DE VILLOTA, Emilio (E)

b. 26 July 1946
2 Grands Prix

A Spanish journeyman who drove in the 1977 Spanish and Austrian GPs in a private McLaren M23. He drove a Williams FW07 in the 1980 Spanish GP (later stripped of its Championship status) where he distinguished himself by tripping up Laffite's Ligier and Reutemann's Williams in their dice for the lead.

DEPAILLER, Patrick (F)

b. 9 August 1944
1 August 1980, Hockenheim
95 Grands Prix; 2 wins
Career span: 1972, 1974–8 (Tyrrell); 1979 (Ligier); 1980 (Alfa Romeo)

This little Frenchman grew up inspired by the example of his compatriot Jean Behra and, like his hero, developed into a racing driver who lived for the moment, a man who believed that everything would work out all right in the end.

A typical example of this devil-may-care attitude was seen by Ken Tyrrell in the autumn of 1973. Having offered Patrick a chance at the wheel of a third car in his F1 team, for the end-of-season North American races, the Frenchman broke a leg while horsing around on a motorcycle. Fortunately, this gaffe did not prevent Patrick from being recruited into Ken's team on a full-time basis the following year, nominally replacing the late François Cevert. For

Depailler

C'est la vie! Patrick Depailler, that quintessential French sportsman cast in the Jean Behra mould.

the next five seasons, Depailler was a loyal and audacious member of the Tyrrell line-up, trying hard on every race outing and being rewarded for his efforts with a fine victory in the 1978 Monaco Grand Prix.

In 1979 he switched to Ligier, winning the Spanish GP at Jarama before suffering serious leg injuries in a hang gliding accident which invalided him out of racing for the rest of the season. He struggled back to fitness for the start of the 1980 season when he joined Alfa Romeo, and had totally recovered by the time he took part in a test session at Hockenheim in preparation for the German Grand Prix. A suspension breakage on the fastest part of the circuit caused him to crash fatally, robbing F1 of a driver totally committed to his profession through an abiding love of sporting values.

More than a decade later, his son Loic reached his eighteenth birthday. Asked by his mother what he would most like as a present, he asked for a dinner party with all his father's former team-mates. It was an enormously popular and emotional reunion.

DOLHEM, Jose (F)

b. 26 April 1944, Paris
d. 16 April 1988, nr St Etienne

Half-brother of Didier Pironi who drove a Surtees in the 1974 United States Grand Prix. He was killed in a private aeroplane crash.

DONNELLY, Martin (GB)

b. 26 March 1964, Belfast
14 Grands Prix

Quiet and introspective away from a racing car, this young Ulsterman was an outstanding performer in junior league single-seaters and won the prestigious 1988 Cellnet award as Britain's most promising driver after finishing third in the British F3 Championship for the second successive season. He drove for Eddie Jordan in F3000 through 1988 and 1989 before being selected to partner Derek Warwick in the F1 Lotus-Lamborghini line-up the following year. He was lucky to escape with his life when he crashed at high speed during practice for the Spanish GP at Jerez, sustaining multiple injuries from which he was still slowly recovering at the start of 1992.

Martin Donnelly's promising F1 career was cut short when his Lotus-Lamborghini crashed in practice for the 1990 Spanish Grand Prix.

Mark Donohue in good company.the versatile Penske driver (second from right) listens in company with Bruce McLaren and John Surtees while Phil Hill (left) holds court.

DONOHUE, Mark (USA)

b. 18 March 1937, Summit, New Jersey
d. 19 August 1975, Graz
14 Grands Prix

One of the great technical drivers of his era, Donohue won the Can-Am Championship in a Porsche and the Indy 500 in a McLaren – both fielded by his friend and mentor, Roger Penske – before the American team owner focused his attention on F1. The team started with its own car, but in mid-1975 switched to a customer March 751. During the race morning warm-up for the Austrian GP, Donohue suffered a tyre failure and crashed heavily on the fast right-hander beyond the pits at Österreichring. Despite initially sitting up and talking, it was soon clear that a blow on the head had inflicted severe brain injuries and Mark died in a Graz hospital three days later. His widow Eden subsequently pursued Goodyear with a multi-million dollar law suit which was later settled out of court.

D'OREY, Fritz (BR)

b. 25 March 1930
d. 1961
3 Grands Prix

A slow Maserati 250F operator who drove the Valerio Colotti revamped Tec-Mec – the final version of this famous front-engined GP car – in the 1959 US Grand Prix at Sebring.

DOWNING, Ken (GB)

b. 5 December 1917, Chesterton, Staffordshire
2 Grands Prix

A wealthy privateer and Lloyds underwriter with other extensive manufacturing, garage and transport interests, Downing drove a Connaught A-type in the 1952 British and Dutch Grands Prix. Now retired to Monaco, his daughter Anne (died 1980) was married to motor racing entrepreneur Paddy McNally, a colleague of contemporary Grand Prix overlord Bernie Ecclestone.

DRAKE, Bob (USA)

b. December, 1924
1 Grand Prix

Drake drove a Tec-Mec Maserati 250F derivative in the 1960 US Grand Prix, positively the last Championship showing for this front-engined Italian classic F1 machine.

DRIVER, Paddy (ZA)

b. 13 May 1934
1 Grand Prix

Driver was a top South African international motorcycle racer who drove a Team Gunston Lotus 72 in the 1974 South African GP at Kyalami.

DROGO, Piero (YV)

b. 8 August 1926
d. 28 April 1973
1 Grand Prix

The founder of the Italian-based coachbuilders which manufactured special bodies for Ferrari and Maseratis in early 1960s, Drogo finished eighth in the 1960 Italian GP at Monza in a F2 Cooper-Climax.

DUMFRIES, Johnny (GB)

b. 26 April 1958
15 Grands Prix

As Earl of Dumfries, heir to the Dukedom, Johnny was anxious to make his own way in life and motor racing was his chosen sport. He won the 1984 British F3 Championship and eventually secured a place alongside Ayrton Senna in the Lotus F1 team for 1986, a deal which he knew was unlikely to last beyond a year. He was right in his judgement, being replaced by Satoru Nakajima in 1987, since when his motor racing activities have been distinctly limited.

EATON, George (CDN)

b. 12 November 1945, Toronto
11 Grands Prix

The blond, baby-faced heir to the Candian department store fortune, Eaton rented a seat in the third works BRM for the 1970 season and proved extremely promising on several occasions. Esssentially a well-heeled amateur, he also had some unproductive outings in the ill-starred BRM P54 Group 7 sports car.

EDWARDS, Guy (GB)

b. 30 December 1942, Macclesfield
11 Grands Prix
Career span: 1974 (Lola); 1976 (Hesketh)

An enterprising and very commercially minded semi-professional, Edwards was a talented 2-litre sports car driver and an outstanding sponsorship negotiator. He raised finance to buy a place in the Embassy Hill Lola team for 1974, only to be summarily dismissed after injuring his wrist in a Formula 5000 accident. He was forced to sue Graham Hill as a result. He briefly drove a Hesketh in 1976 and has more recently concentrated on major sponsorship negotiations for organizations such as the TWR Jaguar sports car and Benetton F1 teams. At the start of 1992 he became Sponsorship Consultant to Team Lotus.

ELFORD, Vic (GB)

b. 10 June 1935, Peckham
13 Grands Prix
Career span: 1968 (Cooper); 1969 (Cooper and McLaren); 1971 (BRM)

This international works Ford rally star finished fourth on his GP début at Rouen in a Cooper-BRM T81C and drove for the team for the balance of that season. He drove the final Cooper GP outing at Monaco in 1969 in the Antique Automobiles-owned Maserati-engineed T81B before switching to a McLaren M7, but crashed heavily in the German GP and broke his arm. Thereafter his sole F1 outing was in a BRM P160 for the 1971 German GP.

EMERY, Paul (GB)

b. 12 November 1916, Chiswick, West London
1 Grand Prix

This indefatigable special builder from the 1950s built a wide variety of cars under the Emeryson banner, and competed in the 1956 British Grand Prix in one such Alta-engined machine.

ENGLAND, Paul (AUS)

b. 28 March 1929
1 Grand Prix

An Australian novice who contested the 1957 German GP at Nurburgring with a F2 Cooper-Climax. He had previously made his name racing in Australia with his superb Holden-engined Auscar sports car, a home-brewed Maserati A6GCH lookalike.

ERTL, Harald (A)

b. 31 August 1948
d. 7 April 1982 near Isle of Sylt
19 Grands Prix

This delightful personality sported an impeccable Inspector Clouseau-like moustache which he somehow managed to squeeze beneath his crash helmet! Basically a motoring journalist and amateur racer, Harald gained sufficient sponsorship to dabble in F1 with Hesketh between 1975 and 1977. He was killed tragically in a light aircraft accident near the Isle of Sylt whilst taking his family to their holiday home in northern Germany.

ESTEFANO, Nasif (RA)

b. 18 November 1932
d. 21 October 1973
1 Grand Prix

A contemporary of Alessandro de Tomaso, Estefano drove a Cooper in the 1960 Argentine Grand Prix and failed to qualify de Tomaso's first F1 car in the 1962 Italian race.

ÉTANÇELIN, Philippe (F)

b. 29 December 1896, Rouen
d. 13 October 1981
12 Grands Prix
Career span: 1950–1 (Talbot); 1952 (Maserati)

A wealthy farmer and wool merchant who won the GP de la Marne as long ago as 1927 for Bugatti, 'Phi-Phi' was always recognizable by his reversed check cap which he wore beneath his goggles in the immediate post-war era before crash hats became mandatory. After the war, he managed a couple of fifth places in a lumbering old 4½-litre Talbot Lago in 1950, and retired after the 1953 Rouen Grand Prix, a non-championship event which took place practically on his doorstep. He was a very active member of the Ançiens Pilote blue blazer brigade right up to his death in 1981.

EVANS, Bob (GB)

b. 11 June 1947
10 Grands Prix
Career span: 1975 (BRM); 1976 (Lotus and Brabham)

A cheerful ex-Formula Fordster, Bob Evans won the 1974 British Formula 5000 Championship at the wheel of a McKechnie team Lola. He briefly drove in F1 with the fading BRM team, plus the Lotus and RAM Brabham équipe before retiring to concentrate on his business activities which included a racewear manufacturing company.

FABI, Corrado (I)

b. 12 April 1961
12 Grands Prix

The younger brother of Teo Fabi, Corrado won the 1982 European F2 Championship at the wheel of a March-BMW, and shared the second Brabham-BMW with his sibling.

FABI, Teo (I)

b. 9 March 1955, Milan
64 Grands Prix
Career span: 1982 (Toleman); 1984 (Brabham); 1985 (Toleman); 1986–7 (Benetton)

Mild mannered and of monk-like mien, Teo shared the 1976 European karting championship with his brother Corrado and the late Elio de Angelis, thereby endorsing a talent which would carry him through to F1 with only fleeting success.

He graduated into front-line international racing via Formula Ford and F2, eventually moving into F1 with the Toleman team at the start of 1982. He stayed there for a single season before being replaced by compatriot Bruno Giacomelli, thereafter turning his hand to the US-based Indy car series and taking the 1983 series by storm. He started on pole position at Indianapolis, won four races and finished runner-up in the championship behind the infinitely more experienced Al Unser.

In 1984 he started the season alternating between Indy cars and F1, but eventually switched back to the Grand Prix scene as a full-time member of the Brabham squad. Disappointingly though, Fabi never achieved much in F1 despite displaying a great deal of promise. He returned to Toleman in 1985 and stayed on after the team was acquired by Benetton, contesting a full programme of Grands Prix throughout the following two years. However, he was eclipsed by team-mates Gerhard Berger and Thierry Boutsen respectively during 1986 and 1987, and eventually opted for a return to Indy cars with Porsche.

FABRE, Pascal (F)

b. 8 January 1960
11 Grands Prix

The first driver for the tiny AGS team in F1 who endured a hopeless season cast in the role as tail-ender throughout 1987.

FAGIOLI, Luigi (I)

b. 9 June 1898
d. 20 June 1952, Monaco
7 Grands Prix
Career span: 1950–1 (Alfa Romeo)

This Italian from a working class background worked his way into the Mercedes Grand Prix team during the early 1930s and then switched to Auto Union in 1937. He joined Alfa Romeo to race 158s in the immediate post-war period, then crashed his Lancia in practice for the 1952 Monaco sports car Grand Prix, breaking a leg. He died of medical complications just over three weeks later.

FANGIO, Juan Manuel (RA)

b. 24 June 1911, Balcarce
51 Grands Prix; 24 wins; World Champion 1951, 1954, 1955, 1956 and 1957
Career span: 1950–1 (Alfa Romeo); 1953 (Maserati); 1954 (Maserati and Mercedes Benz); 1956 (Ferrari); 1957–8 (Maserati)

It is not the fact that Fangio won twenty-four Grands Prix that is so amazing – Jim Clark, Jackie Stewart, Alain Prost, Niki Lauda, Nigel Mansell and Ayrton Senna all exceeded that total – it is the fact that he did so during a career which encompassed only fifty-one races. Thus the calm, serene man from the provincial Argentinian town won over 47 per cent of the Grands Prix he contested – over half of them from pole position – a statistic which will almost certainly remain unmatched in F1 history.

At the time of writing, Fangio has reached his eightieth birthday, yet he is still trim, dignified and radiates considerable presence. His occasional appearance at contemporary Grands Prix is akin to the arrival of royalty. Today's top drivers adopt a respectful demeanour when they shake hands with Grand Prix racing's most respected senior citizen.

Fangio came from humble beginnings. He never forgot them as he climbed the ladder of success, and he established his own racing car museum at Balcarce in recognition of his roots, many years after his retirement. One of the cars included in this collection is a Renault turbo once driven by Alain Prost. It is the great French driver's personal possession, yet Alain was pleased to donate it for display.

Fangio's father was an immigrant Italian who found work variously as a plasterer and a potato farmer. The young Juan went to work in a garage at the tender age of ten and almost succumbed to pneumonia when he was eighteen. Later as a mechanic, then as a driver, he built up his reputation in gruelling cross-country races throughout South America, in 1949 winning the 6,000-mile Grand Prix Nacionale del Norte, a race from Buenos Aires to the Peruvian capital, Lima, and back.

On an exploratory trip to Europe in the summer of 1948, Fangio tried a 1.4-litre Simca-Gordini at Reims, returning for a full programme the following year in a Maserati 4CLT/48 sponsored by the Argentinian government. Before setting off from home he used the car to win at Mar del Plata and then set about establishing a formidable reputation in Europe. Wins at Pau, San Remo, Perpignan, Marseille, Monza and Albi were more than sufficient to guarantee the 38-year-old a place in the works Alfa Romeo team when the red cars from Portello returned to the scene in 1950.

Fangio's first World Championship Grand Prix victory

The great man. Juan Manuel Fangio celebrating the victory of his Mercedes-Benz team-mate Stirling Moss after the 1955 British Grand Prix at Aintree. *Right*: a year later, Fangio looking sombre and thoughtful as he waits on the grid at Silverstone at the wheel of his Lancia Ferrari.

came at Monaco in 1950, followed up by similar successes at Spa and Reims. He finished the year second to his team-mate Farina in the final Championship placings. In 1951 he again won three races, but this time took the title, his first of five.

Alfa Romeo withdrew from Grand Prix racing at the end of 1951, so Fangio threw in his lot with Maserati, intending to start his season for the Italian manufacturer in the Grand Prix of the Monza Aerautodromo on 8 July. Prior to returning to Europe, an early season foray with an F2 Ferrari in Brazil, Uruguay and Argentina had seen him net six victories and he had also committed himself to driving the temperamental 1½-litre supercharged BRM V16 in certain selected events, although by now the World Championship was being run to F2 regulations and there were very few events run for Grand Prix cars proper.

One of these events for BRM was the Ulster Trophy at Dundrod on the day prior to his Monza début for Maserati. He had been promised a flight from Northern Ireland to Italy in Bira's private plane, but the Thai driver did not start and left ahead of him. Fangio eventually strug-

with a subtlety and finesse which others would find difficult to emulate in decades to follow.

In all, Fangio won four Grands Prix during 1955 to take his third Championship, then switched to Ferrari the following year after Mercedes quit motor racing in the wake of the Le Mans disaster. Unfortunately, he would find the Maranello environment disinctly less than congenial. Again, he won three races in Ferrari's bastardized evolution of the glorious Lancia D50, but after taking his fourth title he was only too happy to return to the Maserati fold for 1957 after Moss departed to lead the Vanwall team.

Fangio's last full season netted him wins in Argentina, and at Monaco, Reims and Nurburgring, the last triumph clinching his fifth World Championship as well as being the most amazing performance of his career. He was now forty-six years old, but in an electrifying affirmation of his masterly talent he recovered from a shambolic mid-race pit stop to catch and pass the Ferraris of Mike Hawthorn and Peter Collins, after one of the most sensational displays of driving virtuosity ever seen at Nurburgring or anywhere else.

Fangio started the 1958 season with Maserati, but it was clear that he was losing interest. He was fourth in Argentina and fourth again at Reims in only his second World Championship Grand Prix that season. Immediately after taking the chequered flag, he made his announcement. He would retire from the cockpit and rule off his racing career there and then.

It was a measure of the respect generated by this remarkable man that Mike Hawthorn, storming to victory at Reims in his Ferrari Dino 246, eased off in the closing stages to avoid lapping Fangio's Maserati before the finish. It was a small mark of respect from one of many who knew only too well the calibre of the man he was racing against.

Not that Fangio was soft or oversentimental. He was pragmatic; hard when he needed to be, but a sensitive and rather reserved gentleman away from the cockpit. He expected no favours and delivered few in return, but he had an overwhelming sense of sportsmanship and fair play.

For example, although he was moved almost to tears by Collins's generosity in handing over his Lancia-Ferrari at Monza in 1956, there was no way he would criticize Musso for failing to give up his steed. Encapsulated in that attitude is the essence of a man who remains revered and respected almost a quarter of a century after retiring from the cockpit.

Way back in the early 1950s, even before he drove for the famous German team, Fangio took on the Mercedes-Benz concession for Argentina. It was probably the best investment he ever made. He continues to this day as President of Mercedes-Benz Argentina and, despite heart surgery in the early 1980s, continues to travel the world with the zest of a man half his age.

gled to find a flight to Paris, via London, but Europe was swept by storms that weekend and he was left to drive an overnight marathon in a borrowed Renault to get to Italy in time for Sunday's race. Exhausted, he crashed badly, damaging a vertebra in his back, and was sidelined for the rest of the season.

Fangio came to regard this as a salutary lesson and he never made such a mistake again. By the start of 1953 he had recuperated sufficiently to take up his contract with Maserati and repaid their investment by scoring the only non-Ferrari victory of the season, much to their delight, in the Italian Grand Prix at Monza.

Mercedes-Benz signed him for 1954 and 1955, but he was permitted to drive for Maserati until the German Silver Arrows were ready to race at Reims. He bagged victories in Argentina and Belgium before forsaking the Italian marque and adding another four triumphs to his tally at the wheel of the finely engineered German cars. His second World Championship was now in the bag.

For 1955, Fangio found himself partnered with the young Stirling Moss, and a keen mutual respect, which happily endures to this day, quickly built up between the two men. When Stirling beat the 'Old Man' to win the British Grand Prix at Aintree, Fangio was gracious enough to let everybody believe he had been pipped at the post by his younger colleague. If he chose to concede, he did it

FAIRMAN, Jack (GB)

b. 15 March 1913, Smallfield, Surrey
12 Grands Prix
Career span: 1953 (HWM); 1955–6 (Connaught); 1957 (BRM);
1958 (Connaught); 1959–60 (Cooper); 1961 (Ferguson and
Cooper)

A second division F1 driver, who ran his family's precision
tool manufacturing company, Fairman displayed more
determination than flair and achieved a couple of top six
finishes for Connaught during the 1956 season. He continued racing well into the 1960s, well past the point
where he was realistically competitive.

FANGIO, Juan Manuel

See pages 58–9.

FISCHER, Rudolf (CH)

b. 19 April 1912, Zurich
d. 30 December 1976
7 Grands Prix
Career span: 1951–2 (Ferrari)

A bespectacled Swiss amateur and successful restaurant
owner, Fischer raced his own Ferraris in many non-
Championship races as well as a handful of Grand Prix
outings.

FISHER, Mike (CDN)

1 Grand Prix

Canadian semi-professional who drove a 2-litre Lotus-
BRM V8 in 1967 Canadian Grand Prix at Mosport Park.

FITCH, John (USA)

b. 4 August 1917, Indianapolis
2 Grands Prix

The son of a wealthy building contractor, Fitch competed
in the 1953 German GP in an HWM and the 1955 Italian
Grand Prix in a Maserati. He was an enthusiastic and respected member of the Mercedes-Benz sports car team in
1955 and was heavily involved with Briggs Cunningham's
Le Mans projects.

FITTIPALDI, Emerson

See pages 62–3.

FARINA, Giuseppe (I)

b. 30 October 1906, Turin
d. 30 June 1966, near Chambery
33 Grands Prix; 5 wins; World Champion 1950
Career span: 1950–1 (Alfa Romeo); 1952–5 (Ferrari)

The man who was destined to win the first official World
Championship, 'Nino' Farina was a son of one of the
founders of the Farina coachbuilding company. He
qualified as a doctor of engineering and began his motor
racing career at the wheel of a 1500 Alfa Romeo in the
1932 Aosta-Grand St Bernard hillclimb event. It was not
the most successful of competition débuts. He crashed
heavily, sustaining a broken shoulder and facial lacera-
tions, the first of many accidents which punctuated a long
and successful career.

By the end of 1934 Farina was racing a Maserati 4CM,
winning the Circuit of Biella, and then taking his first
major victory in the voiturette race which acted as
curtain-raiser to the Czech Grand Prix at Brno. He continued campaigning another Maserati the following season before being recruited to drive for the Scuderia Ferrari,
a break which led to him driving the Alfa Romeo 158s in
1938 and 1939. His last victory before racing ceased during the war came at Tripoli in 1940. He picked up the
threads of his career with Alfa Romeo once hostilities were
over, winning the Grand Prix des Nacions at Geneva in
1946 with one of the disinterred 158s.

For 1947 and 1948 he drove as an independent at the
wheel of a 4CLT Maserati, winning the Monaco Grand
Prix in the latter season, and then vaccilating between
Ferrari and Maserati for 1949. In 1950 he rejoined Alfa as
team leader, winning the British Swiss and Italian Grands
Prix to take that first World title.

In 1951 he managed only a single win in Belgium, being
beaten to the Championship by Fangio, and after Alfa's
final withdrawal he joined Ferrari where he stayed to the
end of his career. He retired at the end of the 1955 season
during which he competed in only a handful of races, the
lingering acute discomfort from burns sustained at Monza
the previous year only partly allayed by pain-killing drugs.

He was second at Buenos Aires and third at Spa, but
after an accident in the Mille Miglia he eventually elected
to retire, although he subsequently mounted a couple of
half-hearted assaults on the Indianapolis 500 in 1956 and

FITTIPALDI, Wilson (BR)

b. 25 December 1943, Sao Paulo
35 Grands Prix
Career span: 1972–3 (Brabham); 1975 (Copersucar)

The elder brother of twice World Champion and Indy 500
winner, Emerson, Wilson Fittipaldi displayed a respectable

The first official World Championship title fell to Dr Giuseppe Farina (right) seen here in company with Alberto Ascari (left) and Luigi Villoresi.

1957. In his retirement he was briefly the Jaguar importer for Italy and later became a main agent for Alfa Romeo, the cars he so gloriously campaigned when his racing career was at its zenith.

Farina was widely credited with having pioneered the relaxed, arms-stretched driving style which would later be emulated by Stirling Moss. He was something of a cold fish though, never visiting injured rival drivers in hospital and not expecting them to pay him the compliment either.

He was driving a Lotus Cortina on his way to the 1966 French Grand Prix at Clermont-Ferrand when he was caught out by a slippery road surface in the mountains near Chambery a few months short of his sixtieth birthday.

turn of speed in a works Brabham for two seasons before returning to Brazil to mastermind the Copersucar-backed Fittipaldi team. He drove for the family firm in 1975 before retiring to hand over to his brother the following year. He now looks after the family's Brazilian business interests, including a Mercedes-Benz distributorship. His son Christian won the 1991 International F3000 Championship.

FITZAU, Theo (D)

d. 18 March 1982
1 Grand Prix

A minor league German driver who fielded an AFM-BMW in the 1953 German Grand Prix.

FITTIPALDI, Emerson (BR)

b. 12 December 1946, Sao Paulo
144 Grands Prix; 14 wins; World Champion 1972 and 1974
Career span: 1970–3 (Lotus); 1974–5 (McLaren); 1976–80
(Fittipaldi)

Emerson Fittipaldi led the flood tide of world-class Brazilian drivers who cascaded into Formula 1 during the
1970s, and became the youngest ever World Champion at
the age of twenty-five at the wheel of a Lotus 72. Fittipaldi
had a smooth and delicate touch, balancing great natural
ability behind the wheel with a sense of tactical percep-
tion which earned him a reputation as a strategic racer.

Born in Brazil's bustling industrial second city, Emerson
and his elder brother Wilson Jr grew up with motor racing
in their blood. Their father Wilson Sr was a respected and
experienced motor racing journalist and commentator
who had first come to Europe with the Fangio/Gonzalez
bandwagon in the early 1950s. Two decades later this
silver-haired gentleman would return to chart the F1 progress of his two sons with an understandable sense of
pride.

Emerson made his name in karting and Formula Vee at
home before setting out to Europe at the start of 1969
where he started racing a Formula Ford Merlyn Mk 11A.
His progress through the lesser single-seater ranks was
mercurial and astonishing by any standards. He instantly
asserted himself as a winner, moving through into F3 –
where he again proved immediately competitive – by the
end of the season and was signed with Lotus for a full F2
programme in 1970.

After Piers Courage was killed in the 1970 Dutch Grand
Prix at Zandvoort, Frank Williams tried hard to sign Emerson to drive his de Tomaso for the balance of the season,

Emerson Fittipaldi won his fourth Grand Prix for Lotus and
went on to become the youngest ever World Champion.

FLINTERMAN, Jan (NL)

b. 2 October 1919
1 Grand Prix

This professional fighter pilot with the Dutch air Force
competed in the 1952 Dutch GP at Zandvoort in a Maserati A6GCM.

FLOCKHART, Ron (GB)

b. 16 June 1923, Edinburgh
d. 12 April 1962, Australia
13 Grands Prix
Career span: 1956 (Connaught); 1957–9 (BRM); 1960 (Lotus
and Cooper)

Best known for steering Ecurie Écosse Jaguar D-types to

victory at Le Mans in 1956 (with Ninian Sanderson) and
1957 (with Ivor Bueb). He was third at Monza in 1956 for
Connaught which brought him to the attention of BRM
for whom he plugged away for the next three seasons. He
was killed when his converted Mustang fighter broke up
in turbulence over Australia during a Sydney to London
record attempt.

FOITEK, Gregor (CH)

b. 27 March 1965, Zurich
7 Grands Prix

This abnormally brave youngster (whose father, Karl,
raced a 2-litre Lola sports car with distinction in the early
1970s) made his F1 début with Brabham at the start of
1990 before being replaced by David Brabham after the

but there was no way this was going to happen. Colin Chapman had him locked firmly into a 'Lotus only' contract and quickly affirmed his confidence in his new lad by giving him his F1 début in a Lotus 49C at the British Grand Prix at Brands Hatch.

He scored his first Championship points with a fourth place at Hockenheim in the German race, but then the Lotus game plan suddenly changed dramatically when team leader Jochen Rindt was killed at Monza. With John Miles feeling he no longer wanted to be involved with F1 in general, and the frail Lotus 72 in particular, Fittipaldi found himself propelled into the forefront of F1 attention. In only his fourth race, the United States GP at Watkins Glen, he emerged victorious and set the seal on his F1 future.

In 1971 Emerson lost momentum slightly. He was quite badly knocked around in a road accident and his US GP victory had unrealistically raised expectations. He finished a strong sixth in the World Championship with a second place in Austria and a third in Britain, but really got the hang of the F1 business in 1972 when he romped to his first World Championship victory over Jackie Stewart, a success which owed as much to the well-honed Lotus 72 as it did to Emerson's driving ability.

In 1973 Chapman signed Ronnie Peterson to drive alongside him, a move which not only put Emerson's nose slightly out of joint but resulted in the two men splitting the Lotus wins and allowing Stewart through to take his third World Championship. By the end of the season Emerson had accepted a big money offer to switch to McLaren (now benefitting from plenty of Marlboro support) and demonstrated the wisdom of the switch by taking his second World Championship with wins in Brazil, Belgium and Canada.

For 1975 the Cosworth-engined McLaren M23 was marginally out-gunned by the more powerful Ferrari 312T, but Fittipaldi took a strong second to Niki Lauda in the Championship stakes. He then dropped a bombshell by announcing that he was quitting McLaren to join his brother's fledgeling F1 team which was sponsored by Copersucar, Brazil's state-run sugar marketing cartel.

In retrospect, this move was a case of ill-judged patriotism and family loyalty and was seriously out of focus. It effectively destroyed Emerson's F1 career long before his driving talent had waned. There were a few fleeting moments of promise left, and when Fittipaldi's Copersucar stormed home a strong second to Carlos Reutmann's Ferrari 312T in the 1978 Brazilian Grand Prix at Rio, he was cheered to the echo as a national hero. From then on, however, it was downhill all the way, and although Emerson stopped racing at the end of 1980 to concentrate on team management duties the following year, lack of sponsorship caused the Fittipaldi team to sink into the financial quicksands and they finally closed their doors at the end of 1982.

Emerson then moved to the USA where he became involved first in IMSA sports car racing and latterly CART single-seaters. He proved that there is life after Formula 1 by developing into one of the top contenders in this category, winning the 1989 Indianapolis 500 in a Pat Patrick team Penske before joining the factory Penske team for whom he was continuing to drive through into the 1992 season.

first two events. He switched to the Onyx team, by then controlled by Peter Monteverdi, and his F1 career prospects evaporated when the team pulled out in the middle of the year. He briefly tried Indy car racing in 1992.

FOLLMER, George (USA)

b. 27 January 1934, Phoenix
12 Grands Prix

This tough and versatile racer won the 1972 Can-Am Championship after taking over the Penske Porsche 917/K turbo after Mark Donohue suffered leg injuries. He drove for the UOP Shadow team in F1 during 1973, finishing third at Barcelona where he put François Cevert in his place during an animated discussion on the winner's rostrum, pointing out that if the Frenchman did not like the defensive manner in which he drove, then that was just bad luck!

FORINI, Franco (I)

b. 22 September 1958, Muralto
2 Grands Prix

This talented F3 championship hot shot competed at Monza and Estoril in 1987 at the wheel of a second Osella-Alfa alongside Alex Caffi.

FOTHERINGHAM-PARKER, Philip (GB)

b. 22 September 1907
d. 15 October 1981
1 Grand Prix

A gentleman driver who raced an Alvis at Brooklands before the war and continued in the late 1940s with an ERA and Maserati 4CL which he drove in the 1951 British Grand Prix.

FRÈRE, Paul (B)

b. 30 January 1917, Le Havre
11 Grands Prix
Career span: 1952 (HWM and Gordini); 1953 (HWM); 1954 (Gordini); 1955–6 (Ferrari)

This lean, athletic and urbane Belgian raced on a semi-professional basis for fifteen years, yet this was essentially an adjunct to his profession as a respected and talented international motoring journalist. His racing career really took off when he won the non-title Grand Prix des Frontières at Chimay in an HWM, after which he briefly graduated to the Ferrari F1 team. A second place to Peter Collins in a Lancia-Ferrari at Spa in 1956 was followed four years later by a superb Le Mans victory with Gendebien in a Testa Rossa. Frère, now over seventy years old and living in the south of France, even today remains a fine road driver and is still entrusted with some of the fastest cars in the world for analysis and assessment.

FRY, Joe (GB)

d. 29 July 1950, Blandford
1 Grand Prix

A promising young British driver who was killed at the wheel of the difficult Freikaiserwagen special at the 1950 Blandford hillclimb, less than two months after driving a Maserati 4CL in the British Grand Prix at Silverstone.

GABBIANI, Beppe (I)

b. 2 January 1957, Piacenza
2 Grands Prix

An inexperienced, but quick Italian who had his handful of F1 outings for Osella in 1981 too early in his career to be of much benefit. He later reasserted his reputation as a promising driver with some sterling F2 drives in an Onyx March during the 1983 European F2 Championship, tutored beneficially by former BRM F1 driver Peter Gethin.

GACHOT, Bertrand (F)

b. 21 December 1962, Luxembourg
15 Grands Prix
Career span: 1989 (Onyx); 1990 (Coloni); 1991 (Jordan and Lola)

This cocky, self-confident and amusing personality will, sadly for his own sake, always be remembered for having his 1991 season brutally interrupted by a jail sentence. In August that year Gachot was found guilty of assaulting a London taxi driver with a personal CS gas spray during a traffic incident at Hyde Park Corner. He was back on the grids by the end of the season in a Larrousse-Lola, but tempers ran high and the matter of his incarceration became a *cause celèbre* with the fellow Belgian racers, Thierry Boutsen and Eric van de Poele, picketing the British Embassy in Brussels while Bertrand languished behind bars.

GAILLARD, Patrick (F)

b. 12 February 1952, Paris
2 Grands Prix

A promising French F3 graduate, whose father owned a van

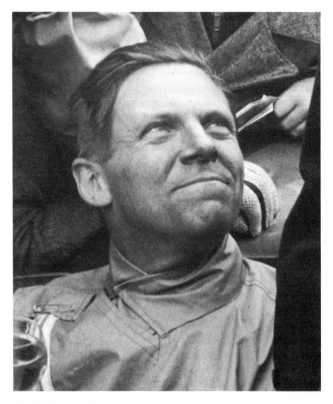

Paul Frère: journalist, road tester and all-round, accomplished high-speed driver.

and truck hire business, Gaillard made his name on the international F3 scene in a Chevron and rented a works Ensign in the 1979 British and Austrian Grands Prix.

GALLI, Giovanni (I)

b. 2 October 1940, Bologna
17 Grands Prix
Career span: 1971 (March); 1972 (Tecno and Ferrari); 1973 (Williams)

'Nanni' Galli was the son of a wealthy textile family who started in touring car racing and made quite a name for himself in a works Alfa Romeo GTA during the mid-1960s. He was also a member of the Autodelta Alfa T33 sports car team and moved into F1 on the back of the Milan company's erratic engine supply deal with March in 1971. In 1972 he drove the flat-12 Tecno and guested for Ferrari in the French GP at Clermont-Ferrand before briefly switching to the Williams Iso-Marlboro squad at the start of 1973. His 'Fruit of the Loom' sportswear brand was briefly a Williams team sponsor in 1978, well after Galli's retirement.

GALVEZ, Oscar (RA)

b. 17 August 1913
d. 16 December 1989
1 Grand Prix

Galvez was one of the greatest Argentinian drivers of all time and was a close rival of Fangio during his early career.

Bertrand Gachot projected an appealing personality, but suffered from an excessive belief in his own point of view.

Italian textile heir 'Nanni' Galli wrestling with the Frank Williams Iso-Marlboro in the 1973 Argentine Grand Prix at Buenos Aires.

He was Argentine national champion in 1947–8 (overall), 1949 (Especiales de Carrera) and 1953–4 (Turismo Carretera). He finished fifth in 1953 Argentine GP in a Maserati.

GAMBLE, Fred (USA)

b. 17 March 1932, Pittsburgh
1 Grand Prix

Gamble was one of the key organizational forces behind ex-airline pilot Lloyd 'Lucky' Casner's Camoradi F1 team. He contested the 1960 Italian GP in the Porsche-Behra F2 special, finishing tenth, and later achieved considerable status as Goodyear's first European racing manager. He now lives in Snowmass Village, Colorado.

GANLEY, Howden (NZ)

b. 24 December 1941, Hamilton
35 Grands Prix
Career span: 1971–2 (BRM); 1973 (Williams); 1974 (March)

A laconic, practical Kiwi whose racing ambitions were fired by a visit to the 1955 New Zealand Grand Prix, Ganley came to Britain in 1961 and used his considerable talents as a mechanic to bankroll his F3 racing – this became really serious from 1967 onwards when he acquired a brand new Brabham BT21. He graduated to F1 with BRM in 1971 via Formula 5000, having driven a McLaren M10B the prevous year. He gained a strong fifth place at Monza in the 1971 Italian GP, but his best placings were fourth at Watkins Glen in that year's US GP, matched by a similar placing in the German GP at Nurburgring the following summer. He drove for Frank Williams in 1973, leading the Canadian GP at Mosport Park for some distance before fading to sixth. Two races for March in 1974 ended his F1 career after which he concentrated on building up his own race car manufacturing company, Tiga, initially in partnership with fellow antipodean, Tim Schenken. In 1987 Howden sold his shares in Tiga and is now involved with Vern Schuppan Racing on a variety of projects.

GARDNER, Frank (AUS)

b. 1 October 1930, Sydney
8 Grands Prix

Arguably the toughest and most versatile saloon car driver ever to appear on the European scene, this former boxing champion took in a programme of Grands Prix during 1965 with a Willment team Brabham-BRM. Thereafter he turned his back on F1 with no regrets and concentrated on just about every other category of international racing.

GARTNER, Jo (A)

b. January 24 1954
d. 1 June 1986, Le Mans
8 Grands Prix

A popular but rather wild Austrian, Gartner drove enthusiastically for Osella in 1984, taking a lucky fifth place in the Italian GP at Monza. He was killed in an inexplicable accident at Le Mans two years later when the Kremer Porsche 962C he was sharing with Sarel van de Merwe and Kunimitsu Takahashi crashed during the night on the Mulsanne straight.

GAZE, Tony (AUS)

b. 3 February 1920
3 Grands Prix

Squadron Leader FAO Gaze, DFC and Bar, RAF was the man who casually inquired of the Duke of Richmond and Gordon as to when a sports car race would be held at the old Westhampnett airfield, on the Duke's Goodwood estate near Chichester, from which the Australian had flown during the war. It was a chance remark which led to the opening of the famous Goodwood track which flourished from 1948 to 1966. Gaze competed in three Grands Prix during the 1952 season in an HWM-Alta and was also a successful Aston Martin sports car driver. For many years he farmed near Ross-on-Wye.

GENDEBIEN, Olivier (B)

b. 12 January 1924
14 Grands Prix
Career span: 1956–9 (Ferrari); 1960 (Cooper); 1961 (Ferrari and Lotus)

Best known as a sports car racing ace of international repute, winning Le Mans for Ferrari on four occasions (1958, 1960, 1961 and 1962), this former wartime resistance fighter came from an aristocratic background. It was during a four-year spell in the Belgian Congo, clearing virgin forest for what was to become the residential area of Stanleyville, that he met a friend who would introduce him to the ways of motorsport as a rally navigator.

His Ferrari F1 outings were widely regarded as a reward for his prowess at the wheel of the Scuderia's sports cars; in 1958 and 1961 his works Ferrari ran at Spa carrying the Belgian national yellow livery under the Équipe Nationale Belge banner. Spa in 1961 marked the occasion of his sole front-row Grand Prix start. Just over a year later he retired from racing, only to be faced with the tragedy of his wife's death a short time afterwards. He subsequently based himself in the USA where he became involved in the cattle rearing business in a big way.

GERARD, Bob (GB)

b. 19 January 1914
8 Grands Prix
Career Span: 1950–7 (ERA and Cooper-Bristol)

Bespectacled Leicester garage owner Frederick Roberts Gerard was one of the dogged British privateers who made quite a reputation in the immediate post-war era with a private ERA, achieving his best result with second place to de Graffenried's Maserati in the pre-Championship status 1949 British Grand Prix at Silverstone. He later switched to Cooper-Bristols and doggedly competed in most British rounds of the World Championship up until 1957.

Finally retiring from racing in 1961, he continued as an owner and entrant through to the early 1970s. His wife Joan was also an accomplished competitor in her own right.

GERINI, Gerino (I)

6 Grands Prix

The chain-smoking pal of Jean Behra, Gerini owned a Maserati 250F and scored his best F1 result when he shared the fourth place Maserati with Chico Landi in the 1956 Argentine Grand Prix.

GETHIN, Peter (GB)

b. 21 February 1940, Ewell, Surrey
30 Grands Prix; 1 win
Career span: 1970–1 (McLaren); 1971–2 (BRM); 1974 (Hill)

The chirpy and popular pint-sized son of successful jockey Ken Gethin, Peter's great moment came in the 1971 Italian Grand Prix at Monza when he forced his BRM P160 into the lead at the last corner, winning the race by one-hundredth of a second at an average speed of 151.634mph (244.025kph). Not only was this the smallest margin of victory in F1 history, but his victory was achieved at a record average speed as well!

Gethin started in junior league F3 and won the first British F5000 title in 1969. He gained promotion to F1 with the McLaren team the following year in the wake of Bruce McLaren's sad death, and made a mid-season switch to BRM in 1971, a matter of weeks before scoring that memorable Monza victory.

He then stayed with BRM through to the end of 1972 after which his F1 career petered to a halt, with only a couple of guest drives in 1973 (BRM at Mosport Park) and 1974 (Hill at Brands Hatch) remaining.

He later became involved in team management, first with F2 March driver Beppe Gabbiani and later for the F1 Toleman team in 1984. He now runs corporate high-

Peter Gethin, seen here in 1983 with his labrador, Dino, won the fastest Grand Prix of all at Monza in 1971.

performance driving school days at the old Goodwood circuit near Chichester.

GHINZANI, Piercarlo (I)

b. 16 January 1952, Bergamo
59 Grands Prix
Career span: 1981–5 (Osella); 1985 (Toleman); 1986 (Osella); 1987 (Ligier)

A pleasant and popular Italian driver who became the first points-scorer for the Osella team at Dallas in 1984.

GIACOMELLI, Bruno (I)

b. 10 September 1952, Brescia
69 Grands Prix
Career span: 1977–8 (McLaren); 1979–82 (Alfa Romeo); 1983 (Toleman)

A chirpy Italian who won the 1978 European F2 Championship in a works March-BMW. He graduated to F1 by way of a third works McLaren in 1977 and 1978 before embarking on a well-paid three-year contract with Alfa Romeo which yielded a third place at Las Vegas in 1981 but precious little else. After a year with Toleman as Derek Warwick's team-mate in 1983, Bruno faded from F1.

Piercarlo Ghinzani tries the cockpit of his Osella for size.

Bruno Giacomelli poses on the cockpit of the McLaren M26 which he drove during the 1978 World Championship season.

GIBSON, Dick (GB)

b. 16 April 1918
1 Grand Prix

A Barnstaple garage owner who campaigned Cooper-Bristol and Connaught machinery before taking part in the 1957 German Grand Prix in a F2 Cooper. He now lives in Mesa, Arizona.

GINTHER, Richie (USA)

b. 5 August 1930, Hollywood, California
d. 28 September 1989, France
52 Grands Prix; 1 win
Career span: 1960–1 (Ferrari); 1962–4 (BRM); 1965–6 (Honda); 1967 (Eagle)

This small, freckle-faced Californian grew up in the same bunch of aspiring racers as Phil Hill, a friend of his older brother. Richie's father worked at the Douglas aircraft factory in nearby Long Beach, and he briefly joined him in 1948 before making his racing début in a Ford-engined MC TC hybrid in 1951. However, on his twenty-first birthday all thoughts of pursuing a racing career had to be shelved as he was drafted to Korea for two years' national service.

On his discharge, he partnered Phil Hill in the 1953 Carrera Panamericana, later managing John von Neumann's Ferrari agency in California before making his Le Mans début in 1957 in a Ferrari 250TR. In 1960 he got the opportunity to become one of the Maranello factory's test drivers, a chance which he seized with both hands. He made his F1 début in a Dino 246 at Monaco in 1960 and impressed the *tifosi* with an assured second place behind Phil in the Italian Grand Prix at Monza, a race boycotted by the leading British teams in protest at the continued use of the bumpy banked circuit.

In 1961 he was part of the squad racing the sensational Dino 156s, putting in a tremendous display to finish second to Stirling Moss's infinitely more agile Lotus 18 through the streets of Monte Carlo. At the end of the season he shrewdly accepted an invitation to join the BRM team as a number two to Graham Hill just as the British 1½-litre V8s were entering their most successful phase.

During his three-year spell with BRM he finished second at Monza in 1962, at Monaco, Monza and Watkins Glen in 1963 and in Germany and Mexico in 1964. He was runner-up in the 1963 Championship behind Graham and fourth in 1964. Immensely reliable, consistent and popular, Ginther was a splendid team man but lacked the aggressive edge to develop into a regular winner.

Replaced at BRM by Jackie Stewart at the start of the 1965 season, he sgined up with the fledgeling Honda F1 team and celebrated this move with a commanding victory in the Mexican Grand Prix, fending off a strong challenge from fellow American Dan Gurney's Brabham-Climax in the final race of the 1½-litre F1. He drove a couple of races for Cooper-Maserati in 1966 before Honda's 3-litre V12 was ready, and was lucky to survive a high-speed shunt at Monza when the bulky Japanese machine flew off the road after a tyre failure.

In 1967 Ginther signed to drive as second driver in Gurney's Eagle-Weslake squad, a deal which also involved a run at Indianapolis. It was at the Brickyard, as he waited in the line-up to do his qualifying run, that it finally dawned on him that he wanted to retire. He did so immediately, without fanfare or fuss.

In the ensuing years, Richie 'dropped out', leading a nomadic existence in the wastes of southern California, living in a motor-home without a clock to remind him of the passing of time. In 1977 he was an honoured guest at Hockenheim to watch Niki Lauda's Ferrari score the 100th Goodyear Grand Prix win, the first of which had been his success at Mexico City.

Another twelve years passed and Ginther, now prematurely frail and very unwell, was invited to Donington Park to become reacquainted with a 1½-litre F1 BRM on the marque's fortieth anniversary. He tried a few laps, but the effort was just too much. A few days later, whilst on holiday in France, Richie succumbed to heart failure at the early age of fifty-nine.

GIRAUD-CABANTOUS, Yves (F)

b. 8 October 1903
d. 31 March 1971
13 Grands Prix
Career span: 1950–1 (Talbot); 1952–3 (HWM)

A Delayahe sports car driver from the immediate post-war period who was originally nominated to race Émile Petit's abortive Dommartin F1 car – the recycled SEFAC pre-war Grand Prix project – and who subsequently switched to Talbot, later closing his professional career with some HWM outings.

GIUNTI, Ignazio (I)

b. 30 August 1941, Rome
d. 10 January 1971, Buenos Aires
4 Grands Prix

A tremendously promising young Italian who made his name driving saloons and sports cars for Alfa Romeo before being recruited into the Ferrari works team at the start of 1970. He drove splendidly to finish fourth in the Belgian GP at Spa on his F1 début and seemed set for a very successful long-term career. At the wheel of the brand new 3-litre Ferrari 312P, he was leading the 1971 Buenos Aires 1,000km race, the opening round of the World Sports Car

Championship, when he collided with the Matra which Jean-Pierre Beltoise was attempting to push back to the pits after it had run out of fuel on the circuit. Giunti sustained unsurvivable injuries and 70 per cent burns, and Italy lost one of its outstanding young racing talents.

GODIA-SALES, Francisco (E)

b. 21 March 1921
d. 1991
13 Grands Prix
Career span: 1951–8 (Maserati)

A wealthy Spaniard from Barcelona, Godia-Sales became one of the band of Maserati 250F driving privateers during the mid-1950s. He is particularly remembered for remarking when Fangio returned to the pits with a badly damaged Maserati 300S Sports car: 'You don't have to be a World Champion to do that. I could have done that!'

GOETHALS, Christian (B)

b. 4 August 1928
1 Grand Prix

A Belgian amateur, Goethals drove a Cooper-Climax in the F2 class of the 1958 German Grand Prix.

GONZALEZ, José Froilan (RA)

b. 5 October 1922, Arrecifes
26 Grands Prix; 2 wins
Career span: 1950 (Maserati); 1951 (Talbot and Ferrar); 1952–3 (Maserati); 1954–5 (Ferrari); 1956 (Maserati and Vanwall); 1957 (Ferrari); 1960 (Ferrari)

Enzo Ferrari once expressed a degree of wonderment as to how Gonzalez drove racing cars so effectively, considering the sweat into which the chubby Argentinian driver seemed to work himself. Yet it was this contemporary of Fangio's – nicknamed 'The Pampas Bull' by the English, yet affectionately called 'El Cabezon' ('Fat Head') by his compatriots – who drove into the Formula 1 history books by winning Ferrari his very first World Championship Grand Prix.

The occasion was the 1951 British Grand Prix at Silverstone. The car was the new non-supercharged 4½-litre Ferrari 375 and the opposition which Gonzales beat in a straight fight was his good friend Fangio in the Alfa Romeo 158. Arms flailing at the wheel, and with his vast bulk overhanging the cockpit sides, Gonzalez caught and passed the supercharged Italian rival machine and pulled steadily away to a momentous victory.

In fact, Gonzalez was far from unfit. The son of a Chevrolet dealer in a provincial town about three hours'

'El Cabezon' – Froilan Gonzalez, winner of the British Grand Prix for Ferrari in 1951 and 1954, at his most expansive!

drive from Buenos Aires, he was a chubby baby who grew into a chubby man. Yet he was a keen athlete from a young age, a first-rate swimmer, a crack shot, a cyclist and a production car road racer just like Fangio. His father set him up in the trucking business, and by 1949 he was ready to join Fangio on their first European tour together.

For the first couple of seasons his results were rather thin on the ground, but when Mercedes resurrected a trio of pre-war two-stage supercharged W163 cars and shipped them to Argentina for a couple of prestigious *formule libre* races at the start of 1951, Gonzalez trounced them in both events in a supercharged 2-litre Ferrari 166. It was his entry to the works Ferrari team for which he would score that splendid Silverstone win a few months later.

In 1952, Gonzalez switched to the Maserati works team in time for the Italian Grand Prix, but he had a big shunt. He then did a full season for the team in 1953 before switching back to Ferrari in 1954. At the wheel of the F2-derived Ferrari 625 he trounced the might of Mercedes to win the British Grand Prix, again on the Silverstone airfield circuit.

Sadly, Gonzalez crashed a sports Ferrari in practice for the Tourist Trophy and only once raced an F1 car in Britain again, coming over for the 1956 British Grand Prix at Silverstone where his guest appearance in a Vanwall ended before it had begun when a driveshaft joint broke on the startline.

Gonzalez's final F1 outing came in a Ferrari Dino 246 in the 1960 Argentine Grand Prix at Buenos Aires where he finished tenth in a race which saw Cliff Allison's best placed sister car end up second to Bruce McLaren's winning Cooper. He still makes the occasional appearance at a Grand Prix outside his own country, carrying his age and weight particularly well.

GONZALEZ, Oscar (RA)

1 Grand Prix

Drove Maserati to sixth place in the 1956 Argentine Grand Prix at Buenos Aires.

GORDINI, Aldo (F)

b. 19 June 1921
1 Grand Prix

The son of Gordini boss Amedee, Aldo took part in the 1951 French Grand Prix at Reims in a Simca-Gordini T11, but also competed in many non-championship events.

GOULD, Horace (GB)

b. 20 September 1921
d. 4 November 1968
14 Grands Prix
Career span: 1954 (Cooper); 1955–8 (Maserati)

Gould was a burly motor trader from Bristol who graduated from a Cooper-Bristol to his own ex-Bira Maserati 250F, then a later similar machine, and based himself for much of the racing season at Modena, scrounging odds and ends from the Maserati factory parts bin. He was an indefatigable, larger-than-life personality with enormous enthusiasm and determination to surmount any set-back. He survived to retire from racing, dying some years later from a sudden heart attack.

GREENE, Keith (GB)

b. 5 January 1938
3 Grands Prix

Keith Greene was the son of Gilby Engineering boss Syd Greene who fielded Maseratis for Roy Salvadori and others during the 1950s. He drove in the 1960 British Grand Prix

in a Cooper-Maserati, the 1961 British GP in a Gilby-Climax and the 1962 German GP in a Gilby-BRM special. He also drove in an extensive non-Championship F1 programme. He subsequently became heavily involved in management duties for a wide variety of teams.

GREGORY, Masten (USA)

b. 29 February 1932, Kansas City
d. 8 November 1985, Italy
38 Grands Prix
Career span: 1957–8 (Maserati); 1959 (Cooper); 1960 (Porsche and Cooper); 1961 (Cooper and Lotus); 1962 (Lotus); 1963 (Lotus and Lola); 1965 (BRM)

The bespectacled, hard-driving heir to an insurance company fortune, Gregory allegedly spent $75,000 during his first two years' racing starting in 1952. He became notorious for shunting cars during his formative years, but matured into a seasoned professional, scoring his best result with a second place in the 1959 Portuguese Grand Prix in

Bespectacled Masten Gregory, seen here sharing the 1965 Le Mans winner's rostrum with Jochen Rindt, had a talent for F1 which was frequently overlooked.

a works Cooper-Climax. His F1 career petered out in 1965, the year he and Jochen Rindt won Le Mans in a NART Ferrari 250LM, and he later became a prosperous Amsterdam-based diamond merchant. A chain smoker, he succumbed to a sudden heart attack at the early age of fifty-three while on holiday in Italy.

GRIGNAUD, Georges (F)

b. 25 July 1905
d. 7 December 1977
1 Grand Prix

This Talbot-Lago stalwart won the non-title Paris GP in 1950 and had a single Championship outing for the team in that year's Spanish GP at Pedralbes.

GROUILLARD, Olivier (F)

b. 2 September 1958, Toulouse
25 Grands Prix
Career span: 1989 (Ligier); 1990 (Osella); 1991 (Fomet)

Olivier Grouillard's driving sometimes proved as wild as his hair style!

A product of the French academy of motor racing, one of the many whose early career was nurtured by the giant Elf petroleum company, this determined young man won the 1984 French F3 Championship before graduating to Formula 3000 with mixed results. After finishing second in the 1988 International Championship behind Roberto Moreno, he graduated into F1 with Ligier, but did not hit it off with the unpredictable team boss and was dropped at the end of the season. The next two seasons with Osella and Fomet produced an unpredictable blend of speed and erratic driving which was set to continue when he signed for Tyrrell at the start of 1992.

GUELFI, André (F)

b. 6 May 1919
1 Grand Prix

This wealthy heir to a Moroccan sardine-fishing business drove an F2 Cooper-Climax at Casablanca in 1958. Married to a niece of the former President Pompidou, he now lives in retirement in Paris.

GUERRA, Miguel-Angel (RA)

b. 31 August 1953, Buenos Aires
1 Grand Prix

An Argentinian F2 graduate whose sole F1 outing with Osella was rewarded with a broken arm and leg when he was elbowed into the wall on the run down towards the Tosa hairpin at Imola on the opening lap of the 1981 San Marino GP.

GUERRERO, Roberto (CO)

b. 15 November 1958, Medellin
21 Grands Prix
Career span: 1982–3 (Ensign/Theodore)

A good natured, quiet and unobtrusively talented young man, Guerrero trained at Jim Russell's Snetterton racing school before racing effectively in F3 up to 1981. With sponsorship from Café do Colombia he bought a seat with Mo Nunn's tiny Ensign team, continuing when it became Theodore Racing the following year. When it became clear that the F1 door was now closed to him, Guerrero relocated to the USA, married his Californian wife Katie, and switched his career to Indy car racing with some success. He gained a fine Indy 500 record with second place to Rick Mears in 1984 and was unlucky not to win the 1989 race. He was in a coma for seventeen days after a testing accident at Indianapolis in 1987, but recovered to resume his career. He qualified his Lola-Buick on pole position for the Indy 500 in 1992.

A talent lost to F1. Despite success in junior single-seater formulae, Roberto Guerrero dialled all the wrong numbers when it came to achieving Grand Prix success.

British F3 Champion in 1985, Mauricio Gugelmin emulated his old pal Ayrton Senna to become yet another Brazilian in F1 only three years later.

GUGELMIN, Mauricio (BR)

b. 20 April 1963, Curitiba
58 Grands Prix
Career span: 1988–91 (Leyton House)

An old friend of Ayrton Senna, Mauricio raced karts against his fellow Brazilian long before either of them became known in European motor racing circles. He began serious kart racing at the age of eight and had already won four junior titles by the time he was twelve. He continued to win seven senior kart championships and the 1980 national title before graduating to cars the following year.

He was soon heading for Europe, and the year after Senna swept everything before him on the British scene, Gugelmin also triumphed in the RAC Formula series. In 1984 he won the European FF2000 title and in 1985 took the British F3 championship which Senna had won two years earlier.

In 1986 and 1987 he tackled Formula 3000, gaining a reputation as a meticulous stylist who could perhaps be accused of lacking a degree of outright aggression. Nevertheless, he won the 1987 F3000 Silverstone International Trophy race and was rewarded for his persistence when the March F1 team took him aboard the following year as a team-mate to Ivan Capelli. Their requirement was for a steady runner who could carry out some of the testing duties and who would not disgrace himself by attempting to run too fast, too soon.

The affable Gugelmin fitted the bill ideally and would stay in the Leyton House ranks through four seasons of wildly fluctuating fortunes. His only podium finish for the team was third in front of his home crowd at Rio de Janeiro in 1989, a performance which suggested there might be more to come from this stylish performer.

GURNEY, Dan (USA)

b. 13 April 1931, Port Jefferson, New York
86 Grands Prix; 4 wins
Career span: 1959 (Ferrari); 1960 (BRM); 1961–2 (Porsche);
1963–5 (Brabham); 1966–8 (Eagle); 1970 (McLaren)

This lanky, affable son of an opera singer may have only won four Grands Prix during his career, but he is remembered beyond question as one of the finest Grand Prix drivers of his generation, one of the few men rated as genuine opposition by the great Jim Clark. He stands shoulder to shoulder with Mario Andretti as the best American F1 driver of all time.

His family moved to California after his father's retirement, and by 1950 Dan was knocking round the Bonneville salt flats with the speed record crowd. His motor racing aspirations were, however, briefly shelved in 1952 when he joined the US Army and was packed off to Korea.

Despite the added responsibilities of a wife and young child, he threw himself into motor racing on his return, starting with a Triumph TR2 and clawing his path up the ladder via a succession of sports cars including a 4.9-litre Ferrari owned by wealthy vineyard owner Frank Arciero. By 1958 he was off to Le Mans as a member of Luigi Chinetti's North American Racing Team, and that led to an invitation to Modena for a test run in a works Ferrari.

By 1960 he was promoted to Ferrari's factory F1 team alongside Phil Hill and Tony Brooks, but found the draconian team discipline and autocratic management style absolutely insufferable. As a result, he made the appalling mistake of switching to BRM for 1961, hurriedly rectifying this move by joining Porsche the following year and

Dan Gurney hurtles round Stavelot in his Brabham-Climax during the 1964 Belgian Grand Prix at Spa – one of many races he led, but so undeservedly failed to win.

winning his first Grand Prix, the French race at Rouen, in their flat-8 cylinder machine.

Between 1963 and 1965 Dan drove for Jack Brabham at the wheel of the fine-handling tubular chassis 1½-litre Climax-engined cars carrying the Australian's name, but while he consistently proved himself almost a match for Clark and the dominant Lotus, time and again he was let down by trifling mechanical failures. He won the French Grand Prix at Rouen again in 1964, and the Mexican race the same year, but never managed to sustain a Championship challenge during his spell with Jack's team.

With the change to the new 3-litre F1 regulations at the start of 1966, Gurney decided to go it alone and start his own F1 team, the first such US effort since Lance Reventlow's abortive Scarab project at the turn of the decade. He established All American Racers at Santa Ana, California, to field cars at both Indianapolis and in the World Championship.

He started the latter programme with an uncompetitive 2.7-litre Climax-engined car, but the sleek Eagles would soon be powered by Weslake V12 engines and, thus equipped, Gurney stormed to victories in the 1967 Race of Champions and Belgian Grand Prix.

Dan would later admit that the Eagle-Weslake was a dramatically underfinanced project: 'We had minimal backing in every area. I think Weslake can be proud of their part in the organization although I think they would concede their end of the operation was a little shy, even though they were working miracles.'

The first Weslake V12 cost $280,000 and each of the six engines built were hand-fettled. Off track, it was a difficult time for Dan. He was attempting to deal with a failing marriage and, rattling back and forth across the Atlantic like a yo-yo, attempting to keep the F1 programme alive whilst at the same time running an Indy car programme, which was taking a disproportionate amount of his time.

The Eagle F1 project finally died in mid-1968, Gurney's enthusiasm for motor racing in general having received a severe dent when Jim Clark was killed in April of that year. In the wake of Bruce McLaren's sad death in the summer of 1970, Dan was drafted back into F1 to fill the void in the McLaren team, but the spark had gone out. He realized that fact, returned to the USA and never raced again.

For the next decade a succession of Eagle Indy car programmes continued, but they too had vanished from the scene by 1983. However, Gurney still continues to be involved in professional motorsport to this day, operating Toyota's racing programme in the US domestic IMSA sports car series. In 1991 he reached his sixtieth birthday, yet still retained the demeanour and character of a man twenty years younger.

HAHNE, Hubert (D)

b. 28 March 1935
3 Grands Prix

BMW's European Touring Car Championship tyro, Hahne drove a Matra-BRM in the F2 class of the 1966 section of the German GP and subsequently contested the same event again in 1967 (in a Lola-BMW) and 1969 (in a BMW 269). After failing to qualify his own March 701 in the following year's German Grand Prix at Hockenheim he instituted legal proceedings against the Bicester constructor, alleging that they had sold him a deficient machine. But when team driver Ronnie Peterson used it to match his own time in a works car round Silverstone, Hahne conceded the point and retired from motor racing.

HAILWOOD, Mike (GB)

b. 2 April 1940, Oxford
d. 23 March 1981, near Tanworth-in-Arden
50 Grands Prix
Career span: 1963–5 (Parnell Lotus); 1971–3 (Surtees); 1974 (McLaren)

Stanley Michael Bailey Hailwood was probably the greatest motorcycle racer in history, so it was sad that his

Mike Hailwood: a fine fellow and a great sportsman, still sorely missed.

transition to four wheels was not marked by the same level of success. 'Mike the Bike' first dabbled in F1 back in 1963–5 when he handled a Parnell Racing Lotus 25 fitted with a BRM V8 engine, his only Championship point coming with sixth place at Monaco in 1964.

After this disappointing foray he did not reappear in F1 for six years, celebrating his return with a storming fourth place for Surtees in the Italian Grand Prix at Monza. He won the European F2 Championship for 'Big John's' équipe and was just poised to grasp the lead in the South African GP from Stewart's Tyrrell when a rear suspension breakage spun him into retirement.

Although Surtees and Hailwood had widely differing temperaments, their background as motorcycle racers bonded them together in a workable alliance. Mike was genial, kindly and totally without any of the pretence one might have expected from a millionaire's son; he could be quite a handful socially when he let his hair down, but there was no doubting his intensely professional approach. Frustrated by lack of success with Team Surtees, he switched to McLaren for 1974 but crashed heavily at Brünchen during the German Grand Prix at Nurburgring, badly breaking a leg.

He retired from racing, returning briefly to two wheels to win a sensational F1 TT on the Isle of Man in 1978 on a 900cc Ducati. The following year he won the Senior TT on a 500 Suzuki before retiring to run a Birmingham-based motorcycle business in partnership with fellow ex-racer Rod Gould.

He was killed in a banal road accident, together with his young daughter Michelle, when their Rover 3500 collided with a lorry which was executing an illegal U-turn on a dual carriageway close to their Warwickshire home. They had just popped out to collect a fish-and-chip supper for the family. Few deaths have stunned the motor racing community more, nor left it reeling with such sincerely felt grief.

HAKKINEN, Mika (SF)

b. 28 September 1968, Helsinki
15 Grands Prix

Having won the 1990 British F3 Championship, this talented young Scandinavian stepped straight into F1 the following year and finished fifth in only his third Grand Prix outing at the wheel of a Lotus-Judd. An absolute natural, with flair, self-assurance and outstanding car control, Hakkinen should be capable of winning Grands Prix before long. In 1992, he continued alongside Herbert in the Lotus squad, nominally number two, but benefiting from the recovery in fortune of the famous British team, which was under new management and using Ford V8 engines again.

HALFORD, Bruce (GB)

b. 18 May 1931
8 Grands Prix
Career span: 1956–8 (Maserati); 1959–60 (Lotus)

This amiable Devonian, whose family owned a Torquay hotel and who bought the ex-Bira Maserati 250F from Horace Gould, led a similarly enterprising, semi-nomadic life, mainly on the non-championship European F1 circuit. He later drove a F2 Lotus before retiring to the family hotel and to boating, his other great enthusiasm, in the early 1960s. By the mid-1970s he was out again driving an old Lotus 16 with great gusto and enthusiasm in historic events.

HALL, Jim (USA)

b. 23 July 1935, Abilene, Texas
11 Grands Prix
Career span: 1960–1 (Lotus); 1963 (BRP Lotus)

This wealthy Texan inherited a $15 million fortune in his teens when his parents and sister were killed in a private plane crash. A couple of US Grand Prix outings in a private Lotus presaged a full season in 1963 alongside Innes Ireland in the BRP Lotus team, and he notched up a fifth and sixth respectively in the German and British Grands Prix. The man behind the famous Chaparral sports cars, which brought high-wing aerofoil technology and backdoor General Motors support to the European racing scene, he is still involved as an Indy car entrant to this day with John Andretti's Lola.

HAMILTON, Duncan (GB)

b. 30 April 1920, Cork, Eire
5 Grands Prix
Career span: 1951 (Talbot Lago); 1952–3 (HWM)

A rumbustious Surrey-based garage owner who flew for the RAF during the war in Lysanders, Hamilton raced Lago-Talbots and HWMs in a handful of Championship Grands Prix. He won the 1953 Le Mans 24-hours with his close friend Tony Rolt in a Jaguar C-type.

HAMPSHIRE, David (GB)

b. 29 December 1917
1 Grand Prix

A company director from Kegworth, near Derby, Hampshire ran in the British and French GPs during 1950 in a Maserati 4CLT/48. He had previously gained considerable success in the immediate post-war period.

HANSGEN, Walt (USA)

b. 18 October 1919, Westfield, New Jersey
d. 7 April 1966, Le Mans
2 Grands Prix

An SCCA sports car racer who graduated to become a polished professional, Hansgen finished fifth with a third Team Lotus entry in the 1964 United States GP. He was killed when he crashed a 7-litre Ford Mk2 in rain during Le Mans tests the following spring.

HARRIS, Mike (RSR)

b. 25 May 1939
1 Grand Prix

This Rhodesian amateur drove an Alfa-engined Cooper T53 in the 1962 South African GP at East London.

HARRISON, Cuthbert (GB)

b. 6 July 1906
d. 22 January 1981
3 Grands Prix

This Yorkshire motor trader raced an ERA in three Grands Prix during 1950, later building up a prosperous Ford dealership and becoming an accomplished trials competitor.

HART, Brian (GB)

b. 7 September 1936, North London
1 Grand Prix

This de Havilland-trained engineer became an accomplished F/Junior and F2 ace in the 1960s and later established one of the most highly respected race engine development businesses in England. He drove one of the super-sleek Ron Harris-entered Frank Costin-designed, wooden chassis Protos-Cosworth cars in the F2 class of the 1967 German Grand Prix.

HASEMI, Masahiro (J)

b. 13 November 1952, Tokyo
1 Grand Prix

This highly successful sports car and Formula Pacific driver handled a Dunlop-shod Kojima special in the 1976 Japanese GP at Fuji. In 1980 he achieved a grand slam in Japan by winning the four major national championships: the All Japan F2 series, the Suzuka F2 series, the Grand Championship series (sports cars) and the All Japan Formula Pacific series. He also shared the winning Nissan in the 1992 Daytona 24-hours.

HAWKINS, Paul (GB)

b. 12 October 1937, Melbourne
d. 26 May 1969, Oulton Park
3 Grands Prix

The son of a racing motorcyclist turned church minister, this tough Australian was a capable single-seater driver, but really made his mark as an outstanding sports car competitor with Ford GT40s and Lola T70s. His Grand Prix début came at East London in the 1965 South African GP in a pushrod 1,500cc Ford-engined Brabham F2, and he then emulated Ascari's trip into the harbour at Monaco during his first time out in an ex-works Lotus 33 owned by English amateur Porsche racer, Dickie Stoop. He was killed when his Lola T70 GT crashed and burned at Island Bend during the 1969 Tourist trophy at Oulton Park.

Hawkins is remembered fondly by his peers as a direct, straight-talking Australian who was as adept an off-track wheeler-dealer as he was behind the wheel of a variety of high-powered Sports Fords, Lolas and Ferraris.

HAWTHORN, MIKE

See pages 78–9.

HAYJE, Boy (NL)

b. 3 May 1949
3 Grands Prix

A Dutch privateer who drove a private Penske PC3 and a March 761 in three races during 1976 and 1977.

HEEKS, Willi (D)

b. 13 February 1922
2 Grands Prix

He drove an AFM-BMW in the 1952 German Grand Prix and a Veritas Meteor in the same event the following year.

HELFRICH, Theo (D)

b. 13 May 1913, Frankfurt
d. 29 April 1978
3 Grands Prix

Helfrich ran in the 1952 and 1953 German Grands Prix in a Veritas-BMW, and the 1954 race in a similarly powered Klenk Meteor special. This motor trader from Mannheim also shared the second place Mercedes-Benz 3000SL at Le Mans in 1952 with Helmut Niedermayer.

HAWTHORN, Mike (GB)

b. 10 April 1929, Mexborough, Yorkshire
d. 22 January 1959, Guildford
45 Grands Prix; 3 wins; World Champion 1958
Career span: 1952 (Cooper); 1953–4 (Ferrari); 1955 (Vanwall and
Ferrari); 1956 (Maserati, BRM and Vanwall); 1957–8 (Ferrari)

Along with Stirling Moss and Peter Collins, John Michael Hawthorn was in the forefront of the wave of British drivers who rose to the status of world-class competitors in sports car and Grand Prix racing during the 1950s. A formidable competitor of his day, Hawthorn had an erratic streak about his driving which may have had its roots in a kidney complaint he suffered from, and which would almost certainly have prevented him from living beyond middle age.

He came into motor racing at the wheel of a Riley sports car, encouraged by his father, Leslie, who had raced motorcycles at Brooklands before World War II. But it was when a friend of the family, Bob Chase, entered him at the wheel of a Cooper-Bristol F2 car in 1952 that he really began to make his name, snatching up impressive fourth place finishes in the Belgian and Dutch Grands Prix, and drawing himself to the attention of the works Ferrari team.

In 1953 he joined Maranello's full-time F1 line-up and made history with a momentous victory in the French Grand Prix at Reims, battling wheel to wheel throughout with Fangio's Maserati in torrid conditions before beating the Argentinian on the final sprint to the chequered flag. In the post-race celebrations, it would later transpire, he conceived a son with a local girl, although this fact would not receive any wider publicity until the early 1990s when a penetrating joint biography of Hawthorn and Peter Collins was published.

Early in 1954 Mike sustained serious burns during the Syracuse Grand Prix in Sicily, shortly after which his father was killed in a road accident when returning from a race meeting at Goodwood. He won his second Grand Prix at Barcelona at the end of the year with the Ferrari type 553 'Squalo', but thereafter decided he would be better off driving for a British team which would enable him to spend more time looking after Tourist Trophy Garage at Farnham, the family business.

Hawthorn was also unfortunately hounded by the sensational end of the British daily newspaper market, being accused of dodging his national service, and this matter concerning one of England's most famous sportsmen was regarded as sufficiently important to prompt discussions in the House of Commons. In fact, Mike's kidney ailment would have rendered him ineligible, but the fact remained that a broad swathe of public opinion could not reconcile this reality with the fact that he was fit enough to race Grand Prix cars.

Above: Mike Hawthorn, seen here in familiar sports jacket and 'papillon', is best recalled for his 1958 Championship-winning exploits in the Ferrari Dino 246. *Top right:* Hawthorn is seen heading for his sole race victory of the season in the French Grand Prix. *Bottom:* Hawthorn with a touch of opposite lock from behind a tinted vizor, heading for the second place at Casablanca which clinched his title.

Unfortunately, the 1955 season turned into a disappointing and tragic fiasco for Hawthorn, for not only did he fall out with Tony Vandervell over what he regarded as the shambolic way the Vanwall team was operated, but he also became implicated in the Le Mans catastrophe when Pierre Levegh's Mercedes vaulted into the crowd and killed more than eighty onlookers.

After being approached by Lancia, who then withdrew from F1 and passed their racing assets over to Ferrari, he briefly drove for Maranello late in the 1955 season and then decided to throw in his lot with BRM for 1956. This proved to be his worst ever season since he started out in F1, and he was happy to high-tail it back to Ferrari for

1957 where he would stay until the end of his career.

Partnering Peter Collins and Luigi Musso, Hawthorn had a grand time throughout 1957 and the first part of 1958, his relationship with his fellow Englishman giving rise to endless off-track pranks and adventures. Yet after Collins was killed in front of him while disputing the lead of the 1958 German Grand Prix at Nurburgring, everything changed for Mike Hawthorn.

Thereafter the balance of the season's racing was regarded as a chore, something to be polished off and then shoved out of his memory. His dominant victory in the French Grand Prix at Reims, scene of his classic first victory over Fangio five years before, represented his sole F1 win of the season, but by dint of a succession of consistent points-scoring performances he pipped Stirling Moss to become England's first World Champion driver. His Ferrari team-mate, Phil Hill, played a crucial role in realizing Mike's ambition when he waved him through into second place during the last race of the season, the Moroccan Grand Prix at Casablanca.

Hawthorn retired from the cockpit at the end of the season, a decision which greatly displeased Enzo Ferrari. Mike had elaborate plans for a joint garage venture with fellow Jaguar dealer Duncan Hamilton, and was on the verge of marriage, when he crashed fatally at the wheel of his Jaguar 3.4 saloon on the Guildford bypass one wet January morning in 1959 whilst indulging in an impromptu race with F1 team owner Rob Walker's Mercedes 300SL.

HENTON, Brian (GB)

b. 19 September 1946, Derby
19 Grands Prix
Career span: 1975 (Lotus); 1977 (March); 1981 (Toleman); 1982 (Tyrrell)

This tough, genial garage proprietor from Castle Donington, near Derby, was an occasional F1 contender in the mid-1970s, later winning the 1980 European F2 Championship for Toleman and moving into F1 full time the following year with their Hart-powered contender which seldom qualified. He showed good form with a rented ride for Tyrrell in 1982, including a questionable fastest lap in the British GP at Brands Hatch. He expanded into property developing in the mid-1980s.

HERBERT, Johnny (GB)

b. 25 June 1964, Romford
15 Grands Prix
Career span: 1989 (Benetton); 1990 to date (Lotus)

This extremely talented young charger seemed on course for a Lotus F1 drive at the start of the 1989 season when he broke his legs in a multiple collision during a Formula 3000 race at Brands Hatch in August 1988. In fact, he still got his F1 opportunity that year with Benetton, finishing an excellent fourth on his début in Brazil, before being

Johnny Herbert: the bright, new British star of the early 1990s.

HILL, Graham (GB)

b. 17 February 1929, London
d. 29 November 1975, Arkley, near London
176 Grands Prix; 14 wins; World Champion 1962 and 1968
Career span: 1958–9 (Lotus); 1960–6 (BRM); 1967–70 (Lotus); 1971–2 (Brabham); 1973–5 (Embassy Hill)

Graham Hill's rags-to-riches success story earned the moustachioed Londoner heroic status during the halcyon days of his Grand Prix career in the 1960s. Extrovert and dapper, he was one of the first F1 drivers to become a multi-media star, as at home on a television quiz show panel as he was behind the wheel of a racing car.

He first sampled the taste of a racing car in 1953, paying £1 for four laps of Brands Hatch in a 500cc F3 car. He was working at Smiths Industries at the time, and his other great passion was rowing, but after those four laps his imagination was fired up to pursue a career in motor racing. By a process of judicious socializing and sheer hard graft, Graham successfully made inroads into the motor racing establishment. He struck a key relationship with Lotus boss Colin Chapman which eventually led to his F1 début at Monaco in 1958.

However, it was Hill's switch to BRM in 1960 that really set him on the road to serious success. He almost won the British Grand Prix at Silverstone, leading in the closing stages until he spun off under pressure from Jack Brabham's Cooper which then went through to win.

BRM had been stumbling along in near-crisis for much of the 1950s, despite substantial financial support from the Owen Organisation, but the development of a new V8 engine for the 1½-litre F1 from 1961 onwards raised their hopes considerably. Nevertheless, the 1962 season started with an ultimatum from the team's owner Sir Alfred Owen that, unless they won at least two Grands Prix, the whole operation would be wound up.

In fact, Hill surpassed their wildest ambitions by notching up confident wins in the Dutch, German and Italian Grands Prix before going on to clinch the World Championship with a fourth victory in South Africa, the final race of the season.

For the next few years Hill and BRM were as closely associated – and as British – as roast beef and Yorkshire pudding. Graham notched up a hat trick of victories at Monaco between 1963 and 1965, and just failed to win the 1964 title after being knocked out of contention in the Mexican Grand Prix by Lorenzo Bandini's Ferrari.

In 1965 he was joined at BRM by the promising young Scot, Jackie Stewart, and, perhaps feeling slightly upstaged by the newcomer, caused a sensation in F1 circles by joining his old rival Jim Clark at Team Lotus in 1967. In fact, this was a Ford-financed effort to assemble the strongest possible driving team in preparation for the arrival of the

Graham Hill's hopes of winning the 1968 British Grand Prix at Brands Hatch end as his Lotus 49 suffers transmission failure and he throws his arm up to warn his team-mate Jack Oliver.

new Lotus 49 with its Cosworth DFV V8 engine which had been financed by the American motor giant.

At the start of the 1968 season Hill found himself increasingly cast in a supporting role to Clark, but the burden of sustaining Team Lotus fortunes suddenly came crashing on to Graham's shoulders when Jimmy was killed in a minor league F2 race at Hockenheim in April. Graham rose to the challenge admirably, winning the Spanish, Monaco and Mexican Grands Prix to ease out Stewart for the title.

In 1969 Graham scored what would be his final Grand Prix success – his fifth triumph at Monaco – before breaking both legs when he was flung from his car in the United States Grand Prix at Watkins Glen. In the wake of this disaster, Hill's gritty determination was taxed as never before, but he forced the pace of his recovery to score a Championship point on his return to the cockpit at the first race of the 1970 season.

Chapman was upset by Hill's accident, but did not allow that to cloud his judgement that Graham was now past his best. For 1970 he engineered him a place at the wheel of a private Lotus fielded by Rob Walker. Graham fought gamely to sustain his reputation, switching to Brabham for 1971 and 1972 before starting his own team in 1973, running a private Shadow DN1.

Remorselessly, he slogged ever onward. A disappointing

1973 season led to a scarcely less successful year in 1974, by which time his team was equipped with Lola chassis. Finally, when Graham failed to qualify at Monaco in 1975, he got the message. At the British Grand Prix he announced that he was retiring from the cockpit to concentrate on furthering the career of his brilliant new signing, Tony Brise.

As Grand Prix racing's senior citizen, an active retirement now beckoned with the prospect of growing old with dignity. He was in a position to lead a comfortable life-style with his wife Bette, daughters Bridget and Samantha and son Damon, and the famous Hill visage, with well-trimmed moustache and saucy wink, had helped him become one of the country's most instantly recognizable sporting stars.

However, behind Graham's beaming public demeanour lurked a less charitable side. Away from his adoring fans, he could be crushingly rude and he was also singularly irresponsible. After he and five other members of his Embassy Hill team, including the talented rising star Tony Brise, were killed when Graham's twin-engined Piper Aztec crashed in fog on Arkley golf course one foggy November night, it was found that the plane was not properly insured. The bereaved families had no alternative to the painful course of suing his estate to obtain financial compensation.

dropped from the team mid-season as it became clear that his injured legs were not fully recovered. Thanks to the faith and loyalty of Peter Collins, then team manager at Benetton and Managing Director of Team Lotus since 1990, Herbert is now an F1 regular and Lotus's fast recovery seems set to repay his dogged determination.

HERRMANN, Hans (D)

b. 23 February 1928, Stuttgart
18 Grands Prix
Career span: 1953 (Veritas); 1954–5 (Mercedes-Benz); 1957–8 (Maserati); 1959 (Cooper-Maserati and BRM); 1960–1 (Porsche F2); 1966 (Brabham F2)

An even-tempered and versatile café proprietor who scored his best F1 result with a third place for Mercedes in the 1954 Swiss Grand Prix. After his F1 career drew to a close he became a regular member of Porsche sports car team, rounding off his career with a Le Mans victory in 1970, sharing a 917 with Richard Attwood, after which he retired.

HESNAULT, François (F)

b. 30 December 1956, Neuilly
19 Grands Prix

A pleasant French F3 graduate who partnered de Cesaris at Ligier in 1984 with little success. He drove as Piquet's number two at Brabham for a few races the following year before being dropped, after a huge testing accident at Paul Ricard, which was witnessed by remarkably few people, and which seriously undermined his confidence. This horrifying accident, which apparently left Hesnault trapped in the Brabham which was rolled up in his protective catch fencing, so unnerved the Frenchman that he retired from motor racing and his place in the team was taken by the Swiss Marc Surer.

HEYER, Hans (D)

b. 16 March 1943
1 Grand Prix

A highly regarded German saloon and sports car driver who started the 1977 German GP at Hockenheim illegally from the pit lane having failed to qualify his ATS Penske PC4. He was subsequently black-flagged off the circuit.

HILL, Graham

See pages 80–1.

HILL, Phil (USA)

b. 20 April 1927, Miami, Florida
48 Grands Prix; 3 wins; World Champion 1961
Career span: 1958–62 (Ferrari); 1963 (ATS); 1964 (Cooper); 1965 (Centro Sud BRM)

Few more intellectual, deep-thinking men ever sat behind the wheel of a Grand Prix car than Philip Toll Hill Jr, who found himself in the right place at the right time to win the 1961 World Championship in one of the distinctive shark-nosed 1½-litre Ferrari 156s.

Phil was brought up in Santa Monica, a genteel, leafy enclave of Los Angeles suburbia fronting on to the Pacific Ocean. He started racing in the late 1940s at the wheel of an MG TC and went to England as a Jaguar trainee in 1949, returning home with one of the Coventry company's famous XK120 roadsters. Quickly establishing his reputation with Jaguar, he was entrusted with a succession of Ferraris owned by the wealthy Allen Guiberson, finishing sixth in the 1952 Carrera Panamericana, a wild and woolly road race through Mexico. A return the following year, sharing a 4.1-litre Ferrari with his friend Richie Ginther (qv) ended with a lucky escape when they slid over a cliff, thankfully emerging unharmed.

Luigi Chinetti, boss of the North American Racing Team – Ferrari's importer for the USA – followed this up by offering Phil drives at Sebring, Le Mans and Reims, and in 1954, again sharing with Ginther, Phil finished second in the Carrera Panamericana behind the Lancia of Umberto Maglioli. Chinetti advised Enzo Ferrari to offer Phil a works drive at Le Mans, and in 1956 to 1957, as an established member of the Maranello sports car team, he enjoyed considerable success in a wide variety of European sports car races.

Phil's Grand Prix début finally came at Reims in 1958 – the final race of Fangio's career – where he drove a Maserati 250F hired from Jo Bonnier into seventh place. This had the effect of hurrying up Ferrari on the F1 front and he duly found his way into the Maranello GP line-up in time to help Mike Hawthorn clinch the World Championship at Casablanca. Running second to Stirling Moss's Vanwall in the Moroccan, he slowed up and waved Hawthorn past, thus ensuring that Mike snatched the title from Stirling's grasp.

In 1959 Phil achieved second places in the French and Italian GPs at the wheel of the uprated Dino 246. He used this car in 1960 when he scored the first of his three Grand Prix victories at Monza in the Italian GP which was boycotted by the British teams after a dispute over the continued use of the bumpy banking.

In 1961 Ferrari was well prepared for the advent of the new 1½-litre F1 regulations, but the outcome of the World Championship was jeopardized by lack of team orders and

Above: The retired 1961 World Champion Phil Hill poses with his 1931 Pierce Arrow – originally bought new by his aunt – outside his home in Santa Monica, California. *Below:* Hill at the wheel of the 1959 Ferrari Dino 246 on his way to second place behind Stirling Moss's Cooper-Climax in the Italian Grand Prix.

Phil stayed with Ferrari through 1962, to be eclipsed totally by the new breed of British V8 challenger from BRM and Coventry-Climax, then made a disastrous career move to the fledgeling ATS team, established by a breakaway group of Ferrari renegades. It almost torpedoed his career for good, but salvation seemed on offer when he was invited to drive alongside Bruce McLaren at Cooper in 1964.

Nothing went right with this relationship either, and when Phil wrote off two cars during the Austrian GP meeting at the Zeltweg aerodrome circuit, John Cooper suspended him. Although reinstated in the team for the last couple of races, Phil was approaching the twilight of his F1 career and some drives in a second-hand BRM, fielded by the Italian Scuderia Centro Sud, finally wound it up during 1965.

Phil continued racing sports cars for another two years, rounding off his 1967 season with a fine victory in the BOAC 1,000km sports car race at Brands Hatch, sharing the distinctive, winged Chaparral 2K with Englishman Mike Spence. At the start of the following year, he suddenly remembered that he had forgotten to renew his international competitions licence and, in his own words, 'found that I had become a retired racing driver'.

That did not worry him at all. He withdrew to Santa Monica to concentrate on his old car restoration business, emerging from time to time over the years to meet up with former colleagues at 'old car' gatherings all over the world. Relaxed and mellow, Phil retains a sharp sense of humour and crystal-clear recall of his halcyon days behind the wheel.

considerable in-fighting between Phil, Richie Ginther and Wolfgang von Trips. Phil won the Belgian Grand Prix at Spa-Francorchamps, later clinching the Championship with a psychologically draining second Monza victory. This was the race in which von Trips was killed along with thirteen spectators, after the German Ferrari tangled with Jim Clark's Lotus and cannoned into the crowd.

HIRT, Peter (CH)

b. 30 March 1910
5 Grands Prix

A wealthy businessman from Kussnacht, near Zurich, who had a precision component manufacturing business and who drove his own private Ferrari in several Grands Prix.

HOBBS, David (GB)

b. 9 June 1939, Leamington Spa
7 Grands Prix

A likeable and enormously versatile driver, Hobbs could turn his hand to anything from F1 to sports cars, and from touring cars to Indianapolis machines. His best F1 Championship result was seventh in the 1974 Austrian GP in a Yardley McLaren M23 replacing Mike Hailwood who had been injured at Nurburgring. He still occasionally races while developing his major talent as a motor racing commentator for the American CBS network.

Happy chappy. David Hobbs never achieved much in F1, but he was a great sports car exponent and remains the most congenial company imaginable.

HOFFMAN, Ingo (BR)

b. 18 February 1953
3 Grands Prix

This handsome Germanic-looking blond raced briefly as Emerson Fittipaldi's team-mate during the 1976 and 1977 seasons in the Copersucar-Fittipaldi team. He was a highly rated driver whose talent was squandered.

A rare outing. Ingo Hoffman testing an early Copersucar-Ford more regularly driven by Wilson Fittipaldi.

HOSHINO, Kazuyoshi (J)

b. 1 July 1947, Shizuoka Prefecture
2 Grands Prix

Nicknamed 'the fastest guy in Japan', Hoshino was Japanese motorcross champion on a Kawasaki before switching to cars as a Nissan works driver in 1969. The multiple national championship winner in F2, sports cars and F3000, he drove a Bridgestone-shod Tyrrell 007 in the 1976 Japanese GP, running as high as third at the height of the torrential downpour, and a Kojima special in the following year. He shared the winning Nissan at the 1992 Daytona 24-hours with Masahiro Hasemi and Toshio Suzuki.

HULME, Denny (NZ)

b. 18 June 1937, Nelson, South Island
112 Grands Prix; 8 wins; World Champion 1967
Career span: 1965–7 (Brabham); 1968–74 (McLaren)

Clive Hulme, father of the 1967 World Champion, won a Victoria Cross at Anzio, and in essence, that is all you need to know about his son, Denis Clive Hulme – 'Denny' to most of his friends, and 'The Bear' to some of those who made the mistake of getting him ruffled. He must claim the distinction of being the most reticent and retiring of all the World Champions covered in this book.

Denny Hulme is a tough old number by any standards. Legend has it that during his youth he was doing some welding in his father's garage when he smelled burning. As it happened, he had trodden on a spark; but had smelled it before he felt the burning sensation in the sole of his foot! Later, he would bear the searing pain and discomfort of methanol burns to his hands – sustained while testing at Indianapolis when a fuel filler cap worked loose on the first McLaren Indy car – similarly without a murmur.

Denny briefly raced an MG TF 1500 in 1957 before switching to an MGA, and graduated into single-seaters in 1959 with a 2-litre Cooper-Climax. He and fellow Kiwi, George Lawton, came to Europe in 1960 for a season's F2 racing, wending a nomadic path around the Continent, but Lawton was killed in an accident at Roskilde and Denny was left to slog on alone.

By 1963 Denny had joined Jack Brabham's fledgeling company as a mechanic and finally got his first F1 drive in the Kanonloppet race at Karlskoga, Sweden, in August 1963 where he finished fourth behind the Lotus 25s of Clark and Trevor Taylor, and his boss in the other works Brabham. His first F1 Championship outing came at Silverstone in the 1965 British Grand Prix and, after Dan Gurney quit the Brabham team to start up on his own at the end of that season, Denny moved in alongside Jack as the team's number two driver for 1966.

Jack won the Championship in 1966, but Denny sustained the momentum of the Brabham-Repco bandwagon by snatching the title from his boss the following year. Hulme believes, in retrospect, that Brabham lost his chance of a fourth World Championship because he tended towards gambling with new and relatively untested technical developments which he hoped would offer an advantage. Hulme was given more proven, reliable equipment and profited accordingly.

Denny won two Grands Prix during his Championship year: at Monaco, the sad event which claimed Bandini's life, and Nurburgring, where he benefitted from the failure of Clark's Lotus 49 and Gurney's Eagle-Weslake. For 1968 he moved to the McLaren team, driving the new Cosworth-engined M7 to victory in the Italian and Cana-

Denny Hulme was the most self-effacing of all World Champions, but never permitted himself the indulgence of celebrity status.

dian Grands Prix to take third place in the final Championship stakes. It had been a shrewd move.

He stayed with McLaren to the end of his career, although Bruce's death in the summer of 1970 devastated Denny's outwardly rock-hard personality. The 1969 season yielded him another win in Mexico, but he had to wait until the 1972 South African Grand Prix for his next victory, then in the Yardley-liveried M19A.

A year later he took the only pole position of his career at the Johannesburg track on the début outing of the striking M23, and also won that year's Swedish Grand Prix at Anderstorp in a late charge which saw him displace Ronnie Peterson's Lotus 72 in a last lap lunge. His final Grand Prix win came at Buenos Aires in 1974 after an archetypal Hulme-style drive: taking things easy in the opening stages, conserving the car and pressing home his attack when the opposition ran into trouble.

At the end of 1974 the manner of his retirement from motor racing was so low key that the F1 community was only convinced he had finally gone when he did not appear at the first race of the following season. For several more years he dabbled in touring car racing, and raced trucks with all the old energy and grit that he used to apply to F1 in his professional heyday.

HUNT, James (GB)

b. 29 August 1947, Belmont, Surrey
92 Grands Prix; 10 wins; World Champion 1976
Career span: 1973–5 (Hesketh); 1976–8 (McLaren); 1979 (Wolf)

The transformation of this Wellington-educated public schoolboy from the ranks of precarious F3 also-ran to World class Grand Prix ace took little more than four years, but even at the pinnacle of his F1 achievement James was out to enjoy life to the full and never made the over-intense error of taking himself too seriously.

The son of a London stockbroker, James cut his teeth in Formula Ford 1600 in the late 1960s before moving into the closely contested F3 category where his oft-impulsive temperament regularly got him into uncomfortable scrapes. Unquestionably, James had the speed, but a succession of accidents caused by trying too hard with uncompetitive machinery brought him close to being written off as a serious contender by the start of the 1972 season.

Just as all seemed lost, he received one of those lucky breaks which can instantly transform a driver's prospects. Support from the enthusiastic Lord Hesketh lifted him into Formula 2 at the wheel of a second-hand March 712M during the summer of 1972, and allowed Hunt to show his true potential against the likes of Ronnie Peterson and Mike Hailwood. For 1973 it was planned that Hesketh would uprate his race programme to give James a full season of European F2, but after some early troubled races it was decided to go the whole hog and dive into Formula 1.

James's first outing in a Grand Prix car had come at the non-title mixed F1/F5000 Brands Hatch Race of Champions where he finished third in a Surtees TS9B. The team then switched to a March 731, engineered by Harvey Postlethwaite (then Ferrari's Technical Director) and he made his Championship début at Monaco. It looked as though he would finish in the points there, only for engine trouble to intervene.

James proved himself to be an instinctive F1 driver. The lack of power in F3 had stifled his talent, but he revelled in the 450bhp developed by a Cosworth DFV V8. Both he and the Hesketh team surged through the summer of 1973 on the crest of a wave. He gained fourth in the British Grand Prix, third at Zandvoort and, finally, a superb second in the United States GP at Watkins Glen where he resolutely tracked Ronnie Peterson's winning Lotus 72 throughout.

For the start of the 1974 season, Postlethwaite produced the straightforward Hesketh 308 design which was plagued with minor mechanical problems for much of the year in addition to some minor errors on the part of the driver. As a result, Hunt failed to sustain his career momentum, but finally won his first Grand Prix the follow-

On the verge of winning the 1976 Championship, James Hunt (left) in company with arch-rival Niki Lauda, Bernie Ecclestone and the late Ronnie Peterson.

ing year with a well-timed triumph over Niki Lauda's Ferrari 312T in the wet/dry Dutch GP at Zandvoort. By the end of the 1975 season, however, the cost of running an F1 team had become prohibitive and Hesketh, unable to find outside backing, withdrew.

After three seasons Hunt was unemployed, but not for long. Within weeks, Emerson Fittipaldi announced that he was leaving McLaren to join the fledgeling Copersucar team run by his brother Wilson. In a flash, McLaren boss Teddy Mayer contacted James and he was signed up to replace the Brazilian in a matter of days.

James was signed to drive alongside the German driver Jochen Mass and immediately stamped his authority on the new situation by taking pole position for his first Grand Prix in Brazil. James won the Spanish GP at Jarama only for his McLaren to be deemed to have infringed the maximum rear track dimensions and be excluded. McLaren appealed and were later reinstated to that victory. Later in the year, after James took the restart in the British Grand Prix at Brands Hatch after the race had been red-flagged after a first corner collision, he was subsequently disqualified and remained so.

His battle with arch-rival and close friend Niki Lauda for the World Championship proved the core of the season's competition. Although outwardly very different personalities, their friendship was genuine, far removed from the cosmetic and transparently insincere chumming-up which would be dished out for public consumption a decade or so later from drivers who really hated each other.

James Hunt in action with the Hesketh 308 in Sweden.

James and Niki had shared flats together in their rip-roaring F2 days, as well as some hair-raising social activities. They knew each other well and understood each other's respective talents. James's Championship hopes were given a major boost when Niki was badly burned in that fiery first lap accident at Nurburgring, but within six weeks the Austrian had forced himself back into the cockpit to resume the title battle.

Confirmation of James's Brands Hatch disqualification meant that he had to overcome a deficit of seventeen points in the last three races if he was going to overhaul Niki for the championship. He did so brilliantly, adding wins in Canada and the USA to his earlier successes in Spain, France and Holland, driving his McLaren M23 with a heady blend of aggression and control. Lauda pulled out of the rain-soaked Japanese Grand Prix at Fuji leaving James to finish third, clinching the title.

In 1977 James again drove well, but the competitive pitch of the McLaren M23 – and its successor the M26 – was quickly undermined by the new generation of Lotus ground-effect F1 machines. He was fifth in the World Championship, but then in 1978 faded to eighth overall after a highly disappointing season.

Seeking rejuvenation, he switched to the Wolf team for 1979, but decided that ground-effect chassis technology reduced the driver's contribution to the point where he was no longer interested. He quit after the Monaco Grand Prix and never regretted it.

Off the track, James was an ever-present item in the gossip columns, never more so than when his first wife Susy went off with Richard Burton. Since his retirement, James has busied himself with various business ventures and stays involved in F1 through his commentating duties with Murray Walker in BBC television. Divorced from his second wife Sarah, he lives in Wimbledon with his collection of budgerigars which have become one of his great passions in life.

Hunt tries his hand in the cockpit of a Williams-Renault in 1990.

87

James in action with the McLaren M23 at Monaco.

HUTCHINSON, Gus (USA)

b. 26 April 1937
1 Grand Prix

An American amateur who drove an ex-works Brabham BT26 in the 1970 United States GP at Watkins Glen.

ICKX, Jacky (B)

b. 1 January 1945
116 Grands Prix; 8 wins
Career span: 1967 (Cooper); 1968 (Ferrari); 1969 (Brabham). 1970–3 (Ferrari); 1973 (McLaren and Williams); 1974–5 (Lotus); 1976 (Williams and Ensign); 1977–8 (Ensign); 1979 (Ligier)

Civilized, articulate and talented, Jacky Ickx's early motor racing achievements marked him down as a potential World Champion long before he ever sat in a Grand Prix car. But somehow the cards never quite fell in the direction of this Belgian driver, despite some quite brilliant drives for Ferrari and Brabham between 1968 and 1972.

The son of the respected Belgian motoring journalist of the same name, Jacky began his career successfully in motorcycle trials events and later raced a Lotus Cortina with great success in saloon car events. He exploded to prominence at the age of twenty-two when he drove a Tyrrell F2 Matra MS7 with remarkable zest in the German GP at Nurburgring, running amongst the leading F1 aces in the top half-dozen before the French machine broke its suspension.

Ickx scored a Championship point on his first GP outing at Monza that same year at the wheel of a Cooper-Maserati, but it was his success in winning the 1967 European F2 Championship for Matra that secured this very formal young gentleman a place in the works Ferrari team the following year. He drove brilliantly to win the French GP at Rouen and was in the running for the World Championship right up to the Canadian GP where a stuck throttle in practice resulted in a broken leg.

For 1969 he shrewdly switched to the Brabham team, winning the German and Canadian Grands Prix, but this move had been massaged by the Gulf Oil Corporation who wanted to have Ickx driving their GT40 sports cars; it was a worthwhile move, however, for he won Le Mans for them! In 1970 he returned to Ferrari where he used the superb new flat-12 312 to win the Austrian, Canadian and Mexican Grands Prix, only just failing to exceed the points total accumulated by Jochen Rindt prior to his death at Monza.

The 1971 season yielded no victories for Ickx, but 1972 saw him win the German Grand Prix at Nurburgring, the last such success of his career. In the middle of 1973 he quit Ferrari and transferred to Team Lotus alongside Ronnie Peterson the following year, but apart from a fine wet weather win in the non-title Brands Hatch Race of Cham-

pions, Ickx now found himself locked into a gradual decline. He quit the team mid-way through 1975 and then squandered what was left of his prestigious reputation with a disastrous foray with the Wolf-Williams team during the first half of 1976.

A brief foray with Ensign in the second half of 1976 went some way to restoring his reputation, but his F1 career petered out in 1979 after he deputized for the injured Patrick Depailler in the Ligier squad.

He subsequently became Clerk of the Course for the Monaco Grand Prix, but had his licence withdrawn in absolutely outrageous circumstances following the 1984 race when he was obliquely accused of favouring Alain Prost's Porsche-engined McLaren which had just emerged victorious as he flagged the race to a premature halt in monsoon conditions. Ickx's links with Porsche made him partial, so the critics said. Truth be told, it was a ludicrous reflection on FISA inability to administer the sport even-handedly. Gentlemen who know their stuff like Ickx were rare gems and badly needed on the administrative side.

He was married for many years to Catherine Blaton, daughter of the wealthy Belgian industrialist Jean Blaton, a regular Ferrari privateer at Le Mans in the 1960s who raced under the pseudonym of 'Beurlys'. Ickx continued with sports cars for several more years, winning Le Mans five times.

IGLESIAS, Jesus (RA)

b. 22 February 1922
1 Grand Prix

This local Argentinian hot shoe drove a Gordini T16 in the 1955 Argentine Grand Prix. Three years later he distinguished himself when his Jaguar-engined special pushed off Stirling Moss's Cooper in the non-title Buenos Aires City GP!

IRELAND, Innes (GB)

b. 12 June 1930, Kircudbright
50 Grands Prix; 1 win
Career span: 1959–61 (Lotus); 1962–4 (UDT-Laystall/British Racing Partnership); 1965 (Parnell Racing); 1966 (Bernard White Racing)

Had it not been for his well-defined sense of obligation, this extrovert, fun-loving Scot might well have enjoyed a career distinguished by many more victories than the single win he achieved in the 1961 United States Grand Prix at Watkins Glen. After being fired in less than gracious circumstances by Lotus boss Colin Chapman a few weeks after scoring the marque's first GP success, Ireland agreed on the spur of the moment to join the UDT-Laystall team operated by Ken Gregory and Alfred Moss (father of Stirling) for the 1962 season.

Robert McGregor Innes Ireland: retired Grand Prix ace, journalist, raconteur, one-time hell-raiser and all-round connoisseur of life.

The following day, he received an invitation to join BRM as Graham Hill's partner, but felt that he must stand by his word to UDT-Laystall and consequently declined the invitation. Hill went on to take the 1962 Championship, and scored a string of other wins throughout the balance of the 1½-litre Formula 1, while Ireland had to content himself with a few wins in non-championship British domestic races – and a lot of hair-raising accidents.

Whether Innes's rumbustious character would have sat comfortably with BRM boss Sir Alfred Owen, a strict Methodist, is another matter. A hedonist, this son of a Kircudbright veterinary lived life in the fast lane throughout his Grand Prix career. But it would be an unfair exaggeration to say that his life passed in a blur of women, booze and cigarette haze, for such a verdict short-changes his unquestionable flair and all-round ability behind the wheel. In his youth he had been apprenticed to Rolls-Royce in Glasgow and London, and later, during his national service, was commissioned in the King's Own Scottish Borderers and seconded to the Parachute Regiment.

Make no mistake, this lean, tough Scot was an accomplished and extremely fast driver, hitting the F1 headlines in 1960 when his Lotus 18 twice beat Stirling Moss's Rob Walker Cooper at Oulton Park and Silverstone.

Innes was shrewd enough to know just how superior his machinery had been on those two occasions, and while he never believed himself to be in Moss's class, he was audacious and frequently fearless. Being dropped by Chapman in such an abrupt fashion left a legacy of bitterness that dominated his life, and it was a matter of enduring regret to Innes that he let a subsequent feud with Jimmy Clark – whom he mistakenly believed was behind his dismissal – continue up to Clark's death in 1968.

The two men never made their peace and Innes, who by then had retired from racing to become Sports Editor of *Autocar* magazine, penned the most moving of all tributes to his fellow Scot. Ireland subsequently severed his connections with racing for over six years, becoming involved in a couple of deep-sea fishing enterprises which yielded little success.

Since the late 1970s he has been back on the F1 scene for many years as a regular contributor to the Californian magazine *Road & Track*. A great raconteur and gentleman, few retired drivers are capable of providing such convivial and amusing company as Innes.

IRWIN, Chris (GB)

b. 27 June 1942
10 Grands Prix

An outstanding product of the British 1-litre F3 scene and a close contemporary of Piers Courage, Irwin made his Grand Prix début in a works 2½-litre Climax-engined Brabham in the 1966 British Grand Prix at Brands Hatch where he finished seventh. His fine fifth place in the following year's French GP at Le Mans represented one of the H16 BRM's few top six finishes. He was badly injured when his Ford F3L sports car somersaulted during practice for the 1968 Nurburgring 1,000km race and never competed again.

JABOUILLE, Jean-Pierre (F)

b. 1 October 1942, Paris
49 Grands Prix; 2 wins
Career span: 1975 (Tyrrell); 1977–80 (Renault); 1981 (Ligier)

This popular Frenchman may not have been the greatest talent in F1 history, but he earned a glorious place in the annals of motor racing when he won the 1979 French Grand Prix at the wheel of a Renault. Apart from the pure nationalistic fervour produced by the occasion, it was the

Jean-Pierre Jabouille struggling with the Ligier-Matra early in 1981, an uphill battle against an inadequately healed leg which he broke the previous season.

first victory for a turbo-charged Formula 1 car, opening the floodgates of turbo success which would last for another ten years.

International success came late in the career of this amiable Danny Kay look-alike, and came only briefly. Jabouille was amongst the first wave of drivers to rise to prominence during France's motor racing renaissance in the late 1960s, working his way through F2 at the wheel of a Matra before joining that team's endurance racing line-up in the early 1970s. He was also a regular F2 contender, winning the European F2 Championship in 1976 at the wheel of an Elf 2.

Jean-Pierre had his maiden F1 outing by way of a one-off run with the Tyrrell team in the 1975 French Grand Prix. Later he had to suffer the brunt of the laughter as the first Renault turbos smoked an unreliable path round the Grand Prix trail in 1977, but by the summer of 1978 France's national racing car had become far less of a joke. Jabouille scored the marque's first Championship points at Watkins Glen that autumn before his historic victory at Dijon-Prenois the following summer.

Jabouille won the 1980 Austrian Grand Prix on the super-fast Österreichring and then badly broke a leg in an accident during the Canadian Grand Prix. He returned to racing with Ligier in 1981, but was still not fully fit and elected to retire after only a handful of outings.

JAMES, John (GB)

b. 10 May 1914
1 Grand Prix

This engineer from Bromsgrove was a keen amateur racer who drove a Maserati 4CLT/48 in the 1951 British Grand Prix at Silverstone.

JARIER, Jean-Pierre (F)

b. 10 July 1946
134 Grands Prix
Career span: 1973 (March); 1974–6 (Shadow); 1977 (ATS); 1978 (ATS and Lotus); 1979–80 (Tyrrell); 1981 (Ligier and Osella); 1982 (Osella); 1983 (Ligier)

This fast, talented, but rather wild French F3 graduate from the late 1960s calmed down his style sufficiently to win the 1973 European F2 Championship in a works March-BMW 732. The same year saw him make his F1 début for March, but it will be for his thrusting performances as a member of the Shadow team in the mid-1970s that he will be most remembered. He had the 1975 Brazilian GP at Interlagos in the bag when his Shadow DN5 retired with a jammed fuel metering unit and, while attempting to restore his career with Lotus in

Jean-Pierre Jarier had all the credentials to be successful, but somehow it never quite clicked. *Below:* a rare shot of the Frenchman in a Shadow DN3 battling with the Can-Am sports Shadows of Jack Oliver and George Follmer in the 'Shadow showdown' challenge event held at California's Laguna Seca circuit late in 1974.

1978, he was similarly dominating the first Canadian GP at Montreal when brake problems intervened. Two further years with Tyrrell failed to produce a worthwhile F1 breakthrough and, into the 1980s, his career gradually entered a downward spiral which hit rock bottom in 1983 with a disastrous season at Ligier. For Jarier, it was the end of the F1 road.

JARVILEHTO, Jyrki (SF)

b. 31 January 1966, Espoo
23 Grands Prix
Career span: 1989 (Onyx); 1990 (Onyx/Monteverdi); 1991 (Dallara)

A protégé of the 1982 World Champion, Keke Rosberg, who advised him to style his name 'JJ Lehto' for professional purposes rather than use his unpronounceable full name, much in the same way as Keke himself had abandoned the christian name 'Keijo'. JJ started his competition career on karts at the age of six, switching to motorcross in his teams only to damage a knee badly enough to require the fitting of an artificial joint. His subsequent intention was to follow the great Finnish

Jyrki Jarvilehto adopted the *nom de course* 'JJ Lehto' on the advice of his manager and mentor, Keke Rosberg.

JOHANSSON, Stefan (s)

b. 8 September 1956, Vaxjo
79 Grands Prix
Career span: 1979 (Shadow); 1983 (Spirit); 1984 (Tyrrell and Toleman); 1985–6 (Ferrari); 1987 (McLaren); 1988 (Ligier); 1989 (Onyx); 1991 (AGS)

This cheerful Swede had all the right credentials when he finally graduated into F1 with the fledgeling Spirit-Honda team in the summer of 1983. A successful kartist, winner of the 1979 British F3 championship and an F1 pace-setter, Johansson was quick, brave and obviously talented. He was also immensely unlucky and, despite spells with Ferrari and McLaren, he never quite got it together for long enough to score that elusive F1 victory.

When Honda switched their engine supply contract to Williams for 1984, Johansson simply filled in as best he could, accepting occasional guest outings with Tyrrell and Toleman. In the Italian GP, standing in for the suspended

Stefan Johansson was always extremely popular, but should have got more out of his time at Ferrari.

tradition and turn his hand to rallying, but with the withdrawal of a prospective sponsor he turned his attention to Formula Ford. By 1986 he had won the European, Scandinavian and Finnish titles and clearly a great future was unfolding ahead of him.

In 1987 he took FF2000 by storm, winning both the British and European titles, then won the closely fought British F3 title in 1988. His subsequent graduation to Formula 3000 was fraught with difficulty, but the Finn's talent had also come to the attention of Ferrari and he enjoyed a worthwhile spell as test driver for the Scuderia during 1989.

Late that season he replaced the excessively outspoken Bertrand Gachot in the second Moneytron Onyx F1 car, staying with the team into 1990 when it passed into the control of Swiss privateer, Peter Monteverdi, and then floundered mid-season with considerable debts. Fortunately the cheerful and gregarious Finn had established a respected F1 reputation by this stage and joined Dallara for 1991, scoring his first podium finish with a third place in the San Marino GP at Imola.

Stefan Johansson's Ferrari F186 leads the Benetton-BMWs of Teo Fabi and Gerhard Berger in the 1986 San Marino Grand Prix at Imola.

Ayrton Senna, he brought the Toleman home in a fine fourth place on the strength of which he earned the number one drive with them for 1985.

Just when it seemed as though he was poised on the threshold of success, the lack of a tyre contract prompted Toleman to shelve their programme. However, Ferrari created a timely vacancy when René Arnoux was dropped from the line-up and Johansson took his place.

He ran competitively throughout 1985, finishing a strong second in both Canada and Detroit, consolidating a reputation which kept him in the Maranello squad. But Ferrari's competitiveness would wane dramatically through 1986 so a succession of mechanical problems and sheer bloody misfortune made it almost inevitable that he would be replaced – Gerhard Berger was the man who took over from him.

Stefan then picked up the prestige number two McLaren ride alongside Alain Prost for 1987, but this was just a question of keeping the seat warm for Ayrton Senna who duly succeeded him in 1988. From then on it was downhill almost all the way via Ligier, Onyx and AGS to a quiet retirement in Monaco and an increasing amount of time spent developing his quite outstanding artistic skills.

JOHNSON, Leslie (GB)

d. 8 June 1959
1 Grand Prix

A stalwart Jaguar sports car racer who took part in the 1950 British Grand Prix at the wheel of an E-type ERA.

JOHNSTONE, Bruce (ZA)

b. 30 January 1937
1 Grand Prix

Johnstone drove a rented BRM in the 1962 South African Grand Prix at East London, and finished ninth, four laps behind winner Graham Hill. He is now living back in Durban where he works for a major Yamaha motorcycle agency.

JONES, Alan

See pages 96–7.

KARCH, Oswald (D)

1 Grand Prix

Contested the 1953 German Grand Prix in a Veritas RS.

KEEGAN, Rupert (GB)

b: 26 February 1955, Westcliff-on-Sea
25 Grands Prix
Career span: 1977 (Hesketh); 1978 (Surtees); 1980 (RAM Williams); 1982 (RAM March)

Rupert Keegan was the fun-loving playboy son of the buccaneering, extrovert airline boss, Mike Keegan, who started on the road to fortune with an ex-RAF Dakota in the Berlin airlift and was widely regarded as the role model for the leading character in the 1981 British television series, *Airline*. Rupert won the 1976 British F3 Championship before embarking on sponsored drives with Hesketh and Surtees, dropping out in 1979, and then returning briefly in 1980 and 1982.

Rupert Keegan: at home against a Monaco backdrop.

KEIZAN, Eddie (ZA)

b. 12 September 1944
3 Grands Prix

This talented South African owner of a Johannesburg alloy sports wheel business drove in his home Grand Prix on three occasions: in 1973 and 1974 in an ex-works Tyrrell and in 1975 in a Lotus 72.

JONES, Alan (AUS)

b. 2 November 1946, Melbourne
116 Grands Prix; 12 wins; World Champion 1980
Career span: 1975 (Hesketh and Hill); 1976 (Surtees); 1977
(Shadow); 1978–81 (Williams); 1983 (Arrows); 1985–6 (Lola)

The son of Stan Jones, a famous hard-living Australian racing star from the immediate post-war era, Alan was fired with a passion for motor racing from an early age. When his father raced Maseratis and Coopers 'down under' in the 1950s, the short-trousered Jones Jr would always be there to watch and, to a great extent, this hard-bitten youngster was spurred on in his ambition to become World Champion by his father's success in Australasia.

It was a long, hard slog for Jones to work himself into a position where becoming a decent F1 driver was a realistic proposition for him. He went to Britain in the early 1970s and struggled through the junior formulae before getting his Grand Prix break at the wheel of a private Hesketh in 1975.

Even at this stage he did not appear to be a natural, but he was obviously endowed with enormous strength and determination. When a lucky break provided him with the chance of a drive in the Shadow team, he underlined his ability by scoring a fine victory in the 1977 Australian Grand Prix.

The partnership immediately clicked, and when Jones got in amongst the leading Ferraris at Long Beach, Williams quickly came to appreciate that he had found himself a rather special new driver. Second place in the United States GP rounded off their first year together and, with designer Patrick Head's superb new Williams FW07 ground-effect chassis in the pipeline for 1979, the following season turned out to be even better.

Although Jones's team-mate Clay Regazzoni won the team's maiden Grand Prix victory at Silverstone, he did so only after Alan's retirement. Jones subsequently made up for that disappointment with victories at Hockenheim, Österreichring, Zandvoort and Montreal.

He sustained this momentum to win the 1980 World Championship with wins in Buenos Aires, Spain (non-championship, as things turned out), Paul Ricard, Brands Hatch, Montreal and Watkins Glen. He might well have retained the title the following year, but for a series of trifling mechanical problems. However, he continued to

Alan Jones was one of the toughest drivers in the F1 business, clinching his 1980 World Championship with victory at Montreal in this Williams FW07. Four years earlier he had really started to show his potential in the Durex-backed Surtees TS19.

drive splendidly, rounding off the season with a victory at Las Vegas.

He then retired, ostensibly to look after his farm and other business interests. He kept his hand in though, driving Porsche sports cars in the 1982 Australian National Championship, eventually concluding that the lure of motor racing at international level was too much to resist.

In the 1983 Long Beach Grand Prix, after a year's absence from the F1 stage, he made his return at the wheel of an Arrows A6. Despite the fact that one of his legs was pinned as the result of a fracture sustained in a horse-riding accident only six weeks earlier, the blunt and uncompromising Australian proved that he still had what it takes.

In 1985 he received a tempting financial offer to re-emerge with the Haas-Lola squad, continuing through to the end of the following season. But the spark had by now dimmed and the glory days with Williams were not to be rekindled.

Alan Jones and the Williams team were thrown together at a time when neither of them seemed to have much to offer. However, the Australian is remembered affectionately by those who worked with him at Williams as a great motivator and a man who lifted everybody's morale, particularly when things were going badly. Chief designer Patrick Head remembers that as a rare quality which is displayed by few top-line drivers.

KELLY, Joe (IRL)

b. 13 March 1913
2 Grands Prix

Kelly was a South American born Dublin-based motor trader who ran an Alta in the 1950 and 1951 British Grands Prix at Silverstone. He was very successful on non-championshp F1 and on the domestic sports car round.

KESSEL, Loris (CH)

b. 1 April 1950
3 Grands Prix

A young Swiss driver who used sponsorship from Tissot watches to buy a place in John MacDonald's RAM Brabham BT44 team during the summer of 1976, qualifying for three Grands Prix.

KINNUNEN, Leo (SF)

b. 5 August 1943, Tampere
1 Grand Prix

This stocky former Porsche racer made his name while paired with Pedro Rodriguez throughout 1970 in works-backed JW/Gulf Porsche 917s. He later contested the thinly supported European Interserie contest for big Group 7 sports cars and made the mistake of renting an uncompetitive Surtees TS16 for the 1974 Swedish GP.

KLENK, Hans (D)

b. 18 October 1919
1 Grand Prix

An occasional Mercedes-Benz test driver, Klenk was later badly injured in this task, and drove a Veritas-BMW F2 in the 1952 German Grand Prix. He was a friend and regular co-driver of Karl Kling on the Carrera Panamericana and Mille Miglia road races.

KLING, Karl (D)

b. 16 September 1910, Giessen
11 Grands Prix
Career span: 1954–5 (Mercedes)

Karl Kling started as a reception clerk in the public relations department of Daimler-Benz in 1936, competing with Mercedes production cars in rallies and reliability trials up to the start of World War II. He serviced planes for the Luftwaffe during the war, and then started racing again in 1946 with a BMW 328 before graduating to Veritas. He was then invited into Mercedes sports car and F1 teams in the early

1950s. A runner-up to Fangio by less than a second on his Mercedes Grand Prix comeback at Reims in 1954, Kling also won the 1952 Carrera Panamericana road race in a Mercedes 300SL with Hans Klenk.

KLODWIG, Ernst (D)

b. 23 May 1903
2 Grands Prix

This German semi-professional drove BMW-engined F2 specials in the 1952 and 1953 German Grands Prix at Nurburgring.

KOINIGG, Helmut (A)

b. 3 November 1948
d. 6 October 1974, Watkins Glen
2 Grands Prix

This very popular, although quite frail, Austrian Formula Super Vee graduate drove a Surtees TS16 very respectably to finish tenth at Mosport Park in 1974. In the next race, the US Grand Prix at Watkins Glen, he was killed in a grisly accident when a slow puncture caused his car to veer out of control and slide beneath insecurely mounted guard rails.

KRAUSE, Rudolf (D)

b. 30 March 1907
2 Grands Prix

A German amateur who drove BMW-engined specials in the 1952 and 1953 German Grands Prix.

LACAZE, Rob (MA)

b. 26 February 1917
1 Grand Prix

Drove a private F2 Cooper-Climax in the 1958 Moroccan Grand Prix, finishing a distant third in the F2 class.

LAMMERS, Jan (NL)

b. 2 June 1956, Zandvoort
21 Grands Prix
Career span: 1979 (Shadow); 1980–1 (ATS); 1982 (Theodores)

Involved in motor racing since he was a teenage instructor at the famous 'skid school' operated at his local circuit by Dutch racer, Rob Slotemaker, pint-sized Jan won the 1973 Dutch Touring Car Championship in 1973, his first year of competition. By 1978 he had added the European F3

LAFFITE, Jacques (F)

b. 21 November 1943
176 Grands Prix; 6 wins
Career span: 1976–82 (Ligier); 1983–4 (Williams); 1985–6 (Ligier)

There was always a happy-go-lucky aspect to the charact of this warm-hearted Frenchman, and his irreverent sen of humour did much to lighten the increasingly inten professional mood which came over Grand Prix racing the late 1970s and early 1980s. Laffite's career in raci began when he acted as unpaid mechanic to fellow Fren racer Jean-Pierre Jabouille. The two men later married tv sisters, thereby becoming related, as well as being tean mates briefly in the Ligier line-up for the first few races 1981.

Jacques graduated through Formula 3, bringing h name to the attention of the F1 world with a victory in tl Monaco F3 classic in 1973 at the wheel of a Martini. Tl following year he got his Grand Prix break with Frar Williams, but in those distant days the British team ha

Happy Jacques! The irrepressible, beaming Jacques Laffite brightened the F1 horizon in the 1970s and early 1980s. *Above:* he is seen here in company with Williams team-mate Keke Rosberg and Technical Director, Patrick Head. *Right:* Laffite on the winner's rostrum after the 1981 Austrian Grand Prix. Second and third place finishers Nelson Piquet and René Arnoux seem distinctly underwhelmed about events!

yet to make its name and was far from achieving the competitive position it was to occupy by the early years of the following decade. On the contrary, it was a financially precarious, hand-to-mouth operation whose cars generally fulfilled a role as also-rans.

For a season and a half, Jacques struggled along for Williams, saving Frank's bacon by surviving to finish second in the 1975 German Grand Prix – producing some much-needed income at an absolutely crucial moment – and the two men developed a healthy respect for each other's talents. Thereafter Laffite accepted an invitation to drive for the new Ligier F1 team at the start of 1976 and he stayed there for several seasons.

Using a Matra V12 engine, the Ligier steadily established itself as a reasonably promising contender, and Jacques managed to score his first GP win in Sweden during the summer of 1977. For 1979 the team switched to Cosworth-Ford V8 engines and Jacques harnessed the new ground-effect JS11 chassis to splendid effect, opening the season with fine victories in the Argentine and Brazilian Grands Prix. Thereafter the car's development became somewhat confused and Jacques failed to score another victory until the summer of 1980 when he won the German GP at Hockenheim.

In 1981, Ligier reverted to the Matra V12 under the Talbot banner. Another moderately successful season ensued with Jacques winning in both Austria and Canada to retain a chance of the World Championship until late in the year.

Thereafter, 1982 proved a sad disappointment and Laffite returned to Williams alongside Keke Rosberg for 1983, the English team now a very different proposition from when he last left it. Jacques and his family moved to England, renting the Stoke Poges mansion previously owned by Vanwall F1 boss Tony Vandervell, the Williams driver developing into a great Anglophile with the local golf course catering for his overriding off-track passion.

Despite the fact he was nearly forty years old, Jacques produced some good drives for the Williams team in the 1983, but when the new Honda-engined FW09 arrived on the scene the following year, the Frenchman found himself unable to match Rosberg's pace and daring, and Williams replaced him with Nigel Mansell for 1985.

Laffite returned to Ligier, the French team now armed with Renault turbo engines. Jacques gave them some excellent runs in both 1985 and the first part of 1986 before a terrible accident just after the start of the British Grand Prix at Brands Hatch saw him sustain two broken legs. 'Happy Jacques' made a full recovery, returning to race saloon cars, but his F1 days were at an end.

99

Championship to his list of successes and moved into F1 the following year with the Shadow team, running alongside Elio de Angelis, with financial support from Samson Shag tobacco. He generally took second billing to the Italian and proved unable to consolidate his Grand Prix career with subsequent intermittent outings for ATS, Ensign and Theodore. Only when he began a long-term association with the TWR Jaguar endurance racing team in 1986 did people begin to appreciate that, after all, a competitive car at the right moment might have delivered Lammers some F1 success.

LANDI, 'Chico' (BR)

b. 14 July 1907
d. 7 June 1989
6 Grands Prix
Career span: 1951–3 (Ferrari and Maserati); 1956 (Maserati)

Francisco Landi was the first serious Brazilian F1 contender in the early 1950s and continued his links with motorsport in his native country up until his death. He ran a car accessory and garage business in Sao Paulo and was the manager of the Interlagos circuit from 1985 until a few months before his death in 1989 when the city's new mayor replaced him in this position.

LANG, Hermann (D)

b. 6 April 1909, Bad Canstatt, near Stuttgart
d. 19 October 1987
2 Grands Prix
Career span: 1953 (Maserati); 1954 (Mercedes)

This great pre-war Mercedes ace, European Champion in 1939, continued racing into the World Championship era, taking a fifth place in the 1953 Swiss Grand Prix at Berne. His last outing at Nurburgring the following year in the new Mercedes W196 was something of a symbolic swansong, but he had won Le Mans with Fritz Riess two years earlier in a 300SL and continued to demonstrate the pre-war W163s for another two decades.

Chico Landi (centre) was Brazil's most successful F1 pioneer from the early 1950s. Here he is photographed at Sao Paulo's Interlagos circuit flanked by his countrymen Emerson Fittipaldi (left) and Ayrton Senna who, between them, would win five World Championships.

Nicola Larini: never in the right car at the right moment.

LARINI, Nicola (I)

b. 19 March 1964, Camaiore
39 Grands Prix
Career span: 1987 (Coloni); 1988–9 (Osella); 1990 (Ligier); 1991 (Lamborghini)

With his father and uncle having raced successfully in saloon cars during the 1960s, it was perhaps to be expected that young Nicola beat a path to the Henry Morrogh racing school at the Magione circuit when he was only nineteen years old. He won on his first outing in Formula Italia and quickly rose to dominate the junior formulae, winning the 1986 Italian F3 title in a Dallara.

After making his F1 début with Coloni (for whom he had driven in F3) at the tail end of 1987, Larini moved to Osella in 1988 and 1989, and his sterling efforts with an uncompetitive car earned him a place in the Ligier line-up for 1990. Although a consistent finisher, he failed to score a single point, and moved to the Lamborghini team for 1991. Seventh placed on his maiden outing for the team at Phoenix proved to be as good as it was going to get.

LARRAURI, Oscar (RA)

b. 19 August 1954
8 Grands Prix

Oscar Larrauri came to F1 relatively late in his career and found no success in an uncompetitive car.

This amiable Argentinian drove a Euro Brun throughout the 1988 season to little effect, partnered by Stefano Modena.

LARRETA, Alberto (RA)

b. 14 January 1934
d. 11 May 1977
1 Grand Prix

An Argentine amateur who took part in the 1960 Argentine Grand Prix in a Lotus-Climax.

LARROUSSE, Gerard (F)

b. 23 May 1940, Lyon
1 Grand Prix

A highly respected endurance racer, Larrousse won Le Mans twice for Matra (1973 and 1974) and drove a Bretscher Team Brabham BT42 in the 1974 Belgian GP at Nivelles-Baulers. He later became competitions chief of Renault and Ligier before establishing his own F1 operation in 1987.

LAUDA, Niki (A)

b. 22 February 1949, Vienna
171 Grands Prix; 25 wins; World Champion 1975, 1977 and 1984
Career span: 1971–2 (March); 1973 (BRM); 1974–7 (Ferrari); 1978–9 (Brabham); 1982–5 (McLaren)

The frail-looking, buck-toothed Austrian boy who rented a works March F2 drive for £8,500 in 1971 grew into one of the most accomplished, deep-thinking and pragmatic Grand Prix drivers of the post-war era – a calm, focused technocrat who clearly demonstrated that honing one's car to technical perfection was every bit as important as the ability to drive it quickly.

The son of a wealthy Viennese dynasty with banking and industrial interests, Niki put himself beyond the pale as far as his family was concerned when he borrowed £30,000 from an Austrian bank, the Raiffeisenkasse, in 1972 to buy a place in the works March F1 team alongside Ronnie Peterson. The uncompetitiveness of the complex March 721X almost sluiced away any chances of continuing a professional racing career and, at the end of the season, it looked as though he had been left high and dry.

With no realistic way of paying off his huge bills, Lauda reasoned he had no choice but to continue. He coaxed BRM into letting him test one of their cars and, after proving quicker than regular drivers Clay Regazzoni and Jean-Pierre Beltoise, he cajoled his way into the team with promises of sponsorship. What he was doing, in fact, was to pay his sponsorship monies with the prize money he had earned in the previous few races, a strategy which would clearly leave him with another notional overdraft by the end of the season.

He came clean with BRM boss Louis Stanley and was allowed to stay on in return for signing a three-year contract. Despite this, when the opportunity presented itself to drive for Ferrari, Lauda seized it with both hands. He eventually had to reach a financial settlement with BRM, but it was a small price to pay for winning two Grands Prix – in Spain and Holland – at the wheel of a Ferrari B3 in 1974.

Lauda motivated Maranello and got the best out of its resources. He forged a strong working partnership with team director Luca di Montezemolo and chief engineer Mauro Forghieri, so when the superb transverse gearbox Ferrari 312T came on to the scene in 1975 it was no surprise that he strode convincingly to the World Championship, winning five races in the process.

In 1976 Lauda's success had made Ferrari overconfident. Montezemolo was replaced as team manager by Daniele Audetto with whom Niki failed to develop such a close relationship. Then came the accident which nearly killed him on the opening lap of the German GP at Nurburgring, caused almost certainly by a broken suspension on the Ferrari 312T2.

Rescued from the burning car thanks to the heroism of fellow drivers Guy Edwards, Arturo Merzario and Harald Ertl, together with a German track marshal, Niki hung between life and death for a few agonizing days. His face and scalp had been burned, but his lungs had also been scorched by the heat and poisoned by toxic fumes from the Ferrari's blazing bodywork. Yet once that initial crisis passed, Niki forced the pace of his physical recovery with an awesome determination which was to earn him worldwide heroic status.

He returned to the cockpit in time for the Italian Grand Prix barely eight weeks later, finishing fourth and setting the second fastest race lap. He defended his title points lead right up to the final race at Fuji, but withdrew from the Japanese race, making no bones about the fact that he was apprehensive about the saturated conditions.

Predictably, certain sections of the Italian press crucified him for his prudent approach. Within the halls of power at Maranello he was regarded by some key personnel as washed up, finished. Lauda knew better. He bounced back in 1977 to win the South African, German and Dutch Grands Prix, retaking his World Championship title and

Halcyon days at Ferrari. *Right*: Niki Lauda leaping the 312T at Brunnchen on his way to second place in the 1975 German Grand Prix at Nurburgring. *Above*: heading the 312T2 towards victory in the 1976 Belgian Grand Prix at Zolder.

quitting Ferrari at the end of the season to join Bernie Ecclestone's Brabham-Alfa équipe.

From a performance standpoint, it was not a good move. He won two races in 1978, both in freak circumstances. The first was with the revolutionary Brabham 'fan car' at Anderstorp, but this technical advantage was later denied to him as the system was banned almost immediately. He was also classed first at Monza, but only after Mario Andretti and Gilles Villeneuve – who finished ahead of him on the road – were penalized for jumping the start.

By the beginning of 1979 it was becoming clear that Lauda's mind was increasingly focused on his airline business. He would spend years battling against government bureaucracy and the Austrian Airlines monopoly for the right to establish his own operation. It was a battle which brought his company – LaudaAir – to the brink of bankruptcy after it was obliged to cancel an option on a DC-10 jetliner in the early 1980s.

Either way, Lauda retired mid-way through first practice for the Canadian Grand Prix at Montreal in September 1979. By the time most journalists had realized what was happening, Niki was on a flight to Long Beach for talks with aeroplane makers, McDonnell-Douglas. It seemed as though a golden chapter in motor racing history was over.

For two years 'The Rat' – as he was affectionately known – put in only an occasional appearance at Grand Prix circuits. Then, for 1982, he was lured out of retirement by McLaren boss Ron Dennis to drive alongside John Watson. People wondered whether he would be quick enough. Even Dennis insisted on a clause enabling Niki to be replaced after four races in the event of him proving insufficiently competitive. But he was so obviously competitive from the outset, winning his third race at Long Beach, that the provision was quickly forgotten.

By 1984, armed with the superb TAG-Porsche turbo V6 engine, and battling against his gifted new team-mate Alain Prost, Niki won his third Championship by the miniscule margin of half a point over the Frenchman. His last Grand Prix victory came at Zandvoort in 1985 after which he retired for good, developing LaudaAir into an internationally respected long-haul operator with routes from Vienna to the Far East and Australia, despite the loss of a Boeing 767 over Thailand in 1991.

Lauda's dry humour, developed in England during the early years of his professional career, stayed with him throughout his time in F1. He was good company, with a keen sense of humour and a no-nonsense temperament which cut through the froth and superficiality which so often surrounds professional sport.

LAURENT, Roger (B)

b. 21 February 1913
2 Grands Prix

This five-times Belgian motorcycle champion drove two Grands Prix during 1952 at the wheel of a Ferrari 500, the best result being sixth place at Nurburgring.

LAWRENCE, Chris (GB)

b. 27 July 1933
2 Grands Prix

A Morgan sports car racing specialist, Lawrence drove the 1966 British and German GPs in a Cooper-Ferrari special entered by J A Pearce Engineering.

LECLERE, Michel (F)

b. 18 March 1947
7 Grands Prix

This very promising young French F2 star drove a third Tyrrell at Watkins Glen in 1975, before getting his full time F1 break with the Water Wolf team at the start of the following year when it was at its lowest ebb. His career was sunk virtually before it began.

LEDERLE, Neville (ZA)

b. 25 September 1938
1 Grand Prix

This outstanding South African national competitor was widely regarded as on a par with John Love by many of his compatriots. He scored a fine sixth place in the 1962 South African GP at East London in his own four-cylinder Climax-engined Lotus 21 a week after making the front row for the non-title Natal GP at Westmead alongside Graham Hill's BRM and Trevor Taylor's Team Lotus 25. He now runs a motor business near Welkom in the Free States gold fields area.

LEES, Geoff (GB)

b. 1 May 1951
5 Grands Prix

Winner of the 1981 European F2 Championship in a Ralt-Honda, Lees enjoyed only occasional F1 outings, a seventh for Tyrrell at Hockenheim in 1979 as Jean-Pierre Jarier's stand-in being his best result. He has since concentrated on building a professional racing career in Japan, and led the Toyota sports car racing team on its 1992 World Championship assault.

Neville Lederle was one of the fastest Lotus privateers on the South African F1 scene in the early 1960s.

LEGAT, Arthur (B)

b. 1 November 1898
d. 23 February 1960
2 Grands Prix

A slow Belgian privateer who drove a Veritas Meteor special in his home Grand Prix at Spa in 1952–1953.

LEHTO, J.J. - Under JARVILEHTO, Jyrki

LEONI, Lamberto (I)

b. 24 May 1953
1 Grand Prix

Leoni won the Misano F2 race with the Trivellato team Chevron-Ferrari V6 at Misano-Adriatico in the summer of 1977 and drove an F1 Ensign in the following year's

Argentine GP. He established FIRST Racing as a Formula 3000 team in 1987.

LESTON, Les (GB)

b. 16 December 1920, Nottingham
2 Grands Prix

Another F3 500cc star, Leston won the 1962 Luxembourg Grand Prix and continued to drive a Connaught at Monza in 1956, and a BRM at Silverstone the following year. He made a fortune during the 1960s with racewear and accessories before relocating to Hong Kong where he made a name as a broadcaster.

'LEVEGH, Pierre' (F)

b. 22 December 1905, Paris
d. 11 June 1955, Le Mans
6 Grands Prix
Career span: 1950–1 (Lago Talbot)

Levegh's true surname was Bouillon, but he took the *nom de course* of 'Levegh' in memory of the pioneer Mors driver of that name who had been his uncle. His handful of F1 Championship outings were at the wheel of the lumbering, outclassed 4½-litre Lago Talbots. A brilliant skater, ice hockey international and tennis player, Levegh was over fifty when Mercedes invited him to drive a 300SLR at Le Mans and was made the scapegoat for the horrifying accident in which he was killed, rather than Mike Hawthorn whose true responsibility it seems to have been.

LEWIS, Jack (GB)

b. 1 November 1936, Stroud, Gloucestershire
9 Grands Prix

The son of a motorcycle dealer who owned H and L Motors in Stroud, this wiry Welshman showed very promising form driving his own Cooper-Climax under the Ecurie Galloise banner in 1962. He switched to a supposedly works-supported BRM V8 in 1962, finishing a strong third in the non-title Pau race, but thereafter became disenchanted with Bourne and quit mid-season, selling the car back to BRM. Then newly married, he and his wife Andrea took a farm near Llandovery where they specialized in horse breeding.

LEWIS-EVANS, Stuart (GB)

b. 20 April 1930, Luton
d. 25 October 1958, East Grinstead
14 Grands Prix
Career span: 1957 (Connaught and Vanwall); 1958 (Vanwall)

This small-framed, rather frail young man (he suffered with a stomach ulcer), only had a brief career in front-line Formula 1, but the statistics fail to do credit to his outstanding ability. He was signed up mid-way through the 1957 season as a third driver for Tony Vandervell's Vanwall team, cementing his position with a brilliant display of high-speed domination in the early stages of the non-Championship F1 race held at Reims a week after the French Grand Prix at Rouen.

A product of the cut-and-thrust world of 500cc F3 racing, Lewis-Evans had come to prominence via some drives in an F1 Connaught and as a member of the Ferrari sports car team. Paired alongside Stirling Moss and Tony Brooks he may nominally have been cast in the role of third driver, but his performances on the circuits certainly never reflected such lowly status. He finished the 1957 season with fifth place at Pescara and was second in the non-championship Moroccan Grand Prix. He also took pole position for the Italian Grand Prix at Monza.

In 1958 he played a significant role in Vanwall's successful onslaught on the Constructors' World Championship, finishing third at Spa and Oporto, and fourth at Silverstone. He displayed a delicate high-speed touch and earned a great deal of admiration and respect from his two senior team-mates. Tragically, on lap forty-two of the Moroccan Grand Prix, the final race on the Championship schedule, he crashed heavily when his Vanwall's transmission locked up, and he sustained serious burns.

He was flown back to Britain in Vandervell's chartered Viscount airliner and immediately admitted to the McIndoe Burns Unit of the East Grinstead hospital where he died six days later. The loss of this mild-mannered, modest and unassuming young driver hit Tony Vandervell very hard and many who knew the gruff industrialist believed he was never quite the same man again.

LIGIER, Guy (F)

b. 12 July 1930, Vichy
12 Grands Prix
Career span: 1966–7 (Cooper); 1967 (Brabham)

Ligier was a highly competitive former rugby player and rowing ace who ran a Ford performance dealership in the shadow of the Eiffel Tower. He was in partnership with his old friend Jo Schlesser and the dealership was managed by Jose Behra, brother of the ex-Ferrari ace who was killed at Avus in 1959. He drove his own Cooper-Maserati T81 and Brabham-Repco V8, scoring a point for sixth place at Nurburgring in the latter, before concentrating on building sports and later F1 cars. All Ligier's cars carry the preface 'JS' in respectful memory of Jo Schlesser who was killed in the air-cooled Honda F1 during the 1968 French Grand Prix. Despite scoring a handful of wins over the years, Ligier's F1 programme has generally been disappointing.

LIPPI, Roberto (I)

b. 17 October 1926, Rome
1 Grand Prix

An Italian amateur who drove a de Tomaso-Osca special in the 1961 Italian Grand Prix at Monza.

LOMBARDI, Lella (I)

b. 26 March 1943
d. April 1992
12 Grands Prix
Career span: 1975–6 (March)

So far the only lady to have registered a top six finish in a World Championship Grand Prix, taking half a Championship point in the prematurely terminated 1975 Spanish GP at Barcelona with her works-tended March. She succumbed to cancer early in 1992 at the age of 48.

LOOF, Ernst (D)

b. 4 July 1907
d. 3 March 1956
1 Grand Prix

This former BMW racing engineer founded the Veritas firm in the early 1950s, building F2 cars initially from basic 328 sports cars supplied by customers and later from scratch.

LOUVEAU, Henri (F)

b. 25 January 1910
2 Grands Prix

Louveau drove Talbot-Lago in the 1950 and 1951 Swiss Grands Prix. He retired from racing following a serious crash at Berne in 1951.

LOVE, John (RSR)

b. 7 December 1924, Bulawayo
9 Grands Prix

Six times South African F1 Champion in the 1960s, this Rhodesian star had originally starred in European F/Junior back in 1961–2 as a member of Ken Tyrrell's Cooper-Austin team. An ill-timed accident at Albi, which resulted in a very badly broken arm, thwarted his chances of moving into full-time F1, but he was a regular South African Grand Prix contestant in his own car. He was leading the 1967 race at Kyalami in his 2.7-litre Climax-engined Cooper when a misfire prompted a precautionary pit stop for extra fuel, dropping him to second behind Pedro Rodriguez.

John Love failed to make F1 in Europe, but dominated that category in South African domestic events for many years.

LOVELY, Pete (USA)

b. 11 April 1926
7 Grands Prix

A Volkswagen dealer from Seattle, Lovely was invited to drive for the works Lotus team in 1960, but when his type 16 arrived too late for him to qualify at Monaco, he hot-footed it back to the USA. He drove a Cooper-Ferrari in that year's US Grand Prix and then reappeared between 1969 and 1972 for a very limited programme conducted at an equally modest pace in his own ex-works Lotus 49.

LOYER, Roger (F)

b. 5 August 1907
d. 24 March 1988
1 Grand Prix

Rented Gordini T16 for 1954 Argentine GP at Buenos Aires, failing to finish.

LUCAS, Jean (F)

b. 25 April 1917, Le Mans
1 Grand Prix

A professional sports car driver and team manager who won the 1949 Spa 24-hours, Lucas drove a Gordini T32 in the 1955 Italian Grand Prix.

LUNGER, Brett (USA)

b. 14 November 1945, Wilmington, Delaware
34 Grands Prix

A scion of the well-to-do industrial family, E I du Pont de Nemours, Lunger's racing aspirations were interrupted in 1968 when he spent thirteen months with the US Marines in Vietnam leading a reconnaissance platoon. His clean-cut image and articulate bearing were popular with motor racing sponsors and he cut a path to F1 via F2 and Formula 5000. He graduated to F1 briefly in 1975 with Hesketh, switched to Surtees in 1976 and then handling privately fielded McLarens, an M23 in 1977 and a later M26 the following year.

MACKAY-FRASER, Herbert (USA)

b. 23 July 1927
d. 14 July 1957, Reims
1 Grand Prix

Mackay-Fraser was the son of an American coffee plantation owner in Brazil and first raced in Europe with his own Ferrari Monza in 1955. He also displayed great form in Colin Chapman's small capacity Lotus sports cars during 1956 and 1957. A week after being given his maiden Grand Prix outing at the wheel of a BRM P25 in the French Grand Prix at Rouen, this popular newcomer became the first works Lotus fatality when he died from injuries sustained after crashing his 2-litre-engined, stripped down Lotus Eleven sports car in the F2 Reims race.

MACKLIN, Lance (GB)

b. 2 September 1919
13 Grands Prix
Career span: 1953–4 (HWM)

Son of the late Sir Noel Macklin, principal of the Cobham-

Brett Lunger at the wheel of his privately entered McLaren M26 in 1978.

based Invicta company, this handsome young English-man was generally regarded as a brilliantly talented driver who never had the urge to apply himself fully. Unreliable HWM machinery prevented him ever scoring a Championship point, and he quit the sport after his Austin-Healey was involved in the Pierre Levegh tragedy at Le Mans in 1955.

MAGEE, Damien (GB)

b. 17 November 1945, Belfast
1 Grand Prix

This lively and gregarious Ulsterman made his name in early 1970s FF1600 and skirted the fringe of F1 non-Championship events, having his one GP outing at Anderstorp in 1974 at the wheel of a Williams.

MAGGS, Tony (ZA)

b. 9 February 1937, Pretoria
25 Grands Prix
Career span: 1961 (Lotus); 1962–3 (Cooper)

The son of a wealthy farmer-businessman, Maggs shot to prominence in Ken Tyrrell's F/Junior Cooper-Austin team in 1961, sharing the European Championship with Jo Siffert. He was invited into the works Cooper F1 team for 1962 and 1963, partnering Bruce McLaren, and finished second in the French GP during both years. He was dropped at the end of 1963 in favour of Phil Hill, drove in three races in the Centro-Sud BRM team during the following year, and completed his F1 swansong in the 1965 South African GP with a Parnell Lotus-BRM. He drove in some F2 races later in 1965 before an accident in a Lotus 22 twin-cam at Pietermaritzburg resulted in the death of a spectating child. Thereafter he quit to concentrate on farming in the Zontspanberg area of Northern Transvaal, surviving a light aircraft accident some years later in which his farm manager was killed.

MAGLIOLI, Umberto (I)

b. 5 June 1928, Biella
10 Grands Prix
Career span: 1953 (Ferrari); 1954 (Maserati and Ferrari); 1955 (Ferrari); 1956 (Maserati); 1957 (Porsche F2)

Maglioli was an occasional F1 Ferrari driver, but enjoyed a distinguished sports car racing careering which really got off the ground in 1954 when he won the Carrera Panamericana and the Targa Florio. He continued racing through to the late 1960s and now has a business based in Lugano making exclusive precision watches.

MAIRESSE, Guy (F)

b. 10 August 1910, La Capelle, L'Aisne
d. 24 April 1954, Montlhéry
3 Grands Prix

Mairesse raced sports and F1 Talbot-Lagos during the immediate post-war period, taking second place at Le Mans in 1950 and 1951, sharing with Pierre Meyrat. When due to drive in the 1954 race with Georges Grignard, he was fatally injured in the Coupe de Paris meeting while avoiding a slower car. He spun through a concrete barrier and killed a six-year-old boy in the process.

MAIRESSE, Willy (B)

b. 1 October 1928, Momminges
d. 4 September 1969, Ostend
12 Grands Prix
Career span: 1960 (Ferrari); 1961 (Lotus and Ferrari); 1962–3 (Ferrari)

The career of this determined and enthusiastic Belgian was punctuated by huge accidents and a terrible reputation for over-driving. Early on, he enjoyed the patronage of Belgium's Ferrari importer, Jacques Swaters, and made his name at the wheel of a Berlinetta during the 1959 Tour de France. He won the Tour de France the following year during which he briefly joined the Ferrari F1 team for three events. He was in and out of the Maranello Grand Prix line-up for the next two years before being signed up as Surtees's number two for the 1963 season.

Painfully burned at Le Mans when fuel which had spilled in the undertray of the Ferrari 250P he shared with Surtees ignited, he struggled back to the F1 cockpit only to crash heavily on the opening lap of the German Grand Prix. That finished his F1 career, but he lingered on in sports car racing until a big shunt in a Ford GT40 at Le Mans in 1968 finally wrung down the curtain on his career. Increasingly distraught as he realized motor racing no longer had any place for him, this tragic figure committed suicide in an Ostend hotel room just over a year later. He was not quite forty-one years old.

MANSELL, Nigel

See pages 110–11.

MANTOVANI, Sergio (I)

b. 22 May 1929, Milan
7 Grands Prix
Career span: 1953–5 (Maserati)

This ambitious young businessman went racing essentially

'Wild Willy' Mairesse practising in his Ferrari 156 for the 1963 German Grand Prix at Nurburgring. It was to be the last F1 race of his career.

as a hobby, sampling a 2½-litre sports Maserati before making the decision to acquire his own 250F Grand Prix car at the start of the 1954 season. He gained a degree of factory support and was effectively integrated as a works team member throughout that season, his smooth and mechanically sympathetic approach earning him fifth places in both the German and Swiss Grands Prix. In the spring of 1955 he crashed the works spare 250F on a wet track during practice for Turin's non-championship F1 race on the Valentino Park circuit, breaking a leg. Unfortunately medical complications set in and the limb had to be amputated, bringing Mantovani's F1 career to an early end at the age of twenty-six. He subsequently learned to walk again with the aid of a stick and artificial leg, staying actively involved in motor racing for many years as a member of the Italian Sporting Commission.

MANZON, Robert (F)

b. 12 April 1917, Marseilles
28 Grands Prix
Career span: 1950–6 (Gordini)

One of the key cornerstones of the Gordini international

racing operation, this diesel equipment distributor from Marseilles joined the team in 1948 after some early success with a privately owned Cisitalia the previous year. His best placing was a third in the 1953 Belgian GP with Gordini, and then he achieved the same result at Reims for the 1954 French GP in a private Ferrari 625. He retired at the end of 1956.

MARIMON, Onofre (RA)

b. 19 December 1932, Cordoba
d. 31 July 1954, Nurburgring
11 Grands Prix
Career span: 1951–4 (Maserati)

Nicknamed 'Pinocchio' because of his facial resemblance to Walt Disney's famous puppet, Onofre Marimon was a cheery, happy-go-lucky protégé of the great Juan Manuel Fangio. He demonstrated great promise in 1953 at the wheel of a 2-litre Maserati A6GCM, the highlight of which was a third place in the Belgian Grand Prix at Spa.

Marimon was recruited to drive for the works team the following year, standing in for Fangio as team leader in several early season non-championship races, and

109

MANSELL, Nigel (GB)

b. 8 August 1954, Upton-on-Severn
165 Grands Prix; 21 wins
Career span: 1980–4 (Lotus); 1985–8 (Williams); 1989–90
(Ferrari); 1991 to date (Williams)

Nigel Mansell's spectacular determination at the wheel of a Grand Prix car propelled him to public prominence in the mid-1980s in much the same way as James Hunt had achieved celebrity status a decade earlier. But while Hunt won the 1976 World Championship, Mansell will be remembered most for his last-minute failure to take the title ten years later.

Across the world, television viewers shared the agony of his disappointment as one of the rear tyres on his Williams-Honda FW11B disintegrated at 190mph (306kph) in the Australian GP as he was poised to take the title.

It was a far cry from his job at Lucas Aerospace in the early 1970s where he had worked on a number of projects, including the RB211 jet engine, before deciding to throw his entire efforts into a motor racing career. From an early age Mansell's interest in motoring had been encouraged by his father, Eric. Nigel cut his teeth in the rough and tumble of kart racing before graduating to car racing in 1976 when he won his first Formula Ford event.

He struggled onwards and upwards into F3, along the way breaking his neck and fracturing a vertebra in his back. But on each occasion he bounced back into play with the resilience and commitment which marked him out as somebody quite special.

These dogged early exploits were eventually brought to the attention of Lotus boss, Colin Chapman, who Mansell impressed considerably during his first test in an F1 car during the summer of 1979. He was duly signed up as a test and development driver, getting his chance to handle a third works Lotus in the 1980 Austrian Grand Prix. It was typical of Mansell's determination that he drove for much of this race in acute discomfort from petrol burns – a result of the fuel cell leaking its contents into the cockpit. He resolutely refused to give up until his engine expired.

In 1981 he was recruited as a full-time member of the F1 team, partnering Elio de Angelis, but Lotus fortunes were then at a low ebb and Grand Prix success continued to elude him. Chapman's faith in his talent never wavered, but when the Lotus founder died suddenly from a heart attack in December 1982, Mansell lost a valuable friend and mentor just when he needed him most.

Nigel stayed with Lotus through to the end of 1984, but his driving sometimes displayed a desperate quality, perhaps reflecting the internal personal tensions between him and team manager, Peter Warr.

'Our Nige'. *Above*: the moustachioed Midlander became one of the most outstanding Grand Prix drivers of the 1980s, prompting a dramatic upsurge of F1 interest in his native land. *Right*: Mansell's Williams-Honda just failing to catch Ayrton Senna's Lotus-Renault for victory in the 1986 Spanish Grand Prix at Jerez.

Serious F1 success did not come his way until 1985, after he had left Team Lotus and joined Williams as a second driver alongside Keke Rosberg. Just as his critics were confirming their view that Mansell would never win a Formula 1 race, he scored a well-judged and overwhelmingly popular victory in the Grand Prix of Europe at Brands Hatch. This was immediately followed up with victory in the South African GP at Kyalami, earning him a final sixth place in the drivers' points table.

These late season successes unlocked the gates to a flood tide of success in 1986. His confidence by now bolstered, Mansell sped to five Grand Prix victories that season, only

losing his chance of the championship with that nerve-racking late-race tyre failure.

Now acknowledged as a world-class driver, Mansell delivered more of the same in 1987, a heady blend of breath-taking speed spiced with a handful of errors and a smattering of mechanical misfortunes. After winning six races in masterly style, an accident in practice for the Japanese GP wrote the dogged Englishman out of the script with two races to go. The championship was handed on a plate to his team-mate Nelson Piquet.

Motor racing politics resulted in Williams being deprived of its Honda engine supply in 1988 and the famous English team fell back on 3½-litre Judd V8s. It was hoped that a light, agile technical package, complemented by the use of computer-controlled 'active ride' suspension would sustain the team's competitiveness. In the event, the season degenerated into a disappointing fiasco with the team failing to score a single victory. Mansell, frustrated and disillusioned, agreed in mid-season to switch to Ferrari for 1989.

Armed with the brand new Ferrari 640, complete with revolutionary electro-hydraulic semi-automatic gear change, he won on his début outing for Maranello. This Brazilian GP victory ensured that he was accorded heroic status amongst the Italian motor racing *tifosi*, and his later victory in the Hungarian race marked a rare defeat for the all-conquering McLaren-Hondas. However, later that season disqualification from the Portuguese GP and suspension from the following weekend's Spanish race tipped his thoughts temporarily towards retirement.

This idea surfaced again more forcefully the following summer when, after his new team-mate Alain Prost reached the mid-season point with four victories to his own tally of zero, Mansell announced that he would quit F1 at the end of the season. It seemed like an emotional over-reaction to his retirement in the British GP at Silverstone, a race he had looked set to win commandingly.

As things transpired, he reversed his retirement decision, but he did not stay with Ferrari. Frank Williams made him an offer he could not refuse and he returned to the British team for 1991, reeling off five victories in the new Renault V10-engined FW14 to finish runner-up in the World Championship yet again.

By the end of 1991 Mansell had consolidated his position as one of Britain's highest-paid professional sportsmen. His cliff-top home on the Isle of Man, purpose built for the family in 1987, was put on the market for over £3 million as he moved with his wife Rosanne and their three children to a similarly magnificent Florida mansion for the winter months. It must have seemed a world away from the days when he and Rosanne had sold their home and moved into rented accommodation in order to finance Nigel's F3 apprenticeship as he struggled to get a foothold on the lowest rung of the motor racing ladder.

He opened the 1992 season with an unprecedented run of five consecutive victories and at last seemed firmly on course for the World Championship.

winning the Rome Grand Prix. He finished third at Silverstone, behind the Ferraris of Gonzalez and Hawthorn, and ahead of his great friend Fangio who was now in the streamlined Mercedes W196, Marimon sharing the joint fastest lap into the bargain.

He seemed cut out for a great future, but crashed heavily on the tricky descent to Adenau Bridge at the Nurburgring whilst practising for the German Grand Prix, and suffered fatal injuries. Those who watched an ashen-faced Fangio consoling a sobbing Gonzalez in the immediate aftermath of their compatriot's death understood vividly what Onofre Marimon had meant to them in particular, and to Argentine motor racing in general.

MARKO, Helmut (A)

b. 27 April 1943, Graz
9 Grands Prix
Career span: 1971–2 (BRM)

Dry witted and even tempered, Marko's teenage years were spent as a hell-raising confederate of Jochen Rindt,

Helmut Marko was rated by some as being potentially more talented than his compatriot Niki Lauda, but a tragic, freak accident cut short his F1 career.

but he calmed down sufficiently to obtain a law degree before pressing on with his own motor racing ambitions. A terrific sports car driver who displayed great natural flair and élan, he was recruited by BRM for Formula 1 during 1971. He was showing great form with the BRM P160 during the 1972 French Grand Prix at Clermont-Ferrand when his vizor was shattered by a flint which embedded itself in one eye. Miraculously, Marko managed to stop the car without a major accident, but he lost the sight in that damaged eye, and a potentially great racing career was at an end. For many years in charge of Renault competition activities in Austria, he more recently established a Formula 3000 team which helped his young compatriot Karl Wendlinger make his name.

MARR, Leslie (GB)

b. 14 August 1922, Durham
2 Grands Prix

Marr was a professional artist who competed extensively in his own private Connaught, finishing thirteenth in the 1954 British Grand Prix, and then failing to finish the following year.

MARSH Tony (GB)

b. 20 July 1931
4 Grands Prix

This British hillclimb ace ran an F2 Cooper-Climax in the 1957 and 1958 German Grands Prix, and then drove a Lotus in two races during 1961. He switched to a 'works-assisted' BRM in 1962 on much the same basis as Jack Lewis, but suffered problems with cracked bellhousings and cylinder blocks which resulted in him taking legal proceedings against the Bourne company after only four non-Championship races. This Chairman of a Petersfield-based engineering company won the British Hillclimb Championship six times with hat tricks during the 1950s in a Cooper-JAP Mk VIII, and in the 1970s with his self-brewed Marsh-Buick special. He recounts with some glee the fact that he still drives to and from work in a Dellow trials car!

MARTIN, Eugene (F)

b. 24 March 1915, Swesne
2 Grands Prix

A wealthy French amateur and successful BMW dealer, Martin drove a Talbot-Lago in the 1950 British and Swiss Grands Prix.

team in time to score the marque's first Championship point with a sixth place at Detroit in 1988.

Since then, Pierluigi has been a consistent and remarkably underrated performer for Minardi, but left at the end of 1991 to join JJ Lehto in the Dallara-Ferrari squad.

MASS, Jochen (D)

b. 30 September 1946, Munich
105 Grands Prix; 1 win
Career span: 1973–4 (Surtees); 1974–7 (McLaren); 1978 (ATS); 1979–80 (Arrows); 1982 (March)

Jochen Mass (popularly nicknamed 'Hermann the German' by the McLaren team with whom he had his most successful F1 years) is a one-time able seaman of tousled appearance who started his racing career competing in sprints and hillclimbs in an Alfa Romeo Giulia Sprint. He gained international prominence with his efforts at the wheel of Ford Capri saloons during the European Touring Car Championship in the early 1970s, but gained admission to F1

Jochen Mass was a popular, gentle and humorous member of the F1 fraternity who perhaps lacked the ruthless, killer instinct.

Tousled Pierluigi Martini was one of the most accomplished drivers produced by Italy during the 1980s.

MARTINI, Pierluigi (I)

b. 23 April 1961, Ravenna
70 Grands Prix
Career span: 1984 (Toleman); 1985, 1988–91 (Minardi)

Pierluigi's uncle was Giancarlo Martini, whose greatest claim to F1 fame was that he managed to crash a borrowed F1 Ferrari 312T on the warming up lap for the 1976 Race of Champions! Pint-sized and curly-haired, 'Piero' has made rather more F1 progress than his uncle, winning the 1983 FIA European F3 title in a Ralt-Alfa Romeo and scoring a terrific second place at Misano on his F2 début in a Minardi-BMW.

These successes led to an F1 test with the Brabham-BMW team, but he did not get the available seat for 1984 and was hardly consoled when he failed to qualify at Monza on a one-off guest outing in the excellent Toleman TG184. In 1985 he began F1 with the Motori Moderni V6-engined Minardi, but was hopelessly inexperienced and dropped back into Formula 3000 for the next two-and-a-half seasons. He was then invited back into the Faenza

Mass

Jochen Mass's McLaren M23 speeds to third place in the 1974 Brazilian Grand Prix at Interlagos.

on the strength of some equally strong showings in F2 single-seaters.

His F1 début came in the 1973 British Grand Prix at the wheel of a Surtees, and he switched to McLaren late in 1974 to drive the last few races in the Yardley-backed M23 which had previously been driven by Mike Hailwood and David Hobbs. He was paired with Emerson Fittipaldi in the Marlboro-McLaren line-up for 1975, winning the tragically shortened 'half points' Spanish GP at Barcelona which was flagged to a premature halt after Rolf Stommelen's Hill GH1 had crashed, killing four onlookers.

After James Hunt's arrival at McLaren the following year Mass progressively fell into a subordinate role, unable to match the Englishman's pace out on the circuit. It was a problem which seemed to get to him. At the end of 1977 he switched to ATS for a disastrous 1978 season which ended prematurely when he fractured a leg during a Silverstone test session. Two years with Arrows followed, then a year off from F1 and a final, unsuccessful Grand Prix assault with an uncompetitive RAM March. From then on, Mass enjoyed considerable success with sports

cars, but this pleasant man had really deserved more from his days in F1.

MAX, Jean (F)

b. 27 July 1943
1 Grand Prix

A French F3 exponent who rented a March 701 for the 1971 French GP at Paul Ricard in which he was placed fourteenth.

MAY, Michel (CH)

b. 18 August 1934
2 Grands Prix

A Swiss engineer who drove a Porsche in the 1961 Monaco GP and a Scuderia Colonia Lotus 18 in the British race at Aintree. He later worked as a consultant on F1 fuel-injection development for the Ferrari team in 1963.

MAYER, Tim (USA)

b. 22 February 1938
d. 28 February 1964, Longford, Tasmania
1 Grand Prix

The brilliant younger brother of Teddy Mayer, later boss of the McLaren F1 team, Tim Mayer drove a third works Cooper-Climax in the 1962 United States Grand Prix at Watkins Glen. He was signed to drive alongside Bruce McLaren in the Cooper F1 line-up for 1964, but he was killed practising for the final round of the Tasman Championship before he could take up the opportunity.

MAZET, François (F)

b. 26 February 1943
1 Grand Prix

A quite promising French F3 Tecno driver from the late 1960s who rented a March 701 for the 1971 French GP at Paul Ricard where he finished thirteenth. Socially well connected, he became right-hand man to Monaco-based Essex Petroleum boss, David Thieme, during his spell sponsoring the Lotus team in the early 1980s. He also drove F2 Brabhams and Chevrons with mixed success in the late 1960s and early 1970s.

McALPINE, Kenneth (GB)

b. 21 December 1920, Chobham
7 Grands Prix
Career span: 1952–3, 1955 (Connaught)

A member of the wealthy McAlpine civil engineering dynasty who bankrolled the Connaught Grand Prix team for almost ten years up until the team closure in 1956. He had his last GP outing at Aintree in 1955 before withdrawing to concentrate on his family's company management.

McDOWELL, Mike (GB)

b. 13 September 1932, Great Yarmouth
1 Grand Prix

This keen amateur racer later managed the Guildford garage business of John Coombs and gained great success on the British national hillclimb scene.

McLAREN, Bruce

See pages 116–17.

McRAE, Graham (NZ)

b. 5 March 1940, Wellington
1 Grand Prix

A top notch Formula 5000 contender from the early 1970s, McRae carried the nickname 'Cassius' and drove one of Frank Williams's uncompetitive Iso Marlboros in the 1973 British GP at Silverstone.

MENDITEGUY, Carlos (RA)

b. 10 August 1917
d. 28 April 1973
8 Grands Prix
Career span: 1953 (Gordini); 1955–8 (Maserati); 1960 (Cooper)

Menditeguy was a talented all-round sportsman who was reckoned to be amongst the world's top six polo players when he came to Europe on the back of the Fangio/Gonzalez bandwagon in the early 1950s. Wild and fearless behind the wheel, he was brutally hard on the machinery. He was an Argentine Grand Prix regular but never spent a full season on the Championship trail.

MERZARIO, Arturo (I)

b. 11 March 1943, Como
57 Grands Prix
Career span: 1972–3 (Ferrari); 1974–5 (Williams); 1976–7 (March); 1978–9 (Merzario)

The skinny, cheerful son of a prosperous building contractor, 'Little Art' made his racing reputation in small capacity sports cars for Abarth before joining the Ferrari endurance racing team in 1970. In 1972 he was promoted mid-season to the F1 team, finishing his first Ferrari drive with a sixth place in the British GP at Brands Hatch. In 1972, he distinguished himself by winning the Targa Florio road race in Sicily, sharing the victorious Ferrari 312PB 3-litre sports car with rally ace Sandro Munari. He remained with Maranello until the end of 1973, after which his services were dispensed with as Lauda and Regazzoni took over at the start of the following year. He then joined Frank Williams and produced some game showings including a sixth at Kyalami and a fourth at Monza. They were his last ever Championship points, for after struggling as a March privateer in 1976 and 1977, he embarked on a programme to build his own Cosworth-engined special for 1978. It was a project which almost bankrupted the popular Italian and wound up his career in F1.

McLAREN, Bruce (NZ)

b. 30 August 1937, Auckland
d. 2 June 1970, Goodwood
101 Grands Prix; 4 wins
Career span: 1958–65 (Cooper); 1966–70 (McLaren)

There were only twelve years separating Bruce McLaren's arrival on the European international motor racing scene from his death in a testing accident at Goodwood. Yet his legacy lives on with his name attached to one of the most prestigious teams Grand Prix racing has ever seen.

Bruce himself would have appreciated the high levels of technical excellence and professionalism which the current management of McLaren International applied to the team throughout the 1980s. For although this quiet New Zealander initially only aspired to a career behind the wheel, the manner in which he shaped the fortunes of the first McLaren Racing company from 1966 up until his death itself represented a significant step towards changing the tempo of professional motor racing.

The son of a successful garage owner from the comfortable Auckland suburb of Remuera, Bruce McLaren grew up with a sunny disposition which an early skirmish with Perthes disease, a potentially debilitating hip condition, failed to extinguish. In 1958 he won the Driver to Europe scholarship promoted by the New Zealand International Grand Prix Association on the strength of some promising performances at the wheel of his own privately run Cooper F2 machine.

That car was duly shipped back to England where the twenty-year-old McLaren lived up to the form predicted by his fellow antipodean, Jack Brabham. A succession of promising Formula 2 performances in his own car earned him promotion to the Cooper factory team for 1959. At the end of that season he won the United States Grand Prix at Sebring, the race which saw team-mate Brabham clinch his first world title.

Bruce opened the 1960 season on a similarly successful note, surviving the broiling heat to win the Argentine Grand Prix at Buenos Aires. He continued to play an unobtrusive supporting role to Brabham throughout the year, finishing second behind the Australian in the final Championship points table.

After Brabham left to establish his own team at the end of 1961, McLaren duly assumed the Cooper team leadership, but life in the once-proud British team was becoming hard going. Cooper had slipped from the competitive high wire and, when Charles Cooper, the ageing, penny-pinching and autocratic patriarch, refused to sanction the construction of two special cars for the 1963/1964 Tasman Championship, Bruce decided to go it alone and build the cars himself.

He formed Bruce McLaren Motor Racing, and this decision eventually led him to quit Cooper at the end of 1965 and pursue his own ambitious plans in a variety of racing categories.

That Tasman adventure at the start of 1964 also had its tragic side, for Bruce's talented team-mate Tim Mayer, a young American rising star, was killed in practice for the final round at Longford, Tasmania. However, his brother Teddy, who had abandoned a career as a lawyer to manage his brother's career, threw in his lot with McLaren to bring in some much needed finance in addition to considerable mental dexterity on the management side.

McLaren Racing blew a breath of fresh air through the stuffy British motor racing establishment during the 1960s at a time when the sport was primed for lift-off into the commercial era. Bruce's tolerant approach acted as a foil to Mayer's often abrasive business edge. The company developed into a well-balanced organization which always thrived on hard work and a no-nonsense approach to any job in hand.

After he won the 1962 Monaco Grand Prix for Cooper, six years would pass before Bruce triumphed again in a World Championship Grand Prix. The next time victory would come at the wheel of a Cosworth-engined car bearing his own name, in the 1968 Belgian Grand Prix at Spa. By this stage his compatriot Denny Hulme had been recruited to drive alongside him and, while Bruce was content to let his friend set the F1 pace, the domination exerted by the rumbling, ground-shaking McLaren-Chevrolet sports cars made the financially lucrative Can-Am series almost their private domain during the second half of the decade.

By 1970 Bruce had established himself as a successful and prosperous businessman. There was talk of retirement from racing, a road car project was nearing completion and the company was now a confident, financially viable business entity which had expanded to launch an assault on that US classic, the Indianapolis 500. Bruce may not have been the fastest Formula 1 driver of his era, but he had gained a reputation for consistency and dependability which was second to none. He also nurtured ambitious plans for a road-going version of his M6 Can-Am sports car, a handful of prototypes being built in 1969–70.

On 2 June 1970, all those plans were ripped asunder with a terrible finality. Testing one of the latest McLaren M8D-Chevrolets in preparation for the forthcoming Can-Am series, an improperly secured rear body section flew backwards off the car as Bruce was lapping Goodwood at speed. The car was pitched out of control and slammed into a disused marshals' post. Bruce could hardly have known anything about it.

Bruce McLaren brought much to F1. He was a steady driver, practical engineer, popular team chief and companionable personality.

MIERES, Roberto (RA)

b. 3 December 1924, Mar de Plata
17 Grands Prix
Career span: 1953 (Gordini); 1954–5 (Maserati)

This scion of a wealthy Argentinian family was an outstanding sportsman, excelling in tennis, rugby, rowing and yachting. He cut his motor racing teeth on such diverse machinery as a 2.3-litre supercharged Alfa Romeo and Mercedes SSK before being invited to go to Europe with Fangio and Gonzalez in the early 1950s. After a couple of preliminary outings his career took off seriously in Europe with three outings in the factory Gordini team during the 1953 World Championship season. In 1954 he bought a new 250F and so impressed the factory with third places in the Swiss and Spanish races that they took him under their wing for 1955. A pleasantly cosmopolitan man who spoke several languages fluently, he eventually retired and returned to his native country at the end of that season.

MIGAULT, François (F)

b. 4 December 1944, Le Mans
13 Grands Prix

A French journeyman who became a member of the Motul BRM team in 1974 and had a handful of guest drives elsewhere.

MILES, John (GB)

b. 14 June 1943
12 Grands Prix
Career span: 1969–70 (Lotus); 1971 (BRM)

John Miles was the bespectacled, scholastic son of thespian Sir Bernard Miles, the driving force behind London's Mermaid Theatre. He was a successful sports car and F3 exponent who gained promotion to Team Lotus F1 ranks in 1969 as the third driver grappling with the experimental 4WD Lotus 63. After Graham Hill was injured at Watkins Glen, he moved into the team as Rindt's full-time number two for 1970, taking fifth place in the South African Grand Prix with a revamped Lotus 49D.

A trained engineer, he became extremely apprehensive about the fragility of the Lotus 72 and, after Rindt's fatal accident at Monza, found his cautious approach rewarded when he was dropped from the team. There is no doubt that Miles was too sensitive and cerebral to fit into Colin Chapman's idea of what a professional racing driver should be, and Miles felt personally traumatized – although inwardly relieved – at the manner in which Chapman dispensed with his services. He drove a handful of non-championship races for BRM the following year, then did some 2-litre sports car events before retiring to concentrate on technical journalism and road testing. He later took up an engineering career with Group Lotus on the road car side of the business and in 1992 expanded his engineering involvement to the Lotus F1 team.

MILHOUX, André (B)

b. 9 December 1928, Bressoux
1 Grand Prix

Milhoux drove a Gordini T32 in the 1956 German Grand Prix at Nurburgring.

MITTER, Gerhard (D)

b. 30 August 1935
d. 1 August 1969
5 Grands Prix

Mitter won the European Hillclimb Championship three times (1966–68) and was an accomplished member of the Porsche sports car team. His F1 debut was in one of de Beaufort's in the 1963 Dutch Grand Prix and thereafter he had four guest drives in his home Grand Prix at Nurburgring. It was there that he was killed practising for the 1969 Grand Prix when his F2 BMW crashed heavily at Flugplatz.

By 1991 Stefano Modena was at the wheel of a Pirelli-shod Tyrrell-Honda, but still his career had not quite taken off.

Stefano Modena arrived in F1 with Euro Brun in 1988.

MODENA, Stefano (I)

b. 12 May 1963, Modena
58 Grands Prix
Career span: 1987 (Brabham); 1988 (Euro Brun); 1989–90
(Brabham); 1991 (Tyrrell)

It was when Modena won the 1986 Monaco F3 race supporting the Grand Prix that his career began to take off, and the romantically named Italian consolidated his reputation with a fine victory in that year's European F3 Championship. The following year he drove outstandingly in an Onyx team March to win the International F3000 title, and graduated full time to F1 the following year with Brun. Two years with Brabham produced a fine third place at Monaco and a switch to Tyrrell produced a second place at Montreal. Apart from that Stefano's career progress has been tidy and unobtrusive to the point of anonymity.

MONTGOMERIE-CHARRINGTON, Robin (GB)

b. 23 June 1915, London
1 Grand Prix

This Eton-educated Gloucestershire farmer raced a second AJB Aston-Butterworth F2 car in the 1952 Belgian Grand Prix. He sometimes had his car entered by his American wife – running in the US blue and white racing colours – which gave rise to some confusion amongst the historians!

MORBIDELLI, Gianni (I)

b. 13 January 1968, Pesaro
19 Grands Prix
Career span: 1990 (Dallara and Minardi); 1991 (Minardi)

The youngest Grand Prix driver of all during the 1991 season, Morbidelli signed a testing contract with Ferrari at the age of twenty-one and made his F1 début shortly after his twenty-second birthday. His father manufactured racing motorcycles, Morbidelli bikes contesting the 125cc and 350cc classes in the early 1970s with Spanish rider Angel Nieto. Gianni graduated directly from karts into F3 at the start of 1987 and eventually clinched the Italian title two years later. He then continued through F3000, making his F1 début as stand-in for Emanuele Pirro at Interlagos in 1990 at the wheel of a Dallara. Later that season he replaced Paola Barilla in the Minardi line-up for the Japanese and Australian Grands Prix, staying on full time in 1991 when the team concluded a deal to use Ferrari engines.

Gianni Morbidelli was another promising Italian to find a full-time F1 berth in the early 1990s.

MOSS, Stirling (GB)

b. 17 September 1929, London
66 Grands Prix; 16 wins
Career span: 1951 (HWM); 1952 (HWM, ERA and Connaught); 1953 (Connaught and Cooper); 1954, 1956 (Maserati); 1955 (Mercedes); 1957 (Maserati and Vanwall); 1958 (Vanwall and Cooper); 1959 (Cooper and BRM); 1960 (Cooper and Lotus); 1961 (Lotus)

When Stirling Moss crashed his UDT-Laystall team Lotus during the non-championship Glover Trophy at Goodwood in the spring of 1962, the entire nation waited with baited breath as he lay unconscious in his hospital bed for a month. For Moss had long since come to be regarded as a British institution, not only for his remarkable racing exploits behind the wheel, but also for his versatility, enthusiasm and general all-round zest for living.

His father Alfred was a prosperous and successful dentist who had raced as an amateur at Indianapolis during the 1920s, and his mother Aileen had been a keen rally competitor with a Marendaz car during the 1930s. It was therefore no surprise that Stirling and his sister Pat – who went on to become the world's leading female rallyist – were raised in a highly competitive, sport-orientated environment. Before cars came into their lives they were both competitive show jumpers, encouraged intently by their enthusiastic parents.

Stirling began his motor sporting career in 1947 at the wheel of a BMW 328, an archetypal medium-fast German sports car. By 1948 he had hurled himself into the turbulently competitive world of 500cc Formula 3, proving the dominant force in this category right through to 1954 when he finally forsook it on the eve of his graduation to front-line F1 with a private Maserati.

Meanwhile, his terrific speed, matchless commitment and remarkable versatility had seen young Moss speed to victory in just about every racing category available. In 1951 he was given the chance to race internationally in single-seaters by the struggling HWM team, whose finances were as brittle as the components that went into their cars.

His form proved so outstanding that he was offered a drive in a works Ferrari in the non-championship Bari Grand Prix, but was furious when he turned up for this Italian domestic event to find that his car had been allocated to Piero Taruffi without any prior debate. It was an experience which soured him against Enzo Ferrari for many years and he would take particular delight in trouncing the scarlet cars from Maranello at every available opportunity.

At the end of 1953 the racing world sprang to attention at the news that Mercedes-Benz would be returning to Grand Prix racing the following year. Alfred Moss and Stirling's manager Ken Gregory approached Mercedes team manager Alfred Neubauer with the suggestion that young Moss might be considered for a place in the team, but Neubauer was not convinced. He wanted to see Stirling at the wheel of a fully fledged Formula 1 car before making such a decision.

As a result, with the generous support of BP, Moss acquired a Maserati 250F and set out to prove himself to Neubauer. By the time the brilliant young English driver had dominated the Italian Grand Prix, his private Maserati pulling away from Fangio's Mercedes until it was sidelined due to failing oil pressure, Neubauer was convinced. Moss was welcomed into the Mercedes fold in 1955 and duly won his first Grand Prix at Aintree.

There was a great deal of the British bulldog about Stirling's whole approach to racing. Fiercely patriotic, he wanted nothing more than to beat the Continentals at the wheel of an English Formula 1 car. However, no such cars existed in the early 1950s, as he found out during his brief dalliance with the 1½-litre supercharged V16 BRM in 1952. There was no choice but to drive for a European team, and he returned to Maserati, now as the works team number one driver, for 1956 after Mercedes withdrew from racing.

During 1956 he added the Monaco and Italian Grands Prix to his victory tally, but in 1957 finally achieved his ambition by signing to drive as team leader at the wheel of a British racing-green Vanwall owned by the grumpy, but similarly patriotic bearing magnate, Tony Vandervell.

Sharing with Tony Brooks, he again won the British Grand Prix at Aintree and also notched up victories at Pescara and, most satisfying of all, at Monza in the Italian Grand Prix where he trounced Maserati and Ferrari in their own personal backyard. In 1958 he sustained the winning momentum, but was pipped to the World Championship by Mike Hawthorn, although the Vanwall team successfully realized their patron's ambition by taking the Constructors' title.

Moss always displayed a well-honed sense of fair play. It was his intervention which prevented the disqualification of Mike Hawthorn in the Portuguese Grand Prix at Oporto and, ironically, helped this rival beat Moss to the Drivers' title. With Vanwall withdrawing from the fray in 1958, Stirling switched to Rob Walker's private team to drive a succession of Coopers and Lotuses through to 1961 when he achieved what was to be his final Grands Prix victories. He beat the much more powerful Ferraris in an example of driving virtuosity at Nurburgring which must be bracketed in the history books with Fangio's performance on the same track four years earlier.

Stirling's continued reluctance to be seduced into driving for Ferrari clearly undermined his possibilities of winning the World Championship. Had he driven for the

A tense moment at Monza. Willing hands help Stirling Moss's Vanwall back into the fray after a routine pit stop in the 1957 Italian Grand Prix, the English star's first overseas win for the magnate bearing Tony Vandervell's team.

Italian team in 1959, 1960 or 1961, the chances are that he would have won the title, but by then he was fast reaching the conclusion that the Championship crown was no accurate barometer of driving talent and the whole thing did not really matter anyway.

Nevertheless, for the 1962 season it was intended that there should be a *rapprochement* between Moss and Ferrari. Stirling was to drive one of their 1½-litre type 156s in the World Championship, entered by Rob Walker and prepared by his master mechanic Alf Francis, but the Goodwood accident wiped out that tantalizing possibility.

In 1963, barely a year after the accident, Moss tested a sports racing car and decided he would retire from racing. He believed his faculties had been irreparably damaged, but today believes he made a premature judgement. It hardly mattered. Within a year or so of his recovery, he had disappeared into a tornado of business activity which would hardly have left any room for racing had he chosen to change his mind and reverse that 1963 decision.

To this day, Stirling remains trim and enormously active, living in the same purpose-built home in Mayfair which he designed to his own specification shortly before the accident which ended his career. Unlike many subsequent F1 prima donnas, his name can still be found in the central London telephone directory!

121

MORENO, Roberto (BR)

b. 11 February 1959, Rio de Janeiro
24 Grands Prix
Career span: 1987 (AGS); 1989 (Coloni); 1990 (Euro Brun and Benetton); 1991 (Benetton and Jordan)

Moreno was a great childhood friend of Nelson Piquet, and originally tried his hand in F1 with a Lotus at Zandvoort in 1982. After a patchy period of disappointing results, he restored his reputation by winning the 1988 European F3000 title in a Ralt-Honda. Recruited by Benetton after Nannini was badly injured in a helicopter accident late in 1989, he cemented his place in the team for a following year by finishing second to Piquet in a Benetton 1–2 win at Suzuka. Question marks about his fitness, allied to a keenness amongst the Benetton management to recruit the dynamic young Michael Schumacher, saw him dismissed from the team less than a week after finishing fourth at Spa. He was consoled by a couple of runs for Jordan before his F1 career dried up, apparently for good.

In fact, Roberto was to be thrown a lifeline in 1992 when he was invited to drive for the Andrea Moda team on a race-to-race basis, giving the small Italian team a timely morale-booster by qualifying at Monaco.

MORGAN, David (GB)

b. 7 August 1944
1 Grand Prix

This energetic F3 and F2 racer from the early 1970s drove a Surtees TS16 in the 1975 British Grand Prix. He later made his name as an F3000 and F1 engineer, working on Eric van de Poele's F1 Lamborghini in 1991. In 1992, he continued in F1 as engineer to financially strapped Brabham team – again working with van de Poele – although the cars rarely made the cut.

MOSER, Silvio (CH)

b. 24 April 1941, Zurich
d. 26 May 1974, Monza
12 Grands Prix

A pint-sized Swiss who made his name in F3 during the mid-1960s and had his first GP outing in the 1967 British race in an uncompetitive Cooper-ATS. He acquired an ex-works Brabham-Repco in which he took his best ever result with a fifth at Zandvoort in 1968, keeping the car through to the following season before switching to a hopeless Bellasi F1 special. He was signed to drive Brabham BT42s for the Bretscher team in 1974, but sustained fatal head injuries as he toured round to the pits in his Lola T292 sports car during the Monza 1,000km race,

having failed to refasten his harness after an incident out on the circuit.

MOSS, Stirling

See pages 120–1.

MUNARON, Gino (I)

b. 2 April 1928
4 Grands Prix

This Italian privateer drove an elderly Maserati 250F in the 1960 Argentine Grand Prix and an equally uncompetitive Cooper-Castellotti in the French, British and Italian races in the same year.

MURRAY, David (GB)

b. 18 December 1909
d. 5 April 1973
4 Grands Prix

An Edinburgh accountant who raced his own private Maserati in a handful of Grands Prix before becoming involved as one of the driving forces behind Ecurie Écosse, the famous Scottish Jaguar racing sports car team. He relocated to the Canary Islands in the 1960s and died in straitened financial circumstances.

MUSSO, Luigi (I)

b. 29 July 1924, Rome
d. 7 July 1958, Reims
24 Grands Prix; 1 win (shared)
Career span: 1953–5 (Maserati); 1965–8 (Ferrari)

The death of this educated and cultured man as he fought to keep pace with team-mate Mike Hawthorn in the opening stages of the 1958 French Grand Prix robbed Italy of its last front-line Formula 1 driver of the decade. Born in Rome, the youngest of three sons of an Italian diplomat who had spent much time in China, 'Luigino' not only became an accomplished racing driver, but was also a fine horseman, a crack shot and a talented fencer.

In the early 1950s he progressed gradually through sports car racing, first with a 750 Stanguellini and later a 2-litre Maserati which benefited from a degree of works assistance. For 1954 he purchased a Maserati 250F in which he won the non-championship Pescara race and finished second in the Spanish Grand Prix. In 1955 he was second at Bordeaux, Naples and Syracuse and finished third in the Dutch Grand Prix before transferring to

Ferrari for 1956. He started his Maranello career on a high note by sharing the winning Lancia-Ferrari with Fangio in the Argentine Grand Prix.

A crash in the Nurburgring 1,000km sports car race caused him to miss the balance of the season with a broken arm, but in 1957 he won the non-title Marne Grand Prix at Reims. However, he increasingly found himself under psychological pressure from Hawthorn and Collins as they went into 1958. The prize fund at Reims was considerably greater than at many other Grands Prix and success in this race may have led Musso to over-drive. An infusion of cash would have been beneficial at the time to shore-up a particularly shaky business enterprise. Perhaps he just tried too hard as a result.

NACKE, Bernhard (D)

d. 1980
1 Grand Prix

This German club racer fielded a BMW-Eigenbau special in his home Grand Prix at Nurburgring in 1952.

NAKAJIMA, Satoru (J)

b. 23 February 1953
74 Grands Prix
Career span: 1987–9 (Lotus); 1990–1 (Tyrrell)

The first Japanese to become an F1 regular, Nakajima's inclusion in the second works Lotus alongside Ayrton Senna in 1987 was part of the deal which gained the Hethel team access to Honda engines. He stayed with Lotus until the end of 1989, then switched to Tyrrell for two seasons – again paid for by Honda – until deciding to retire. A pleasant and popular man who never made any waves, he was a good test driver and not at all disgraced by some of his performances; notably he gained a fourth place in the pouring rain in the Lotus-Judd at Adelaide in 1989.

NANNINI, Alessandro (I)

b. 7 July 1959
77 Grands Prix; 1 win
Career span: 1986–7 (Minardi); 1988–90 (Benetton)

This good-natured, chain-smoking Italian always used to joke that he would never be the most famous member of his family. His sister Gianna was firmly established as one of their country's leading rock singers by the time Sandro assumed the number one seat in the Benetton-Ford team on Thierry Boutsen's departure to Williams at the start of 1989.

The following two seasons proved that Sandro's re-

Satoru Nakajima became the first Japanese driver to tackle F1 on a full-time basis between 1987 and 1991.

marks had done him rather less than justice. The previous year, following two seasons' struggle with an uncompetitive Minardi, he had received what many regarded as his long-overdue reward by being promoted to the Benetton-Ford line-up. It was a selection Sandro fully justified by producing a succession of mature performances, the most outstanding of which were third at a rain-soaked Silverstone, and a chase through to ninth at Monza after losing a lap at the start with mechanical problems.

Nannini's competitive career on four wheels had started when he went rallying behind the wheel of a Citroën Dyane, a somewhat unlikely choice of car. From then he switched to a Lancia Stratos and in 1980 made the switch to circuit racing, graduating to F2 with Minardi in 1982 and staying with them through to the end of 1987.

He won the 1989 Japanese GP after Senna's exclusion and was on course to win in Hungary the following year before Ayrton's McLaren elbowed him off the circuit. Then came tragedy. A week after finishing third in the Spanish GP at Jerez, one of Sandro's forearms was severed in a horrifying helicopter accident within the grounds of

123

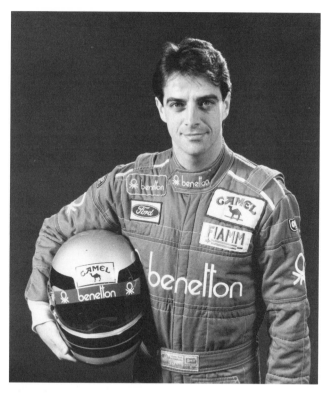

Sandro Nannini was a hugely popular star in the making, but although he was lucky to survive a 1990 helicopter accident, his F1 career was at an end.

the family villa near Siena. Thanks to miraculous micro-surgery and lots of determination, the limb was reattached and saved. His F1 days were over but he returned to drive Alfa Romeo touring cars in the Italian Championship at the start of 1992.

NATILI, Massimo (I)

b. 28 July 1935
1 Grand Prix

Natili was another of that large band of Italian domestic F1 racers who successfully qualified an ageing Centro-Sud Cooper-Maserati as Lorenzo Bandini's team-mate for the 1961 British GP at Aintree.

NAYLOR, Brian (GB)

b. 24 March 1923, Salford
7 Grands Prix

Naylor was a Stockport motor trader who raced extensively in club events and tried a handful of Grands Prix, initially in an F2 Cooper-Climax and later his Maserati-engined JBW special. His best result was achieved with the

latter machine when he was thirteenth in the 1960 British Grand Prix at Silverstone.

NEEDELL, Timothy ('Tiff') (GB)

b. 29 October 1951, Havant
1 Grand Prix

Started his career by winning a Formula Ford Lotus 69F in a competition run by *Autosport* magazine at the start of 1971. He was refused a Super-Licence by FISA in 1979 when he was offered a drive with Ensign in F1 – Patrick Gaillard got the seat – but drove for the team in the 1980 Belgian Grand Prix. Since then he has built a reputation as a sports car driver and broadcaster.

NEVE, Patrick (B)

b. 13 October 1949
10 Grands Prix

This ambitious Belgian drove for the RAM Brabham and Ensign teams in 1976 before switching to the fledgeling Williams Grand Prix Engineering operation the following year with a private March.

NICHOLSON, John (NZ)

b. 6 October 1941
1 Grand Prix

An engine preparation wizard whose company – Nicholson McLaren – fettled the McLaren team's special Cosworth DFVs in the mid-1970s, John Nicholson was also an accomplished semi-professional racer at Formula Atlantic level. He drove in the 1975 British Grand Prix in his Lyncar special – with home-brewed Cosworth power, of course.

NIEDEMEYER, Helmut (D)

b. 19 November 1919
d. 3 April 1985
1 Grand Prix

Niedemeyer drove an AFM-BMW in the 1952 German Grand Prix at Nurburgring, the same year in which he shared the second place Mercedes-Benz 300SL at Le Mans with Theo Helfrich.

NIEMANN, Brausch (ZA)

b. 7 January 1939
1 Grand Prix

A regular South African national racing contender who drove Ted Lanfear's Lotus 22 F/Junior, fitted with a 1,500cc pushrod four-cylinder engine, in his home GP in 1963 at East London.

NILSSON, Gunnar (s)

b. 20 November 1948
d. 20 October 1978
31 Grands Prix; 1 win
Career span: 1976–7 (Lotus)

This very promising Swedish driver developed into one of the stars of the British Formula 3 scene during the mid-1970s and was prompted into the Lotus Grand Prix team at the start of 1976 as part of a deal which saw Colin Chapman release Ronnie Peterson to return to the March F1 team.

Nilsson proved a willing apprentice, eager to learn the ropes from team leader Mario Andretti with whom he was paired through to the end of the 1977 season. Armed with the ground-effect Lotus 78, Nilsson also grasped a great

Gunnar Nilsson battled vainly against the onset of cancer with all the determination he applied to his efforts behind the wheel.

opportunity to win the rain-soaked 1977 Belgian Grand Prix at Zolder after Andretti took John Watson's Brabham-Alfa off the road on the first lap, eliminating both cars.

By the end of the season Gunnar was starting to feel unwell rather too regularly for his own comfort. But his confidence and optimism were undaunted and he signed to drive for the fledgeling Arrows team alongside Riccardo Patrese at the start of the 1978 season. However, it was clear that he would not be fit enough to start the season and while the team considerately announced that they would keep the drive open for him until he recovered, it was soon clear that Gunnar was suffering from terminal cancer.

He lingered until the autumn before succumbing to the disease, by which time he had given great impetus to the Gunnar Nilsson Cancer Treatment Campaign which was supported in his memory by many members of the motor sporting fraternity.

NUCKEY, Rodney (GB)

b. 26 June 1929
1 Grand Prix

A Cooper-Bristol privateer whose family ran the Warrior Tap and Die Company in South Mimms, Hertfordshire, Nuckey competed in the 1953 German Grand Prix. He now lives in retirement in Australia.

O'BRIEN, Robert (USA)

1 Grand Prix

This American amateur drova a Simca-Gordini T15 in the 1952 Belgian Grand Prix at Spa, finishing fourteenth, six laps behind Ascari's winning Ferrari 500.

OLIVER, Jack (GB)

b. 14 August 1942, Romford
50 Grands Prix
Career span: 1967–8 (Lotus); 1969–70 (BRM); 1973 (Shadow); 1977 (Shadow)

Oliver was a cocky Essex lad who fought his way up through F3 into F2 with an ex-works Lotus 48 in 1967, and was in the right place at the right time when Jim Clark was killed in the spring of 1968. Drafted into the Lotus F1 team alongside Graham Hill, he blotted his copybook with Colin Chapman by shunting at both Monaco and Rouen, but his 49B was leading the British Grand Prix at Brands Hatch when the transmission failed.

He rounded off the season with a third in Mexico City, but by then had been dropped in favour of Jochen Rindt for 1969. Oliver then joined BRM on a two-year contract which only yielded a couple of top six finishes – sixth at Mexico in 1970 and fifth at Österreichring the following year. Dropped by the team for 1972, he had a guest drive in the British Grand Prix, only returning to full-time F1 with the new Shadow team in 1973. He finished third in the Canadian Grand Prix at Mosport Park, a chaotic wet/dry race where even the official lap charts exploded – to this day the author believes Oliver was actually cheated out of a victory on that dank, dismal day!

Thereafter he worked in a management role for Shadow, driving a couple of events for the team in 1977 (the Race of Champions and Swedish Grand Prix) before he and a group of colleagues broke away to establish the rival Arrows équipe for 1978. Sued by Shadow boss Don Nichols in the London High Court, it was established that Oliver and his pals had infringed Shadow design copyright with their new Arrows A1 design and were forced to make recompense. He is still a director of the Arrows team which was renamed Footwork following takeover by a Japanese businessman at the end of 1990.

ONGAIS, Danny (USA)

b. 21 May 1942
4 Grands Prix

This Indy car hot shot from Hawaii managed to get himself involved driving a Penske PC4 for Ted Field's Interscope Racing team in the 1977 US and Canadian GPs. He also drove a works Ensign in the first two races of the 1978 season, in Argentina and Brazil.

OWEN, Arthur (GB)

b. 23 March 1915
1 Grand Prix

This amateur racer and hillclimber from Jersey competed in the 1960 Italian GP with a Cooper-Climax.

PACE, Carlos (BR)

b. 6 October 1944, Sao Paulo
d. 18 March 1977, near Sao Paulo
72 Grands Prix; 1 win
Career span: 1972 (Williams); 1973–4 (Surtees); 1974–7 (Brabham)

This debonair and charming Brazilian was a contemporary and close rival of the Fittipaldi brothers, and made his way to Britain in 1970 where he showed splendid form at the wheel of an F3 Lotus 59. In 1971 he moved up into F2 with Frank Williams, winning a non-championship race at Imola, before gaining promotion into the Williams F1

ranks the following year driving a March 711 alongside team leader Henri Pescarolo.

Despite having a long-term contract with Williams, he switched to Team Surtees for 1973, a move which may have seemed smart at the time, but which collapsed in contractual disagreement mid-way through 1974. Carlos then made another change, joining the Brabham team under Bernie Ecclestone's patronage. The greatest moment of his F1 career followed early in 1975 when he took his Brabham BT44B to a fine victory over Fittipaldi's McLaren M23 in the Brazilian Grand Prix. It was to be his sole Grand Prix victory.

In 1976, in contrast to team-mate Carlos Reutemann, he was suffused with optimistic enthusiasm when it came to Brabham's change-over to Alfa Romeo engines. He put all his speed and commitment into getting the best out of the new partnership, and a second place in the 1977 Argentine Grand Prix at Buenos Aires suggested that progress was being made in the right direction. Tragically, after the first three races of the season he was killed in a light aircraft accident near Sao Paulo.

In 1990 the Brazilian GP returned to Interlagos after a decade's absence and the track was renamed the Autodromo Carlos Pace in memory of this popular man.

PAGANI, Nello (I)

b. 11 October 1911
1 Grand Prix

This Moto-Guzzi and Gilera rider twice won the Pau Grand Prix for Maserati in 1947 and 1948. He later became manager of the legendary MV Agusta motorcycle racing team, and took part in the 1950 Swiss Grand Prix at Bremgarten in a Maserati 4CLT/48.

PALETTI, Riccardo (I)

b. 15 June 1958
d. 13 June 1982, Montreal
2 Grands Prix

This pleasant, bespectacled novice died from injuries sustained when his Osella slammed into the back of Didier Pironi's stalled pole position Ferrari at the start of the 1982 Canadian GP. Paletti, who had started from the back of the grid, was doing well over 100mph (160kph) on impact.

PALM, Torsten (S)

b. 23 July 1947
1 Grand Prix

A competitive F3 and F2 competitor who drove a rented Hesketh 308 in the 1975 Swedish GP at Anderstorp.

Jonathan Palmer at speed in the Tyrrell 017 during 1988. This promising Englishman never quite made the grade in F1.

PALMER, Jonathan (GB)

b. 7 November 1956, London
84 Grands Prix
Career span: 1984 (RAM); 1985–6 (Zakspeed); 1987–9 (Tyrrell)

A level-headed and pragmatic young man who completed his medical training and qualified as a doctor, Palmer held two hospital posts before opting for a full-time career in professional racing.

He made his single-seater name in Formula Ford and won the 1982 British F3 Championship before graduating to F2 with the Ralt-Honda squad, winning the 1982 European Championship. He also had his F1 début that year, driving a Williams FW08C in the GP of Europe at Brands Hatch. He graduated full time to F1 with the RAM team in 1984, but this and the German Zakspeed team for whom he drove in 1985 and 1986 were small and underfinanced.

Nevertheless, Jonathan quickly gained a reputation as a cool and methodical racer whose orderly mind and clear-sighted approach helped him to develop into a fine test and development driver. His three subsequent seasons with Tyrrell yielded little in terms of hard results and in 1990 he capitalized on his testing reputation by becoming official test driver for the World-Championship-winning Honda Marlboro McLaren team.

PARKES, Mike (GB)

b. 24 September 1931, Richmond, Surrey
d. 28 August 1977, near Turin
6 Grands Prix
Career span: 1966–7 (Ferrari)

Son of a former chairman of the Alvis company, Mike Parkes was born into a world of cars and motor racing, and rose to become a long-distance sports car driver of considerable status. He also briefly enjoyed a spell as a Ferrari F1 driver, the highlights of which were second place to Scarfiotti in the 1966 Italian Grand Prix and victory in the following year's Silverstone International Trophy.

He trained as an engineer with the Rootes Group in Coventry, staying with them until 1962 by which time his professional racing career had started. He joined Ferrari in 1963 as a test and development engineer, being promoted

127

to the F1 team after a string of international sports car successes following the departure of John Surtees with whom he had a somewhat strained personal relationship.

An enormous accident on the opening lap of the 1967 Belgian Grand Prix left him lying beside his upturned Ferrari with head injuries and a badly broken leg. The accident virtually finished his career, for although he subsequently had some sports car drives, the old magic had deserted him.

After his retirement he managed the Filipinetti private Ferrari team and operated a team of Fiat 128s contesting the European Touring Car Championship. After that he became involved in the management of the Lancia rally team for whom he was still working when he died in a road accident near Turin.

PARNELL, Reg (GB)

b. 2 July 1911, Derby
d. 7 January 1964
6 Grands Prix
Career span: 1951 (Alfa Romeo and Maserati); 1951 (Ferrari and BRM); 1952 (Cooper); 1954 (Ferrari)

Had it not been for World War II, this farmer and haulage contractor from Derby might well have matured into one of Britain's great Grand Prix drivers. As it was he gained a reputation as a steady, dogged and supremely versatile runner in almost every category. He retired to the post of team manager at Aston Martin at the end of the 1954 season and later ran the Yeoman Credit/Bowmaker teams from which he developed Reg Parnell Racing at the start of 1963. He died of peritonitis following medical complications after a routine appendix operation.

PARNELL, Tim (GB)

b. 25 June 1932
2 Grands Prix

The popular, roly-poly son of Reg Parnell, Tim Parnell took part in the 1961 British and Italian GPs in his own privately run Lotus 18 as well as an extensive non-Championship programme. He retired after a handful of events in 1962, later managing Parnell Racing after his father's death in 1964 and eventually becoming BRM works team manager from 1970 to 1974. He is now a pig farmer near Derby.

Reg Parnell tries the BRM V16. Even the rugged professional from Derby could make little sense of this British racing disaster.

PATRESE, Riccardo (I)

b. 17 April 1954, Padua
224 Grands Prix; 5 wins
Career span: 1977 (Shadow); 1978–81 (Arrows); 1982–3 (Brabham); 1984–5 (Alfa Romeo); 1986–7 (Brabham); 1988 to date (Williams)

The transformation of Grand Prix racing's one-time *enfant terrible* from an immature, supercilious youngster to one of the most charming and relaxed personalities on the Formula 1 stage was a process which took place gradually over a period of more than a decade. Riccardo drove his first World Championship race at Monaco as long ago as 1977 and has been a consistent points scorer ever since with the exception of a catastrophic 1985 season during which he scored not one top six finish in a painfully unreliable Alfa Romeo.

Patrese is also a statistical phenomenon within the Grand Prix community. He holds the outright record for World Championshp Grand Prix starts, matching Graham Hill's previous maximum of 176 as long ago as the 1988 Australian GP. He has been a points scorer for longer than any other driver in F1 history and has the longest winning record – ten seasons between his first victory at Monaco for Brabham in 1982, and his most recent at Estoril for Williams in 1991.

After running his first season with the Shadow team he switched to the newly established Arrows squad the following year where he displayed a heady blend of brash aggression and considerable potential. Sadly, he was erroneously labelled with the blame for the pile-up at Monza which resulted in the death of Ronnie Peterson. He was later totally absolved of any responsibility, but not before the other drivers held what amounted to a disgraceful 'kangaroo court' to ban Patrese from taking part in that year's United States GP as punishment. Riccardo was seriously wronged by this shameful episode.

Switching to Brabham for 1982, he finally scored his maiden Grand Prix victory through the streets of the Mediterranean principality, five years to the day after his début. The following season he won the South African GP at Kyalami after which he spent a long time in the F1 wilderness. A switch to Alfa Romeo for 1984–5 was largely fruitless, and a move back to Brabham-BMW for the next two seasons was hardly much better.

It was something of a surprise when Frank Williams signed Riccardo as Nigel Mansell's team-mate at the start of the 1988 season, but it was a move which proved to be the making of the Italian driver. After a difficult time in 1988 when he wrestled with the Judd-engined Williams FW12, Patrese was right back on the pace in 1989 with the

Probably the most popular man on the contemporary F1 scene, Riccardo Patrese only recently achieved sustained success as a member of the Williams-Renault line-up.

Renault V10-engined FW12B and FW13. In 1990 he won the San Marino GP followed by the Mexican and Spanish races in 1991, and he proved an admirable team-mate to Mansell, being only a fraction slower than the Englishman on many occasions.

Relaxed and self-assured, Patrese has a natural air about his character which makes him one of the easiest contemporary F1 drivers to deal with. He lives with his wife Susy, son Simone, and twin daughters Beatrice and Maddalena in Padua, and maintains a flat in Cortina for skiing expeditions. Away from the circuits, his great passion is collecting precision scale-model trains manufactured by the German Marklin company.

Patrese evokes memories of less successful days, struggling with the Brabham BT55-BMW during 1986.

This collision between Alain Prost's Renault RE30 and Nelson Piquet's Brabham-BMW in the 1983 Dutch Grand Prix at Zandvoort was a key factor behind the Frenchman's failure to win that year's title.

130

PEASE, Al (CDN)

b. 15 October 1921
2 Grands Prix

A privateer who drove the original 1966 Eagle F1, fitted with a 2.7-litre Climax four-cylinder engine, in the 1967 and 1969 Canadian Grands Prix.

PENSKE, Roger (USA)

b. 20 February 1937, Shaker Heights, Ohio
2 Grands Prix

This sleek graduate of Lehigh University was little more than an ambitious semi-professional racer when he drove privately entered Coopers in the 1961 and 1962 US Grands Prix at Watkins Glen. He retired early to concentrate on a business career and is now one of America's most successful multi-millionaire business tycoons with a huge automotive empire, and runs the most successful ever Indy car racing team.

PERDISA, Cesare (I)

b. 31 October 1932
7 Grands Prix
Career span: 1955–6 (Maserati); 1957 (Ferrari)

A Maserati 250F privateer whose family were wealthy publishers, owning the respected Italian motor magazine, *Quattrorotte*. He used to unnerve Stirling Moss by his habit of cracking raw eggs and then swallowing them in one gulp – sometimes when sitting in the cockpit on the grid!

PERKINS, Larry (AUS)

b. 18 March 1950
11 Grands Prix
Career span: 1976 (Ensign); 1977 (Brabham)

Larry Perkins was a bespectacled Australian who made his name in Europe with some heady performances in early Ralt F3 machinery. He showed credible F1 form in a private Ensign and then a Brabham-Alfa in the latter half of 1976 before any further progress was terminated in a disastrous partnership with the dead-on-its-feet BRM équipe at the start of the following year. To this day he remains a highly competitive contender on the Australian national touring car scene.

PERROT, Xavier (CH)

b. 1 February 1932, Zurich
1 Grand Prix

A popular Swiss garage owner who drove his private

Brabham in the F2 class of the 1969 German F2 at Nurburgring.

PESCAROLO, Henri (F)

b. 25 September 1942, Paris
57 Grands Prix
Career span: 1968–70 (Matra); 1971–2 (Williams); 1974 (BRM); 1976 (Surtees)

The son of one of France's leading surgeons, 'Pesca' was a medical student himself until motor racing got in his way and he was carried forward on the flood tide of French nationalism along with Matra and Jean-Pierre Beltoise during the mid-1960s.

French F3 champion in 1966, he soon moved into F2, but his long-term career prospects were nearly jeopardized when he suffered unpleasant facial burns while testing a Matra sports car at Le Mans in the spring of 1969. He returned to the cockpit in time to win the F2 section of that year's German GP and was promoted into the works Matra F1 team alongside Beltoise the following year, the highlight being a superb third place at Monaco.

In 1971 he switched to Frank Williams's team, finishing fourth at Silverstone in a March 711, but after a rather disappointing second season with the team he dropped out of F1 before gaining restoration in 1974 as part of the underfinanced Motul BRM squad. He was out again in 1975, but raised private finance to drive a Surtees TS19 in 1976, again without any success.

Formal, distant and ascetic, Pescarolo never achieved the level of success in F1 that his earlier single-seater success hinted at. However, he was a top line sports car driver and scored a hat trick of Le Mans victories for Matra in 1972 (sharing with Graham Hill) and in 1973 and 1974 (partnered with Gerard Larrousse).

PESENTI-ROSSI, Alessandro (I)

b. 31 August 1942
3 Grands Prix

This over-ambitious but uncompetitive Italian privateer drove a Gulf Italy-backed private Tyrrell 007 in three races during 1976.

PETERS, Josef (D)

b. 16 September 1914
1 Grand Prix

Peters drove a Veritas RS-BMW in the 1952 German Grand Prix at Nurburgring.

PETERSON, Ronnie (s)

b. 14 February 1944, Orebro
d. 11 September 1978, Milan
123 Grands Prix; 10 wins
Career span: 1970–2 (March); 1973–6 (Lotus); 1976 (March);
1977 (Tyrrell); 1978 (Lotus)

One of the most exciting seat-of-the-pants talents ever to sit in a racing car, this son of a provincial Swedish baker enlivened the 1970s with his mind-boggling exploits in a variety of Grand Prix cars. A tall, mild-mannered, blond Swede cast in the classic mould, out of a car he could be reticence personified. But when the starting signal was given and the vizor on his helmet snapped down, Ronnie was transformed into a dazzlingly spectacular acrobat whose performance was just as likely to end in a major shunt as a race victory.

Peterson knew only one way to drive a racing car – flat out. He demonstrated this quality early on as he battled his way to the top of European karting before switching to cars. It was there that he helped put the Italian Tecno company on the map as a winning force in the hotly contested 1-litre Formula 3 category. To this day, his battle with compatriot Reine Wisell in the 1969 Monaco GP supporting F3 classic is recalled with awe by those who witnessed it.

Ronnie came into F1 on a three-year contract with the newly established March Engineering organization at the start of 1970. For his first season he learned the ropes in a works-operated 701 sponsored by Colin Crabbe's Antique Automobiles concern, and gained promotion into the works team for the following year. March would remain his spiritual home throughout his F1 career. He had a strong relationship with its three surviving directors, Max Mosley, Robin Herd and Alan Rees, all of whom developed a rapport and understanding with the blond lad who grew up with the team and who was regarded as 'their baby'.

In 1971 Ronnie demonstrated his world-class talent with a string of five second places which earned him the position of runner-up to Jackie Stewart in the World Championship. It was a season in which his star quality was emphasized by victory in the European F2 Trophy series. He was ready to win Grands Prix, but he would have to wait until 1973 when he switched to Lotus before he at last broke his duck.

After emerging triumphant in the 1973 French Grand Prix at Paul Ricard other victories quickly followed at Österreichring, Monza and Watkins Glen. He finished the season by taking third place in the World Championship and stayed with Lotus the following year, hauling the now ageing 72 to three more wins in Monaco, France and Italy.

The failure of the Lotus 76, intended as a replacement for the type 72, meant that Team Lotus continued to rely on a five-year-old design through to the start of the 1976 season when Chapman's organization made another design blunder with the 'all adjustable' type 77. After the first couple of races, Peterson quit the team and returned to March where the solid, uncomplicated 761 chassis helped him to a morale-boosting victory in the Italian Grand Prix at Monza.

For 1977 he accepted a big money offer to join Ken Tyrrell's team where he would sample the latest version of the revolutionary P34 six-wheeler. It was a disaster. No wins were forthcoming and Ronnie was frequently outclassed by his team-mate Patrick Depailler. By now questions were being aired about the Swede's talent. Had he lost his edge?

Ronnie was absolutely confident that he still had winning ability and he got the chance to prove that in 1978, restoring his reputation as Mario Andretti's number two in the pace-making Lotus 79 line-up. Accepting second billing to Andretti might have been hard for some, but Ronnie deferred willingly. The way he saw it, he was being given another chance in a top car – and the reason the Lotus 79 was such a competitive tool was largely due to the test and development work which Andretti had so conscienciously carried out.

The strategy worked perfectly. Ronnie restored his reputation with a succession of superb drives, often following Mario round a few feet from the American's exhausts, winning in South Africa and Austria after Andretti hit trouble. He did enough to earn himself the offer of the number one McLaren seat for 1979, but sustained serious leg injuries in a multiple accident just after the start of the Italian Grand Prix at Monza.

Although it seemed as though his life was not threatened by these injuries, Ronnie slipped into a deep coma that Sunday evening as a bone marrow embolism got into his bloodstream. Just before breakfast-time the following morning this gentle giant of a man slipped away, leaving a great void on the contemporary Formula 1 scene.

His wife Barbro was left to care for their three-year-old daughter Nina, but there was more tragedy to come for the family. In December 1987 Barbro Peterson was found dead in the bath at her Cookham Dean home in Berkshire. Thereafter, Nina went to live with the family of Ronnie's brother Tommy back in Sweden.

Right: Peterson on his way to a brilliant 1974 Monaco Grand Prix victory with the ageing Lotus 72.

PICARD, François (F)

b. 26 April 1921, Villefranche-sur-Saône
1 Grand Prix

This French sports car driver from Nice was very badly injured when he crashed Rob Walker's F2 Cooper-Climax in the 1958 Moroccan Grand Prix at Casablanca, spinning off on oil spilled by Tony Brooks's expiring Vanwall. Happily, he subsequently made a full recovery from those injuries.

PIETERSE, Ernest (ZA)

b. 4 July 1938

A South African privateer who drove his own Climax four-cylinder Lotus 21 in his home Grands Prix at East London in 1962 and 1963.

PIETSCH, Paul (D)

b. 20 June 1911
3 Grands Prix

A reserve driver for Auto Union in 1935, Pietsch is now boss of the publishing house which owns the respected German motoring magazine, *Auto Motor und Sport*. His post-war racing high spot was a works Alfa 159 outing in the 1951 German GP. His first wife Ilse's affair with the legendary Achille Varzi before the war led to the Italian driver's morphine addiction which he later conquered.

PILETTE, André (B)

b. 6 October 1918, Paris
9 Grands Prix
Career span: 1951 (Talbot); 1953 (Connaught); 1954 (Gordini); 1956 (Ferrari and Gordini); 1964 (Scirocco)

A semi-professional Belgian journeyman whose son Teddy would later become an accomplished F5000 performer in the 1970s.

PILETTE, Teddy (B)

b. 26 July 1942, Brussels
1 Grand Prix

Son of André Pilette, this pleasant Belgian drove a Brabham BT42 in the 1974 Belgian Grand Prix at Nivelles-Baulers, but was better known for his F5000 and Can-Am exploits in cars entered by Stella Artois brewery millionaire Count Rudi van de Straaten's Team VDS. He won the European Championship for Formula 5000 cars in both 1973 and 1975, but his career never progressed much beyond this second-division level.

PIOTTI, Luigi (I)

6 Grands Prix

This middle-aged Italian privateer was typical of the many well-heeled customers who kept Maserati in business during the mid-1950s. His biggest claim to fame was when he pushed Stirling Moss's 250F round to the pits at Monza when he ran out of fuel, thereby saving the Englishman's victory in the 1956 Italian Grand Prix!

PIPER, David (GB)

b. 2 December 1930, Edgware
2 Grands Prix

Piper came from farming family who made a fat profit when the M1 motorway was driven through their land. He raced a Lotus 16 in the 1959 and 1960 British Grands Prix, but then concentrated on sports cars, becoming Ferrari's most successful private campaigner. He lost part of one leg in an accident while filming *Le Mans* in 1970, but still races in historic events.

PIQUET, Nelson

See pages 136–7.

PIROCCHI, Renato (I)

b. 26 May 1933
1 Grand Prix

The Italian semi-professional who drove Cooper-Maserati in the 1961 Italian Grand Prix, finishing twelfth, five laps behind Phil Hill's winning Ferrari.

PIRONI, Didier (F)

b. 26 March 1952
d. 23 August 1987, off the Isle of Wight
70 Grands Prix; 3 wins
Career span: 1978–9 (Tyrrell); 1980 (Ligier); 1981–2 (Ferrari)

This dour, calculating Frenchman was highly motivated by a desire to become his country's first World Champion, and brought a clinical and objective approach to his motor racing career. He was a man who always seemed to have his temperament under tight control and seemed set to realize his ultimate ambition after assuming the Ferrari team leadership after the death of Gilles Villeneuve early in 1982.

Sadly, Pironi's own Championship challenge came to an end when he was involved in a massive accident during practice for the German Grand Prix at Hockenheim.

In heavy rain and spray, his Ferrari cartwheeled over the back of Alain Prost's Renault, leaving Didier with serious leg injuries which ended his racing career.

Inspired by the racing exploits of his cousin, the late José Dolhem, Pironi's professional career began in 1972 when he finished sixth in the French national Formula Renault Championship. Aided by his country's strong motor racing infrastructure, he battled up through into Formula 2 in 1977, the year in which he won the Monaco F3 classic in a guest drive for the Martini team. This attracted the attention of Ken Tyrrell who snapped him up to partner Patrick Depailler in his F1 team for 1978.

He signalled his potential by scoring Championship points in four of his first six races in a season which also saw him win Le Mans for Renault. In fact, the French national team wanted him to drive for them in 1979, but Tyrrell would not release him, so Pironi spent a second year with Ken's team before switching to Ligier for 1980.

For Ligier he won the Belgian Grand Prix in command-

Didier Pironi tries a Ligier for size during tests at Paul Ricard. This tough nut survived a huge accident in a Ferrari only to be killed in a powerboating tragedy.

ing style, comfortably beating Alan Jones's Williams. He also led Jones again at Monaco before retiring and finished a strong second to the Australian in the French GP. At the end of that season he was recommended as a Ferrari candidate to succeed Jody Scheckter, a challenge which he willingly assumed. However, as partner to Villeneuve, Pironi seldom looked in the same class as the French-Canadian and a fourth place at Monaco was the best he could manage in a year when Villeneuve achieved two Grand Prix victories.

The 1982 season began on a promising note with Ferrari dominating the thinly supported San Marino GP, but when Didier slipstreamed past Villeneuve to take the lead on the last lap, the relationship between the two men was at an end. Villeneuve believed Pironi, a man he had hitherto regarded as a friend, to be guilty of breaching team orders. The tragic rift between the two men was never resolved as Villeneuve was killed while practising for the following race in Belgium.

Pironi went on to win the Dutch Grand Prix in masterful style before that tragic Hockenheim accident cut short his season. Ahead lay dozens of painful operations over the years to repair his damaged legs, and predictions about a return to the cockpit seemed ever more optimistic.

Restless for a sporting challenge, Didier turned his hand to the equally spectacular sport of powerboat racing. Off Cowes in the Solent, he barrelled through the wake of a passing oil tanker without easing back on the throttles. The powerboat flipped over, killing Pironi and his two crew members, journalist Bernard Giroux and former F3 racer Jean-Claude Guenard.

PIRRO, Emanuele (I)

b. 12 January 1962, Rome
37 Grands Prix
Career span: 1989 (Benetton); 1991 (Dallara)

Pirro began competing in karts at the age of eleven and, by the time he was fifteen, he had won the first of four Italian titles. In 1980 he moved into car racing, winning the Formula Italian title at the age of eighteen. Then it was straight into F3 for the 1981 Italian Championship during a year which started with a drive in a Jolly Club Lancia Montecarlo to a class win in the Daytona 24-hours, and finished with an invitation from Cesare Fiorio to drive a works Lancia in the endurance race at Kyalami. There followed a long apprenticeship in F3, F2 and F3000 before he was invited to test a Brabham-BMW BT54 in the summer of 1984. Thereafter, he built up a reputation as an outstanding BMW saloon car driver and was drafted into the Benetton-Ford team as Johnny Herbert's successor in 1989. In 1990 he switched to Dallara where he remained for two seasons before losing his place in the F1 business.

135

PIQUET, Nelson (BR)

b. 17 August 1952, Rio de Janeiro
204 Grands Prix; 23 wins; World Champion 1981, 1983 and 1987
Career span: 1978 (Ensign and Brabham); 1979–85 (Brabham); 1986–7 (Williams); 1988–9 (Lotus); 1990–1 (Benetton)

Nothing gave Nelson Piquet more pleasure and satisfaction than going out on to a starting grid knowing that he had a technical or performance advantage over his rivals. It was a calculating approach perhaps, which may have ruffled the feathers of some purists, but the Brazilian quickly came to appreciate that World Championships are often won by consistently garnering points rather than by sheer heroism behind the wheel.

As the record book reveals, his way works. Yet, if his father's ambitions had prevailed, Nelson might well have made his mark on the centre court at Wimbledon rather than the race track at Rio. During his teenage years, his father packed him off to California for an intensive bout of tennis coaching. However, it was the lure of cars, karts and motorcycles which finally swayed his long-term ambitions.

Having made a name for himself on the domestic Brazilian Formula Super Vee scene, Nelson embarked for Europe at the start of 1977 to launch his international F3 programme. Driving a Ralt, he would finish third in that season's European Championship before switching his attentions to the British scene the following year. In 1978 he won a total of thirteen races, clinching the BP championship and attracting a great deal of attention on the part of F1 team managers.

Nelson's Grand Prix début came at Hockenheim in 1978 at the wheel of an Ensign and he also handled a private McLaren M23 in the Austrian, Dutch and Italian races. In the last race of the season he drove a third works Brabham-Alfa as a preliminary to joining Niki Lauda in the Bernie Ecclestone-owned team the following year.

Niki Lauda's sudden – and, as things transpired, temporary – retirement from F1 late in 1979 elevated Nelson to the position of Brabham team leader. The following year he won his first Grand Prix at Long Beach with the Cosworth V8-engined Brabham BT49, following this up with further successes in the Dutch and Italian races. His novice status notwithstanding, he finished runner-up in the championship behind Alan Jones.

The following year Nelson duly bagged his first world title, edging out an over-tense Carlos Reutemann in a sweltering finale under the scorching Nevada sun in Las Vegas. Then, for 1982, Brabham switched to BMW turbo power, heralding a mechanically troubled year and only a single win for Nelson. But his shrewd commitment to the Brabham-BMW development programme reaped dividends in 1983 when he snatched his second championship title in a down-to-the-wire battle with Renault's Alain Prost.

Two relatively bleak seasons followed this success and, frustrated by Brabham's fruitless switch to Pirelli rubber in 1985 and Ecclestone's reluctance to pay him what he believed to be his market value, Piquet stunned the racing world by switching to the Williams-Honda camp for 1986. He almost won the title again in his first year with Williams, blaming his failure on the team's unwillingness to encourage Nigel Mansell to play a supporting role, something which quite clearly was not part of either man's contract.

Being edged out by Prost for the championship in the very last race clearly irked Piquet enormously, even though his tactical approach would continue to pay off as he eased through to take his third title in 1987. He was no happier with the Williams *modus operandi*, however, and moved to Lotus in 1988, a switch which contributed to Frank's team losing its Honda engine supply contract as well as being the beginning of the end for Nelson's own front-line F1 career.

Above: Nelson Piquet was a shrewd, tactical and intelligent performer who won three World Championships through stealth and common sense. *Right:* at the wheel of the Williams-Honda FW11 at Adelaide in 1986, a day when he nearly won what would have been his fourth such title.

Even with a Honda V6 turbo engine, Nelson found the Lotus 100T hopelessly uncompetitive as compared with the world-beating McLaren MP4/4s. Things were even worse when the team had to use Judd V8s the following year after Honda withdrew their engines. Nelson was reduced to the role of a midfield runner at best. In such a situation, his motivation suffered.

Two years with Benetton in 1990–1 saw Piquet revelling in an Indian summer, notching up a total of three wins. When the car was on the pace, he would do just what was needed. But he was approaching forty now, with more than a decade of F1 competition already under his belt.

By the end of 1991 the offers from top teams were no longer coming his way and he did not need them. He was not prepared to drive for peanuts and turned away from F1 to try his hand at the 1992 Indianapolis 500, in practice for which he was involved in a serious accident, suffering extensive foot injuries which almost certainly spelled the end of his racing career. A millionaire, with a luxury yacht in the Mediterranean and a Hughes chopper to keep the grass from growing on his helicopter pad, it was difficult to argue that Nelson Piquet had not adopted the right strategy in life!

POLLET, Jacques (F)

b. 2 July 1932
5 Grands Prix

This loyal Gordini campaigner dovetailed a limited World Championship programme in 1954 and 1955 with a wider programme of minor league F1 events.

PON, Ben (NL)

b. 9 December 1936
1 Grand Prix

This Porsche sports car racer drove one of Carel de Beaufort's Ecurie Maarsbergen Porsche four-cylinders in his home Grand Prix in 1962.

POORE, Dennis (GB)

b. 19 August 1916
d. 12 February 1987
2 Grands Prix
Career span: 1952 (Connaught)

An outstanding force on British hillclimb scene in an ex-Hans Ruesch Tipo 8C-35 3.8-litre Alfa Romeo which he retained to his death after winning the British Championship in 1950. A wealthy boss of the Manganese Bronze company, Poore provided the financial backing to get *Autosport* magazine off the ground in 1950, and his company also sought to save the British motorcycle industry – unsuccessfully as it transpired – by buying Nortons from the receivers.

POSEY, Sam (USA)

b. 26 May 1944, New York
2 Grands Prix

A prosperous driver whose father was killed during the war, Posey made quite a reputation on the North American scene as a versatile F5000 and Trans-Am saloon competitor. He had two Surtees F1 drives in 1971 and 1972, later retiring to become a respected motor racing commentator.

POZZI, Charles (F)

b. 27 August 1909
1 Grand Prix

Pozzi drove a Talbot-Lago in the 1950 French Grand Prix at Reims, but later became much better known as Ferrari's French *concessionaire*, entering cars at Le Mans for many years.

PRETORIOUS, Jackie (ZA)

b. 22 November 1934
3 Grands Prix

Drove three times in his home Grands Prix at Kyalami, on the final occasion (1973) at the wheel of a Frank Williams Iso-Marlboro.

PROPHET, David (GB)

b. 9 October 1937
d. 29 March 1981, near Silverstone
2 Grands Prix

A British national level racer, this Birmingham motor trader took part in the 1963 and 1965 South African Grands Prix in a 1,500cc pushrod engined Brabham-Ford. He was killed in a helicopter accident shortly after taking off from a fog-bound Silverstone circuit.

PROST, Alain

See pages 140–1.

PRYCE, Tom (GB)

b. 11 June 1949, Ruthin, Clwyd
d. 5 March 1977, Kyalami
42 Grands Prix
Career span: 1974 (Token); 1975–7 (Shadow)

This gentle, reticent son of a Welsh policeman won a Lola FF1600 car in 1970 through a competition in the *Daily Express* newspaper. An accomplished F3 contender, he moved into F1 with the Token F1 special during 1974, financed by shipbroker Tony Vlassopulo and Lloyds underwriter Ken Grob. The Monaco GP organizers declined his entry on the basis of Tom's inexperience, so he switched to the F3 supporting race and walked away with that instead. Promoted to F1 in 1974 following Brian Redman's withdrawal from the Shadow team, he showed considerable speed and flair from the outset. He won the non-title Brands Hatch Race of Champions and started the British GP from pole position in 1975. His best placings were a third in the 1975 Austrian and 1976 Brazilian Grands Prix. He was killed when he hit a marshal who was crossing the track during the South African Grand Prix in 1977 in one of the most bizarre of motor racing accidents.

Tom Pryce (second from right) in company with Shadow team manager Alan Rees (left), Goodyear racing engineer Bert Baldwin and UOP's Jim Durham after finishing fourth in the 1975 German Grand Prix.

PROST, Alain (F)

b. 24 February 1955, St Chamond
183 Grands Prix; 44 wins; World Champion 1985, 1986 and 1989
Career span: 1980 (McLaren); 1981–3 (Renault); 1984–9
(McLaren); 1990–1 (Ferrari)

The Grand Prix history books must surely assess this Charles Aznavour look-alike as the pivotal personality of the 1980s. By the end of 1991 the pleasantly unassuming Frenchman had won three World Championship titles and, with forty-four Grand Prix victories to his credit, was eleven wins ahead of his closest pursuer Ayrton Senna.

Unquestionably, Prost displayed the Midas touch from the very start of his career. He won the 1973 karting World Championship, three years later displayed a similar mastery of the European Formula Renault series and in 1979 clinched the European F3 Championship. The way was clear ahead for Grand Prix stardom and, after McLaren offered him a test drive at the end of 1979, team director Teddy Mayer signed him on the spot.

Although 1980 was one of the most disappointing seasons in F1 McLaren history, Alain scored championship points on his first two outings for the team. However, when he was offered a Renault seat alongside René Arnoux for 1981, he snatched the opportunity with both hands, despite a certain amount of legal wrangling with McLaren. Almost immediately he began to reel off the victories, yet the Drivers' title consistently eluded him. The cars were frequently unreliable and, after a major falling-out with the management, he left the French team at the end of 1983.

It was a timely decision. Back at McLaren, which had now been transformed by the takeover from Ron Dennis and John Barnard, driver John Watson had not yet finalized his contract for 1984. Watson lost out as the team management quickly offered Prost the chance of running alongside Niki Lauda.

With the new Porsche-made TAG turbo engine ready to race, the 1984 McLaren proved to be in a class of its own. But although Alain won seven races to Niki Lauda's five,

Two faces of Alain Prost, separated by a decade. *Above:* the fresh-faced Renault newcomer of 1981. *Left:* the seasoned triple World Champion Ferrari team leader of ten years later.

Prost's McLaren-TAG chases Michele Alboreto's Ferrari during the 1987 Monaco Grand Prix.

the Austrian took the title by the margin of half a point.

In 1985 Prost left nothing to chance, winning five Grands Prix to clinch that long-awaited title. He did it again the following year to become the first driver since Jack Brabham (1959–60) to take consecutive titles. Prost's velvet touch behind the wheel, allied to quite remarkable mechanical sensitivity, cast him the role of Lauda's successor as the best all-round F1 technocrat in the business.

In 1987 lack of development on the TAG/Porsche engine left Prost significantly handicapped, but he drove brilliantly through the year to win three more races. In the last of them, at Estoril, he relentlessly hounded Gerhard Berger's Ferrari into a spin only three laps from the finish, surging through to beat Jackie Stewart's thirteen-year record of twenty-seven wins.

Then, in 1988, Prost found himself facing the biggest challenge of his career when Ayrton Senna was signed to drive alongside him and McLaren switched to Honda power in the final year of the turbo formula. The combination of these two great drivers and the new McLaren-Honda conferred such an advantage over the opposition that the two men turned the World Championship into their own personal playground, winning fifteen out of sixteen races.

Prost was forced to raise the standard of his game to get on terms with his new, younger team-mate, even though he took fewer calculated gambles in heavy traffic than his rival and found it impossible to conceal his dislike of racing in the rain. In 1989 he continued to be highly competitive and won the Championship for the third time, although the circumstances surrounding his collision with Senna in the Japanese GP clouded the whole season for both men.

Either way, it was the end of the road for Prost and McLaren. By the middle of the 1989 season Alain had become so disillusioned over his personal dealings with Senna, whom he felt he could no longer rely on, that he told team chief Ron Dennis that he would be leaving. He also had personal problems which aggravated his somewhat jaundiced view of F1 and Dennis counselled him earnestly not to be too hasty, even suggesting that he took a paid year's sabbatical with a view to returning to McLaren in the future.

It was not what Prost wanted. He signed for Ferrari and helped transform the team into a position where it could realistically challenge for the World Championship. Prost went into the 1990 Japanese GP still with a good chance of taking his fourth Championship, only to be shoved off the road by Senna at the first corner, a move which guaranteed that the second straight season ended in acrimony at the Suzuka circuit.

This was as close as Prost would get to winning a Ferrari World Championship. The team went off the boil in 1991, a season blighted by Prost's pseudo-political trial of strength with team director Cesare Fiorio. It ended with Fiorio being relieved of his post, but the poison chalice was eventually pushed under Prost's nose towards the end of the season. After some outspoken criticism of the way in which the team was operated, Alain found himself dismissed shortly after finishing fourth in the Japanese GP.

It was a sad way for this chirpy, surprisingly sensitive little man to leave the F1 stage at the end of the first season in a decade which had not seen him mount the top spot on any victory rostrum. The following winter saw Prost testing a Ligier-Renault extensively before finally making a decision to sit out the 1992 season.

PURLEY, David (GB)

b. 26 January 1945
d. 2 July 1985, off Sussex coast
7 Grands Prix

This immensely popular, larger-than-life former paratroop officer, who saw service in Aden, hailed from Bognor Regis where his father Charlie founded the successful Lec Refrigeration company. A dashing, all-round sportsman, David made quite a name for himself in F3 before first dabbling in F1 at the wheel of a March 731. He was awarded the George Medal for his heroic, but tragically vain, efforts to rescue former March driver Roger Williamson from his upturned, blazing car in the 1973 Dutch Grand Prix at Zandvoort. Purley later built his own car – the Lec CRP1, incorporating his father's initials – but was invalided out of racing with multiple fractures after a horrifying accident at Silverstone during practice for that year's British Grand Prix. His enthusiasm for daredevil escapades undaunted, Purley switched his attention to aerobatics and was killed when his Pitts Special biplane crashed into the sea off the Sussex coast.

An all-English hero, David Purley was a great sportsman and a hugely popular man.

QUESTER, Dieter (A)

b. 30 May 1939
1 Grand Prix

A seventh place in the 1974 Austrian GP at Österreichring in a Surtees TS16 was the sole F1 outing for this talented, versatile saloon F2 driver. He made his name in the mid-1960s with BMW and married Juliane, daughter of the Munich company's engine development chief, Alex von Falkenhausen.

RABY, Ian (GB)

b. 11 September 1921
d. 7 November 1967
3 Grands Prix

This enthusiastic Brighton garage owner made his name in a Formula 3 500cc Cooper and ventured into F1, first with a Gilby and later a private Brabham-BRM in 1964. He crashed his F2 Brabham during the European Championship race at Zandvoort in 1967, succumbing to multiple injuries many weeks later.

RAHAL, Bobby (USA)

b. 10 January 1953, Chicago
2 Grands Prix

Now one of Indy car racing's most popular exponents – and winner of the Indy 500 in 1986 – Rahal drove the 1978 United States and Canadian Grands Prix for Walter Wolf's team.

RAPHANEL, Pierre-Henri (F)

b. 27 May 1961
1 Grand Prix

A promising F3000 graduate who missed the F1 boat, qualifying for his sole Grand Prix start at Monaco in 1989 at the wheel of the Coloni.

REBAQUE, Hector (MEX)

b. 5 February 1956, Mexico City
42 Grands Prix
Career span: 1977 (Hesketh); 1978 (Lotus); 1979 (Lotus and Rebaque); 1980–1 (Brabham)

This well-heeled and quite promising Mexican came into F1 after some feisty US F/Atlantic outings, trying his hand first with Hesketh and then with his own private Lotus. His 1979 season was complicated when he commissioned his own Lotus 79 facsimile, but he returned to full-time F1 in the middle of 1980 when he replaced Ricardo Zunino in the Brabham F1 ranks alongside Nelson Piquet. He brought sponsorship from the Mexican petroleum company, Pemex, and would probably have shown better form in European races had he not insisted on jetting home to Mexico between each event.

REDMAN, Brian (GB)

b. 9 March 1937, Burnley, Lancashire
12 Grands Prix
Career span: 1968 (Cooper); 1972 (McLaren); 1974 (Shadow)

One of the great sports car racing drivers of his era, a versatile all-rounder with an enormously attractive, straightforward personality, Brian Redman's fleeting F1 outings in fact served as a seemingly irrelevant footnote to a glittering career in almost every other international racing category. Brian's early career was closely linked with the rise of the Bolton-based Chevron sports car company and his first F1 involvement with Cooper in 1968 ended when he broke his arm following a front suspension failure which caused the machine to vault the guard rail at the tricky Les Combes left-hander during the Belgian Grand Prix. A brief sojourn in retirement in South Africa at the start of 1971 was followed by a return to full-time international racing, including terrific 1972 and 1973 seasons in Ferrari's endurance racing team as Jacky Ickx's regular partner. A handful of races with McLaren also came along that year, but he withdrew from F1 from choice in the summer of 1974, fed up with the high-pressure environment after three races for the Shadow team. He is still racing Chevron sports cars in historic events to this day, and won an historic F1 race at Watkins Glen in 1991 at the wheel of a Surtees TS16.

REES, Alan (GB)

b. 12 January 1938
3 Grands Prix

Taciturn son of a road haulage contractor from Monmouth, Alan Rees became one of the most accomplished minor league single-seater racers of the mid-1960s, capable of matching Jochen Rindt on occasion in the Winkelmann F2 team for which he was driver/manager. Two German GP outings (1966 and 1967) in F2 Brabhams and a Cooper-Maserati ride at Silverstone in 1967 helped convince Rees that he did not have what it took to make the top grade, but he took until the end of the following year before finally deciding to retire. Later one of the founders of March Engineering with Robin Herd, Max Mosley and the late Graham Coaker (then team manager of Shadow and Arrows), he remained with Footwork as its factory-based manager into 1992.

REGAZZONI, Gianclaudio (CH)

b. 5 September 1939, Lugano
132 Grands Prix; 5 wins
Career span: 1970–2 (Ferrari); 1973 (BRM); 1974–6 (Ferrari); 1977 (Ensign); 1978 (Shadow); 1979 (Williams); 1980 (Ensign)

A rough, tough and uncompromising Swiss from the province of Ticino, 'Clay' Regazzoni was cast in the heroic mould of a bygone age. At a time when the safety movement was gathering momentum in motor racing circles, Regazzoni was something of a maverick, interested only in racing at all costs – and racing hard.

During the late 1960s he carved a spectacular swathe through F3 and F2, controversy snapping at his tail for much of the time. In 1968 he was implicated in the fatal accident involving Englishman Chris Lambert's Brabham after a collision with his Tecno during the Dutch round of the European F2 Trophy at Zandvoort, but was subsequently exonerated. Many people thought this incident would blight his career progress, but it did not prevent him from graduating into F1 as an occasional member of the Ferrari F1 team in 1970.

Clay Regazzoni was a winner, but admitted that he raced just for the hell of it.

Regazzoni

A splendid victory in the Italian Grand Prix at Monza cemented his position as regular team-mate to Jacky Ickx for the next couple of seasons, but his efforts yielded no more victories for that immediate period. A barren season with BRM followed in 1973, but he returned to Ferrari to partner Niki Lauda in 1974 and won the German GP in fine style. The following year he won at Monza and in 1976 he swept away the first Long Beach Grand Prix in the Ferrari 312T.

At the end of the 1976 season he was replaced by Carlos Reutemann and found a berth with the tiny British Ensign team for 1977. Clay's sheer enthusiasm for racing meant that it was no hardship to him driving for a small constructor. He just loved being in F1 driving the cars, and fifth places for Ensign at Monza and Watkins Glen proved just as satisfying as victory at the wheel of a Ferrari.

In 1978 he drove for Shadow – unsuccessfully as it turned out – and was then snapped up by Frank Williams to partner Alan Jones in 1979. Everything clicked for the rugged Swiss who stormed to victory in the British Grand Prix at Silverstone to give Frank's team its first World Championship success.

Clay thereafter would always hold a special place in Frank's heart, but there was no such sentiment when it came to replacing him with Reutemann for 1981. Williams was a young, thrusting team and required two world-class drivers. Regazzoni did not quite fit that bill.

Unconcerned, Regazzoni returned to the Ensign stable, again happy to continue his F1 career. In the 1980 Long Beach race a brake pedal snapped and Clay's car went careering down a slip road to slam into a parked Brabham which had retired earlier in the race. Clay sustained back injuries which invalided him out of the sport. Thereafter, partially confined to a wheelchair – he can stand, but not walk – he sustains an active presence at most European Grands Prix commentating for Swiss television.

REVENTLOW, Lance (USA)

b. 24 February 1936, London
d. 24 July 1972, Colorado
1 Grand Prix

The pampered only son of Woolworth heiress Barbara Hutton by her marriage to the irascible Danish nobleman Count Court Haugwitz-Reventlow, this rich young American – who was briefly married to actress Jill St John – bankrolled the highly ambitious Scarab F1 project which arrived on the scene at the start of 1960. Sadly, the front-engined monsters were by then outdated by the smaller, more agile, central-engined machines from Cooper and Lotus. Lance qualified only at Spa after which the project proved short lived. He was killed as a passenger in a single-engined Cessna 206 which crashed into a wooded hillside in Colorado's Rocky Mountains.

REUTEMANN, Carlos (RA)

b. 12 April 1942, Santa Fe
146 Grands Prix; 12 wins
Career span: 1972–6 (Brabham); 1976–8 (Ferrari); 1979 (Lotus); 1980–2 (Williams)

This serious-minded Argentinian driver remained some thing of a distant enigma throughout a long and dis tinguished Grand Prix career during which he combined flashes of dazzling genius with disappointingly lacklustre showings. Away from the cockpit his gentle, thoughtful and charming personality was often concealed behind a mask of deep thought and intense concentration.

Reutmann, nicknamed 'Lole', first came to Europe in 1970 as a member of the Formula 2 Brabham team fielded by the Automobile Club of Argentina. He only just lost out to Ronnie Peterson in the battle for the 1971 European F2 Trophy, and quickly moved up into F1 with Bernie Ecclestone's Brabham team at the start of the following season.

However, it was not until 1974 that Brabham designer Gordon Murray produced a machine that could do justice

Right: Carlos Reutemann's Ferrari 312T3 heading for victory in the 1978 United States Grand Prix at Watkins Glen. *Above:* the beaming countenance of this gentle, gifted and complex man.

Reutemann's expanding talent. This was the elegant T44 in which he chalked up impressive victories in the South African, Austrian and United States Grands Prix. The following year he would win the German GP at Nurburgring in the Brabham BT44B derivative, but when the team concluded a deal to use the Alfa Romeo flat-12 engine for 1976, Reutemann seemed to lose his motivation.

He was disappointed with the performance of the new cars and negotiated a release from his Brabham contract to sign with Ferrari. He raced only once for the new team, at Monza, but lined up alongside Niki Lauda for the 1977 season. The two men did not hit it off together, perhaps because of their diametrically opposed personalities, and Reutemann won only the Brazilian Grand Prix.

Reutemann's prospects improved in 1978 once Lauda moved to Brabham, and the Argentinian won the Brazilian, Long Beach, British and United States GPs in fine style. An unproductive season at Team Lotus in 1979 was followed by a move to Williams where he was recruited as team-mate to Alan Jones.

Once more, Carlos found himself paired alongside a man with whom he had little in common. Whereas Jones was extrovert and outgoing, Reutemann was introverted and, perhaps, somewhat over-sensitive. Either way, he was certainly too talented to be content with his nominal number two status at Williams. In 1980, he scored a solitary victory at Monaco only after Jones and Didier Pironi's Ligier retired ahead of him, but in 1981 he would mount the strongest Champsionship challenge of his career.

He started the season by winning the Brazilian Grand Prix against team orders, ignoring pit signals to drop back behind Jones. He was penalized financially, but Carlos could not have cared less. In his view, he was a racer, and racers do not thrown away victories.

After a succession of good performances, including another victory in Belgium, he arrived at Las Vegas for the final race of the season on the threshold of the Championship. A blindingly quick qualifying lap earned him pole position, but when the starting light blinked green, Reutemann unaccountably seemed to capitulate. In reality, slight changes to his car's set-up had conspired to undermine his confidence and he faded to eighth place, the title going to Brazil's Nelson Piquet.

Two races into the 1982 season, Carlos Reutemann retired from the cockpit for good. He never went back on that spontaneous decision, even though he subsequently acknowledged that he had given up too soon. Quite why he did so is a secret that will probably never be revealed, but it certainly deprived the sport of one of its front-line stars. In 1991 Reutemann was elected Governor of Argentina's Santa Fe province.

REVSON, Peter (USA)

b. 27 February 1939, New York
d. 22 March 1974, Kyalami
30 Grands Prix; 2 wins
Career span: 1964 (Parnell Lotus); 1971 (Tyrrell); 1972–3
(McLaren); 1974 (Shadow)

Scion of the Revlon cosmetics empire, this handsome
American was briefly ensnared by the Parnell Lotus-BRM
équipe in 1964. He then scampered back across the Atlantic to build his reputation in Can-Am and other US-based
categories before sampling a Tyrrell-Ford in the 1971 US
Grand Prix at Watkins Glen. It was an inauspicious return
as the clutch failed almost at the start, but it did not prevent him from being signed up by the Yardley McLaren
squad for the following two years.

Revson surprised many of his critics. He was a solid,
reliable performer whose turn of speed proved quite an
eye-opener. He was a regular points scorer and, armed
with the McLaren M23 in 1973, won the British and Canadian Grands Prix. He also hit the society headlines when
he started dating the then Miss World, American model
Marjorie Wallace.

Despite his success, he had a slightly strained relationship with McLaren Managing Director Teddy Mayer with
whose late brother Timmy he had been a classmate with
at Cornell and a fledgeling Formula Junior team-mate in

Peter Revson was never short on confidence and radiated a
patina of superiority which not everybody found attractive.
Here he waits for the start of the 1973 British Grand Prix, the
race in which he scored his first F1 win.

the early 1960s. Thus for 1974 he switched to the promising Shadow team only to be killed during testing in preparation for the South African Grand Prix when his car
suffered a front suspension failure and ploughed into a
guard rail at Kyalami's tricky downhill Barbecue bend.

RHODES, John (GB)

b. 18 August 1927
1 Grand Prix

RINDT, Jochen (A)

b. 18 April 1941, Achum, Germany
d. 5 September 1970, Monza
60 Grands Prix; 6 wins; World Champion 1970
Career span: 1964 (Brabham-BRM); 1965–7 (Cooper); 1968
(Brabham-Repco); 1969–70 (Lotus)

The spectacularly talented, hard-nosed heir to a German
spice fortune, Rindt's career path led him through production cars and Formula Junior to burst into public prominence by winning the 1964 London Trophy at Crystal
Palace in his own F2 Brabham. That summer afternoon he
beat all the established stars and put his name in the frame
for future F1 success.

Rindt's parents had been killed in a bombing raid on
Hamburg when he was a few weeks old after which he had
been cared for by his maternal grandparents in the Austrian city of Graz. He grew up with a wild and rebellious
streak which made him an acutely independent operator
throughout his career, brimming with self-confidence and
natural talent. He made his F1 début in Rob Walker's
Brabham-BRM in the first Austrian Grand Prix to be held
on the Zeltweg aerodrome, thereafter signing a three-year
deal with Cooper which would see him perform with
great *brio*, but little success, to the end of the 1967 season.

At this point he switched to Brabham, an apparently
ideal move to judge by the team's World Championship-
winning form in 1966 and 1967. Sadly, the team's latest
four-cam Repco V8 engine proved a technical disaster.
While Jochen bagged a third place in the 1967 car at
Kyalami, he could not look forward to only one other top-
six finish through the balance of the season – third in the
German GP at a mist-shrouded Nurburgring, miles behind
Jackie Stewart's victorious Matra.

Jochen liked working with Jack Brabham. He trusted the
pragmatic Australian and his engineering confederate Ron
Tauranac, feeling safe and secure at the wheel of the
team's cars. Yet he had been an F1 competitor since 1964
and, despite gaining a reputation as the uncrowned king
of Formula 2, was frustrated that he had been unable to
duplicate that success in the sport's most senior category.

mini racing hot shot of the mid-1960s, Rhodes had a one-off run in the 1965 British GP with a Cooper-Climax ielded by Bob Gerard.

RIBEIRO, Alex (BR)

. 7 November 1948
0 Grands Prix

'his Brazilian raced in British F3 during 1976 before con-cluding an unproductive March rent-a-drive deal for F1 the following year, finishing eighth in Germany and Canada. Devoutly religious, Ribeiro's cars regularly carried the legend 'Jesus Saves' on their bodywork in addition to his sponsorship identification.

RIESS, Fritz (D)

b. 11 July 1922, Nuremberg
1 Grand Prix

Thus, when Colin Chapman came shopping at the end of 1968, a season which had seen Team Lotus suffer the devastating loss of Jim Clark, Rindt rallied to the cause. Backed by lashings of Firestone cash, Chapman was in a position to out-bid Brabham and Goodyear, so Rindt left to join Graham Hill in the Lotus line-up.

Chapman found Rindt something of a culture shock after so many years working with Jimmy. With Clark he had built up a brotherly, once-in-a-lifetime rapport which bordered on the telepathic. Rindt was more aloof, distant and with an abrasive edge to his personality. He was not terribly confident about Chapman's engineering and even less so about his organization – particularly after the British Grand Prix at Silverstone when first a loose rear wing end-plate, and then shortage of fuel, wiped out his chances of scoring his first victory.

Respected journalist Denis Jenkinson, Continental correspondent for *Motor Sport* magazine, went as far as betting his beard that Rindt would never win a Grand Prix. However, Jochen duly obliged with the Lotus 49B at Watkins Glen towards the end of 1969. Off came Jenks's beard, much to Jochen's amusement, for he never really hit it off with the compact, trenchant scribe anyway!

Brabham and Goodyear tried to lure Rindt back into their fold for 1970, but despite really wanting to drive for Jack again, Jochen simply could not ignore the financial and technical resources Chapman had at his disposal. He started the 1970 European season with a heart-stopping last lap victory at Monaco, squeezing his Lotus 49D into the lead at the last corner after Brabham ironically slid into the straw bales.

Then Chapman took the wraps off the sensational Lotus 72. With its torsion bar suspension, side radiators and sleek aerodynamics, it rewrote the parameters of contemporary F1 car design. Of more immediate importance to Jochen, it enabled him to sustain his winning momentum. The Dutch, French, British and German Grands Prix all fell to the combination of Rindt and the superb Lotus 72, although by mid-season he was psychologically bruised by the deaths of his close friends Piers Courage and Bruce McLaren.

He was surrounded by rumours of impending retirement. His wife Nina – a former international model and daughter of the wealthy Finnish amateur racer Curt Lincoln – was certainly apprehensive about Jochen continuing in racing. Practising for the Italian Grand Prix at Monza, her worst fears were realized when Jochen crashed under braking for Parabolica and sustained fatal injuries. He died leaving a daughter Nina – just three years old – and an unassailable Championship points tally which ensured that he became the sport's first posthumous champion.

Jochen Rindt was one of the titans of F1. Arrogant, confident and bursting with talent, the Austrian became the sport's sole posthumous World Champion to date.

Riess drove a Veritas-BMW in the 1952 German Grand Prix, the same year in which he partnered Hermann Lang to win Le Mans in a Mercedes-Benz 300SL.

RISELEY-PRITCHARD, John (GB)

b. 17 January 1924, Hereford
1 Grand Prix

John Riseley-Pritchard drove a Connaught A-type in the 1954 British Grand Prix, but this Lloyds broker's greatest claim to fame is that he gave Tony Brooks his first serious motor racing opportunity.

ROBARTS, Richard (GB)

b. 22 September 1944
3 Grands Prix

This successful FF1600 and F3 driver was sponsored by a wealthy estate agent friend to drive alongside Carlos Reutemann in the Brabham team at the start of 1974. Unfortunately the arrangement did not work out and he was dropped from the line-up after only three Grands Prix to be replaced by Rikky von Opel. He still lives at Steeple, in rural Essex, and is a director of a large, specialist coachbuilding company.

RODRIGUEZ, Pedro (MEX)

b. 18 January 1940
d. 11 July 1971, Norisring
55 Grands Prix; 2 wins
Career span: 1963 (Lotus); 1964–5 (Ferrari); 1966 (Lotus); 1967 (Cooper); 1968 (BRM); 1969 (BRM and Ferrari); 1970–1 (BRM)

It was always rumoured that Don Pedro Rodriguez, father of the two brilliant Mexican racing brothers, was head of his country's secret service. He was certainly head of the country's police motorcycle patrols and, either way, amassed considerable wealth and influence from property dealings and other business interests.

Along with his younger brother Ricardo, Pedro Rodriguez raced motorcycles in his early teens. Their father indulged them from an early age with plenty of expensive high-performance cars in which they established their reputations well before reaching their seventeenth birthdays. Pedro was just twenty and Ricardo eighteen when Luigi Chinetti brought them to Le Mans to share a Ferrari 250TR in 1960. There they put the fear of God into the Maranello works team and would have won if the hard-pressed V12 had lasted the course.

Both youngsters were competing in Mexican F/Junior races by the start of 1961, but while Ricardo accepted the invitation of a renta-drive deal in a works F1 Ferrari later

that year, Pedro's business commitments forced him t[o] decline the opportunity. After Ricardo's death while pra[c]tising for the 1962 Mexican Grand Prix, Pedro's interna[]tional racing career developed in less spectacular style.

After a succession of one-off drives for Ferrari and Lot[us] in North American Grands Prix, he finally got his full-tim[e] F1 break with the Cooper-Maserati team for 1967. Wit[h] luck and reliability on his side, he won the South Africa[n] Grand Prix at Kyalami on his début for the team, and the[n] switched to BRM in 1968. After the tragic death of Mik[e] Spence at Indianapolis, Pedro lifted the battered BR[M] team morale with a succession of feisty drives, but fe[ll] back into a part-time F1 role the following year whe[n] John Surtees took over as number one.

In 1970, Pedro's talent blossomed into full flower. H[e] returned to lead the Bourne line-up, now driving the fine[] handling P153 with which he produced a brilliantly disc[i]plined victory in the Belgian Grand Prix at Spa. He ha[d] also assumed the crown as king of the sports car driver[s] and his lurid antics with the JW/Gulf Porsche 917s earne[d] him a glowing and fully justified reputation as one o[f] motor racing's great all-round professionals.

He developed into a great Anglophile, living happily i[n] Bray-on-Thames, driving round in a Bentley S1 saloo[n] and wearing a deerstalker. Yet the relaxed life of a[n] English country gentleman was not for Pedro; he wante[d] to race, race, race as often as possible. Into 1971, and no[w] partnered with Jo Siffert, it looked as though the BR[M] team was set to lift off for a period of renewed success.

Sadly, the week before the British Grand Prix, he ac[]cepted an offer to drive Swiss entrant Herbert Muller['s] Ferrari 512M at an inconsequential Interserie sports ca[r] race at Norisring. Going like hell, jousting for the lead, [a] slower car moved Pedro into the wall and the Ferrar[i] erupted into flames. He died an hour or so later.

RODRIGUEZ, Ricardo (MEX)

b. 14 February 1942
d. 1 November 1962, Mexico City
5 Grands Prix
Career span: 1961–2 (Ferrari); 1962 (Lotus)

Ricardo Rodriguez stunned the Ferrari fans by qualifying hi[s] Ferrari 156 second on the grid, a whisker away from vo[n] Trips's pole-winning sister car, at Monza for the 1961 Italia[n] Grand Prix. He was nineteen years old, absolutely fearles[s] and confident in his belief that nothing could touch him.

In 1962 he was a full-time member of the Maranello [F1] squad, but the team was now entering an uncompetitiv[e] trough and the best he could manage was fourth place a[t] Spa and sixth at the Nurburgring. However, he drove [a] Dino 246SP to victory in the Targa Florio, sharing wit[h] Willy Mairesse and Olivier Gendebien.

Ricardo clearly had a glittering career mapped out ahea[d]

The fearsomely talented, but sadly short-lived, twenty-year-old Ricardo Rodriguez battling his Ferrari 156 in the 1962 Dutch Grand Prix at Zandvoort.

of him, although many people felt that he was in the wrong environment at Ferrari where young and inexperienced drivers so frequently found themselves under intense pressure too early in their careers. He was slightly irked when Ferrari declined to send a car to contest the first non-title Mexican Grand Prix at the end of the season, but fixed up a run in Rob Walker's Lotus 24 instead. Annoyed that John Surtees had posted a quicker time in the similar Lotus he had borrowed from Jack Brabham, Ricardo overdid things as he tried to redress the situation, slamming over the outer lip of the banked Peraltada right-hander just before the startline. He suffered multiple injuries and died shortly afterwards.

ROL, Franco (I)

b. 1908
d. 5 June 1977
5 Grands Prix

Rol drove a Maserati A6GCM in the 1950 Monaco, French and Italian Grands Prix. He switched to an Osca 4500G for the 1951 Italian race, and reverted to his Maserati at Monza the following year.

ROLT, Tony (GB)

b. 16 October 1918, Bordon, Hampshire
3 Grands Prix

Major A.P. Rolt distinguished himself by attempting to escape from Colditz whilst a POW during the war. He won Jaguar's first victory at Le Mans in 1951, later becoming a regular Connaught F1 driver, but with few Championship Grand Prix outings.

Subsequently he established the Coventry-based FF Development, specializing in Ferguson-based four-wheel-drive systems. His son Stuart raced Ford Capris to good effect during the 1970s.

ROOS, Bertil (S)

b. 12 October 1943
1 Grand Prix

This Swedish up-and-comer made a name in North American F/Atlantic before being invited to have a guest outing in a Shadow DN3 in the 1974 Swedish GP at Anderstorp.

149

ROSBERG, Keijo (SF)

b. 6 December 1948
114 Grands Prix; 5 wins; World Champion 1982
Career span: 1978 (Theodore); 1979 (Wolf); 1980–1 (Fittipaldi);
1982–5 (Williams); 1986 (McLaren)

When Alan Jones took the decision to retire abruptly at the end of the 1981 season, the Williams team faced a major problem recruiting a successor to the brilliant Australian. Eventually Williams signed up 'Keke' Rosberg, the Swedish-born Finn who had established a spectacular reputation in the lower echelons of the sport, but who had been hampered by the lack of a competitive car while serving out a two-year stint in the under-financed Fittipaldi F1 team.

Rosberg's early experience had been gained in Formula Vee single-seaters, and he gradually worked his way up the international motor racing ladder, scoring a significant victory in streaming wet conditions at the 1978 Silverstone International Trophy meeting. The Finn's lightning reflexes and tremendous wet-weather skills were highlighted in this performance at the wheel of the Theodore F1 car.

Even though Keke had achieved this success in his second F1 race, he vanquished opposition of only a modest standard and his triumph could be regarded mainly as an interesting pointer to possible future form.

Happily for the Williams team, Rosberg had lost none of that instant flair by the time he started the 1982 season armed with a competitive car. At one stage it seemed as though he might become the first World Champion to take the title 'on points' without scoring a single Grand Prix victory, but he squeezed in a good win at the Swiss Grand Prix and clinched the title after beating off a challenge from Ulsterman John Watson in the final race of the year at Las Vegas.

The Williams team was late picking up the threads of turbo engine development and had no such powerful unit available in 1983. Nevertheless, Keke managed to reward them with a brilliant victory in the Monaco Grand Prix. Gambling correctly that the rain-slicked track surface

Left: Keke Rosberg with Niki Lauda; he always believed in calling a spade a spade. *Above:* Rosberg's victory at Dallas in 1984 was the first for the Williams-Honda alliance and confirmed his role as one of the great improvisers behind the wheel of a Grand Prix car.

would dry out quickly, he started the race on slick tyres and out-ran the more powerful opposition in an awesome display of raw car control. He failed to win another race that season, but by dint of some heroic motoring kept the naturally aspirated Williams within sight of the turbos on all but the fastest circuits.

Rosberg was armed with turbo power at last in 1984, thanks to the Williams-Honda alliance. He fought an up-hill battle against the all-conquering McLaren-TAGs, but gave the Williams team its first turbo-charged win in the one-off Dallas Grand Prix. As most of his front-line opposition slid into the walls or collapsed with heat exhaustion beneath the boiling Texas sun, Rosberg kept his cool to notch up probably his most impressive victory of all.

At the start of 1985 Keke was distinctly apprehensive about the prospect of Nigel Mansell joining Williams as his team-mate. With characteristic openness, he voiced these reservations, but later acknowledged that he had been too hasty in reaching such a judgement. He won at Detroit and Adelaide, but then decided to switch to McLaren in 1986 for one final stab at the title.

That final season was a disappointment. 'I thought I was the fastest driver in the world until I went to McLaren with Alain Prost,' he would later remark. No wins came his way, but the chain-smoking Finn did not reverse his decision to retire. He kept away from racing for almost four years before signing to drive for the Peugeot team in the Sports Car World Championship. He did a full season in 1991 before switching to drive an AMG Mercedes-Benz 190E 2.5 in the 1992 German Touring Car Championship.

ROSIER, Louis (F)

b. 5 November 1905
d. 29 October 1956, Montlhéry
38 Grands Prix
Career span: 1950–1 (Talbot); 1952–3 (Ferrari); 1954 (Maserati and Ferrari); 1955–6 (Maserati)

A dogged, tactical old stager, Rosier won many post-war non-Championship races in a Talbot-Lago as well as Le Mans in 1950 (sharing with his son Claude) and the French Championship from 1949 to 1952 inclusive. He was fatally injured when he crashed his Ferrari sports car during the Coupe du Salon meeting at the Paris track.

ROTHENGATTER, Huub (NL)

b. 8 October 1954, Bussum
25 Grands Prix

This enterprising Dutch entrepreneur drove for Osella and Zakspeed, with little in the way of hard results, in 1984 and 1985. He is now a sponsorship consultant to the Philips electrical company with whom he first made contact after taking a full page advertisement in a Dutch national newspaper inviting them to sponsor his own career!

RUBY, Lloyd (USA)

b. 12 January 1928, Wichita Falls, Texas
1 Grand Prix

This great Indy car contender raced an ex-Jim Hall square-bodied Lotus 18 in the 1961 US Grand Prix at Watkins Glen entered by J Frank Harrison. He retired after seventy-six laps with magneto drive failure. Eight years later he was poised to win the Indy 500 when he pulled away slightly prematurely from a pit stop with the fuel hose still connected, causing the fuel filler nozzle to pull away from the chassis and dump the tank contents all over the pit lane.

RUSSO, Giacomo (I)

b. 23 October 1937, Milan
d. 18 June 1967, Caserta
2 Grands Prix

This talented young Italian F3 ace raced under the pseudonym of 'Geki' and drove a third works Lotus at Monza in 1965 and 1966. He was killed in a multiple pile-up in a national level F3 race in the summer of 1967 on the challenging Casenta road circuit, at a time when such tracks had only the most primitive of safety facilities.

RUTTMAN, Troy (USA)

b. 11 March 1930, Mooreland, Oklahoma
1 Grand Prix

The youngest ever winner of the Indianapolis 500 (in 1952 when aged twenty-two) Ruttman tried a Maserati 250F in the 1958 French Grand Prix at Reims, having stayed over after the Race of the Two Worlds at Monza the previous weekend.

RYAN, Peter (CDN)

b. 10 June 1940
d. 2 July 1962, Reims
1 Grand Prix

Ryan drove an ex-works Lotus 18 in the 1961 United States GP under the J Wheeler Autosport banner, coming to Europe the following year for a full season of F/Junior. An outstandingly promising youngster who showed his potential by winning the Canadian sports car Grand Prix at Mosport Park in a Lotus 19 the previous September, beating Stirling Moss's similar machine, he was killed at Reims in an Ian Walker Racing Lotus 22.

SAID, Bob (USA)

b. 5 May 1932, New York
1 Grand Prix

An American amateur sports car racer and property developer who registered the final World Championship GP start for a Connaught with a B-type 'toothpaste tube' at Sebring in 1959.

SALA, Luis (EP)

b. 15 May 1959
26 Grands Prix

An accomplished Formula 3000 performer who won the rain-soaked 1986 Birmingham Super-Prix before enjoying a season and a half as a member of the Minardi team (1988–9).

SALAZAR, Eliseo (RCH)

b. 14 November 1954, Santiago
24 Grands Prix

A cheerful Chilean who tried F3 in 1979 before contesting the British F1 National Championship in an RAM Williams FW07 the following year. His intermittent F1 career continued with RAM March, Ensign and ATS, but little came of it. Most famous for being thumped by Nelson Piquet – an incident televised worldwide – after the two collided in the 1982 German Grand Prix.

SALVADORI, Roy (GB)

b. 12 May 1922, Dovercourt, Essex
47 Grands Prix
Career span: 1954–6 (Maserati); 1957–8 (Vanwall and Cooper);
1959 (Aston Martin); 1960–1 (Cooper); 1962 (Lola)

Born in England of Italian parents, Salvadori's racing career began in 1947 with a 2.9-litre Alfa Romeo. He graduated to Formula 1 via a succession of other cars, including a 2-litre Maserati sports car which he drove for Sidney Greene's Gilby Engineering team.

From 1954 to 1956 Roy handled a Maserati 250F owned by Greene, taking a succession of good placings in predominantly non-championship events before being asked to drive for the works Cooper team, and later the abortive front-engined Aston Martin DBR4 which did not arrive on the scene until 1959. He later drove for the Yeoman Credit team, in whose Cooper he almost won the 1961 United States Grand Prix – he was closing on Innes Ireland's victorious Lotus in the closing stages when the Cooper's engine broke!

At the end of 1962 he retired from F1 and quit sports car racing a couple of years later. A successful motor trader, he became heavily involved in the Cooper-Maserati F1 squad as team manager before retiring to Monaco in the late 1960s.

Handsome and charming, Salvadori was always a great hit with the ladies. The best story told about him in this respect comes from Rob Walker. It took place at Le Mans in 1954 when Prince Bira, who had now married for the second time, was also driving for the Aston Martin sports car team. One evening Bira said to Roy: 'Would you mind taking my sister-in-law to bed tonight?' Salvadori retorted mischievously, 'I'd rather have your wife!' Bira pondered this for a moment, before replying: 'No, I don't think that's on, Roy. It's either my sister-in-law or nothing.'

Roy Salvadori at the wheel of the Bowmaker Lola-Climax in 1962. He was another who deserved Grand Prix success but failed to achieve it.

SANESI, Consalvo (I)

b. 28 March 1911
5 Grands Prix

This Alfa Romeo factory test driver was occasionally included in the works 158/159 team in 1950 and 1951, his
best placing being fourth at Bremgarten in the latter season. He raced on in sports cars to the mid-1960s.

SCARFIOTTI, Ludovico (I)

b. 18 October 1933, Turin
d. 8 June 1968, Rossfeld
10 Grands Prix; 1 win
Career span: 1963–7 (Ferrari); 1967 (Eagle Weslake); 1968
(Cooper)

This patrician, impeccably mannered nephew of Fiat boss
Gianni Agnelli captured the hearts of his countrymen
with an enormously popular win in the 1966 Italian
Grand Prix at Monza at the wheel of a Ferrari 312. An able
and versatile performer, he was not out of the top drawer
as far as F1 competition was concerned, but on that September afternoon he did not put a foot wrong in the blis-
tering conditions.

Little over a decade earlier, Scarfiotti had started his
career at the wheel of a Fiat 1100 saloon. In 1957 he won
his class in the Mille Miglia, then continued to develop a
burgeoning reputation with some consistently respectable
showings in Osca sports cars. Scarfiotti also developed
into one of the best hillclimb specialists in the business at
a time when this branch of the sport attracted a great deal
of international prestige, with Ferrari and Porsche jousting for European Championship honours.

Ludovico took the appropriately named European
Mountain Championlship in 1962 and 1965 with a Ferrari
Dino sports car. He also made his F1 début as early as
1963, standing in for the injured Willy Mairesse to finish
sixth in the Dutch GP at Zandvoort, a couple of weeks
after sharing the winning 250P with Bandini at Le Mans.
A week after that he shunted the F1 car in practice for the
French GP at Reims, and suffered leg injuries.

For the next two seasons he was only an occasional
member of the Ferrari F1 squad, but was reinstated for
some races as a third-stringer, alongside Bandini and Mike
Parkes, after Surtees quit mid-way through 1966. That
timely win at Monza seemed to have sealed his position as
a regular Ferrari F1 team member for 1967, but the New
Year started with Bandini, Parkes and newcomer Chris
Amon on Maranello's books, so in the Commendatore's
best traditions everyone was kept guessing . . .

When Parkes was badly injured after upending his Ferrari 312 on oil dropped by Stewart's BRM H-16 on the
second lap of the Belgian Grand Prix, Scarfiotti – already
depressed by the death of Bandini at Monaco the previous

Ludovico Scarfiotti may not have been the greatest F1 driver,
but his 1966 Italian Grand Prix triumph ensured that his
name is enshrined in the memories of his countrymen.

month – virtually gave up. He returned to F1 the following year as a member of the Cooper-BRM works team,
but also signed to drive a Porsche in his old stamping
ground, the European Mountain Championship.

He was practising at Rossfeld, virtually in the shadow of
Hitler's 'Eagle's Nest' at Berchtesgarten, when his Porsche
Bergspyder slammed off the road into a clump of trees. A
stuck throttle was blamed for the accident which claimed
the life of this charming Italian gentleman, although
stories persist to this day that Scarfiotti deliberately drove
off the road to avoid another injured competitor (killed
many years later in a US sports car accident) who had
crashed shortly before and was lying in the road.

SCARLATTI, Giorgio (I)

b. 2 October 1921
12 Grands Prix
Career span: 1956 (Ferrari); 1957–9 (Maserati); 1960 (Maserati
and Cooper); 1961 (de Tomaso)

A steady Italian privateer, Scarlatti made his modest reputation driving F1 and sports cars for Maserati. He shared a Porsche RSK in the 1958 Targa Florio with Jean Behra, the Frenchman who firmly believed that they would have won if Scarlatti had been able to drive a little faster.

SCHECKTER, Ian (ZA)

b. 22 August 1947, East London
18 Grands Prix

The elder brother of 1979 World Champion, Jody Scheckter, whom he followed to Europe after winning the 1972 Formula Ford 'Sunshine Series' and the Driver to Europe award that went with it. His F1 début was in the 1974 South African GP at Kyalami in a Team Gunston Lotus 72, and subsequently he was a regular in his home race. He had a couple of outings for Williams in Europe during 1975, then a full programme with a works March, sponsored by Rothmans in 1977. It led nowhere, apart from back to South Africa for domestic-level F/Atlantic races.

SCHECKTER, Jody

See pages 156–7.

SCHELL, Harry (USA)

b. 29 June 1921, Paris
d. 13 May 1960, Silverstone
55 Grands Prix
Career span: 1950 (Cooper-JAP and Talbot); 1951–2 (Maserati); 1953 (Gordini); 1954–5 (Maserati, Ferrari and Vanwall); 1956 (Vanwall and Maserati); 1957–8 (Maserati and BRM); 1959 (BRM); 1960 (Cooper)

This charismatic, immensely popular semi-professional was born of a French father, pre-war Delahaye racer Laury, and his feisty Irish-American wife Lucy O'Reilly Schell. Tremendous value for money, the stories about Schell's racing pranks are legion, but he was a fine driver and his performance at Reims in 1956 when he harried a trio of Lancia-Ferraris with his lone Vanwall signalled that Tony Vandervell's cars were really to be taken seriously. He was also a great Maserati 250F privateer before and after his fleeting Vanwall involvement.

SCHENKEN, Tim (AUS)

b. 26 September 1942, Sydney
33 Grands Prix
Career span: 1970 (de Tomaso); 1971 (Brabham); 1972 (Surtees); 1973 (Williams)

Harry Schell was a fun-loving dilettante, but that did not prevent him from being quite a performer at the wheel of a Grand Prix car.

This chirpy Australian demonstrated outstanding FF1600 and F3 form in the late 1960s before gaining promotion to the Brabham team in 1971, scoring a strong third place in the Austrian Grand Prix. He switched to Surtees the following year because he had doubts that Brabham team's new owner Bernie Ecclestone might not do a good enough job! His last GP outing (for Williams) was at Mosport Park in 1973. He is now Clerk of the Course for the Australian Grand Prix at Adelaide.

SCHERRER, Albert (CH)

b. 28 February 1908
d. 5 July 1986
1 Grand Prix

This businessman from Basle raced a Jaguar XK120 on an amateur basis and an HWM in the 1953 Swiss Grand Prix.

SCHECKTER, Jody (ZA)

b. 29 January 1950, East London
112 Grands Prix; 9 wins; World Champion 1979
Career span: 1972–3 (McLaren); 1974–6 (Tyrrell); 1977–8
(Wolf); 1979–80 (Ferrari)

This curly-haired South African was quickly accorded the nickname 'Fletcher' after the baby seagull in the book *Jonathan Livingstone Seagull* who tried to fly at too early an age and kept crashing into the cliff face. Jody was unquestionably World Champion material, but on the strength of some of his early F1 performances it was really a question of whether he would live long enough to achieve that aim.

Jody arrived in Britain at the start of 1971 having won the prize as South Africa's most promising young racing driver. He breezed through FF1600 and F3 to such great effect that he was in a works McLaren M19A in time for the following year's United States Grand Prix at Watkins Glen. This dazzling progress continued, and in 1973 he led the French Grand Prix at Paul Ricard with the new McLaren M23 before being pushed off by Fittipaldi's Lotus.

A couple of weeks later, trying too hard on the first lap of the British Grand Prix at Silverstone, Scheckter ran wide coming out of Woodcote corner and triggered the spectacular multiple pile-up which resulted in the race being red flagged to a halt!

Jody Scheckter in conference with Wolf designer Harvey Postlethwaite. In 1977 he would win the Monaco Grand Prix for the team (*opposite*), but switched to Ferrari to take the title two years later at the wheel of the flat-12 engined 312T4 at Zandvoort (*below*) .

For 1974 he was signed to lead the Tyrrell team in the wake of Jackie Stewart's retirement, and began to calm down. He won the Swedish and British Grands Prix, finishing third in the final Championship points table. In 1975 he won his home Grand Prix at Kyalami, and in 1976 he won the Tyrrell P34 six-wheeler at Anderstorp.

Reasoning that he was going to make little further progress with Tyrrell, he signed for the newly reorganized Walter Wolf Racing outfit in 1977. This was effectively a brand new one-car team based round a Cosworth V8-engined package penned by former Hesketh designer Harvey Postlethwaite, organized by Peter Warr and bankrolled by Austro-Canadian oil man Walter Wolf.

Scheckter almost won the 1977 World Championship, bagging the Argentine, Monaco and Canadian Grands Prix, and eventually finishing second behind Niki Lauda. It was an encouraging start but the team failed to sustain this momentum through 1978 and Jody accepted an offer from Ferrari to lead the team in 1979.

Many observers felt that the combination of Ferrari's collective Latin temperament and Scheckter's sometimes abrasive South African frankness would be a recipe for disaster. Jody knew full well that life might be difficult at Ferrari, particularly as he would be paired with such an outstanding new star as Gilles Villeneuve, but he was absolutely confident he had made the correct decision.

Even when Villeneuve beat him into second place at Kyalami and Long Beach, Jody showed himself to be happily free of the psychological hang-ups which affected many of his colleagues in such situations. His moment came when he won the Belgian and Monaco Grands Prix in quick succession and he duly clinched his World Championship with a third win in the Italian Grand Prix at Monza, a race in which Villeneuve abided by team orders in honourable fashion and followed him in second place.

For 1980, Ferrari form plummeted as the 1979 car was revamped into the 312T5 and proved hopelessly uncompetitive. Villeneuve tried his hardest, but Jody was demoralized and knew inwardly that his spark of motivation was beginning to dim. He retired at the end of the season.

Today Jody Scheckter lives in Atlanta with his second wife Claire and runs a business specializing in high-technology security systems.

157

SCHILLER, Heinz (CH)

b. 25 January 1930
1 Grand Prix

This Porsche dealer from Geneva drove a BRM V8-engined Lotus 24, entered by Ecurie Filipinetti, in the 1962 German Grand Prix.

SCHLESSER, Jean-Louis (F)

b. 12 September 1952
1 Grand Prix

A highly successful sports and saloon car driver who became team leader of the Mercedes-Benz Group C team, Jean-Louis is the nephew of Jo Schlesser who was killed at Rouen in 1968. Sometime test driver for the Williams F1

The dynamic Ronnie Peterson (left) in conversation with his close friend Tim Schenken.

team, his sole Grand Prix outing came at Monza in 1988 as stand-in for Nigel Mansell, where he tripped up race leader Ayrton Senna's McLaren in a collision which was certainly not all his responsibility. He is married to the former tennis star Mariana Simonescu whose first husband was Wimbledon champion Bjorn Borg.

SCHLESSER, Jo (F)

b. 18 May 1928, Madagascar
d. 7 July 1968, Rouen
3 Grands Prix

The enormously popular sports car racing friend of Guy Ligier, Schlesser ran an F2 Matra in the sub-class of the 1966 and 1967 German Grands Prix. Desperate to get into F1 at the advanced age of forty, he accepted an invitation to drive the untested air-cooled Honda RA302 in the 1968 French Grand Prix at Rouen. He crashed on the second lap and was killed when the car caught fire.

SCHNEIDER, Bernd (D)

b. 20 July 1964
9 Grands Prix

An enthusiastic German F3 graduate whose F1 career was virtually written off, thanks to a catastrophic season driving a Zakspeed-Yamaha in 1989.

SCHOELLER, Rudolf (CH)

b. 27 April 1902
d. 7 March 1978
1 Grand Prix

A German-based Swiss also-ran who drove a private Ferrari 212 in the 1952 German GP.

SCHROEDER, Rob (USA)

b. 11 May 1926
1 Grand Prix

He drove a Lotus 24 entered by Texan oil millionaire, John Mecom, in the 1962 US Grand Prix at Watkins Glen, finishing tenth, seven laps behind Jim Clark's winning Lotus 25.

SCHUMACHER, Michael (D)

b. 31 September, Kerpen
6 Grands Prix

Schumacher was rated as the next Aytron Senna when he

exploded on to the Grand Prix scene in the late summer of 1991 after signalling his talent with outstanding drives in the Mercedes-Benz Group C sports car team. He qualified seventh on his maiden F1 outing for Jordan at Spa only to switch to Benetton, amidst much legal acrimony, in time for the Italian GP at Monza. A man whose talent shines out like a beacon, Schumacher found himself at the centre of the second legal row in four months when the Swiss Sauber team, which had built and fielded the Mercedes sports car entries, claimed he was bound by a contract to drive their new F1 car when it makes its competition début in 1993. Benetton's lawyers vigorously reject this contention.

SCHUPPAN, Vern (AUS)

b. 19 March 1943
8 Grands Prix

A popular Australian who drove occasionally for Ensign, Hill and Surtees during the mid-1970s before pursuing a more successful sports car career which included a Le Mans victory in a works Porsche. He is now one of the top Porsche preparation experts, specializing in the manufacture of carbon-fibre composite chassis for the 962 and its derivatives.

SCHWELM CRUZ, Adolfo (RA)

b. 28 June 1923
1 Grand Prix

Schwelm Cruz started racing in Italy during 1949 with an Alfa Romeo 2300 before débuting in Argentina two years later when he was national sports car champion. He drove a Cooper-Bristol in the 1953 Argentinian GP.

SCOTT-BROWN, Archie (GB)

b. 13 May 1927, Paisley
d. 19 May 1958, Spa
1 Grand Prix

This great little Scottish driver with a withered right arm achieved fame with his exploits at the wheel of Lister-Jaguar sports cars, but had one Grand Prix outing at Silverstone in 1956 with a Connaught B-type. He was badly injured at Spa when his Lister-Jaguar crashed at the same spot which claimed Dick Seaman's Mercedes in 1939, and died the following day.

SCOTTI, Piero (I)

b. 11 November 1909, Florence
1 Grand Prix

A successful Florence-based Italian privateer who owned an import-export and mineral water business. He took part in the 1956 Belgian Grand Prix at the wheel of a Connaught.

SEIDEL, Wolfgang (D)

b. 4 July 1926
d. 1 March 1987
10 Grands Prix

This German amateur spread his limited Championship programme across ten seasons, starting with a Veritas RS in the 1953 German Grand Prix and rounding it off at Aintree in the 1962 British GP where he drove a Lotus 24-BRM V8.

SENNA, Ayrton

See pages 160–1.

SERAFINI, Dorino (I)

b. 22 July 1909
1 Grand Prix

A former Gilera motorcycle ace who shared the second place Ferrari 375 at Monza in 1950 with Alberto Ascari.

SERRA, Chico (BR)

b. 3 February 1957
18 Grands Prix

Regarded by many as the great Brazilian F1 talent that was allowed to slip away, Serra was a terrific FF1600 performer in British national events and proved a strong rival to Nelson Piquet for the 1978 British F3 honours, even though he was using a less competitive March chassis. He joined Fittipaldi for F1 in 1981, but his Grand Prix aspirations died with the team the following year. He still races saloon cars back home in Brazil today.

SERRURIER, Doug (ZA)

b. 9 December 1920
2 Grands Prix

An enterprising South African enthusiast who built his own F1 special, the LDS, powered by an Alfa Romeo four-cylinder engine driving through a Porsche five-speed gearbox. He used it to contest the 1962 and 1963 South African GPs at East London.

SENNA, Ayrton (BR)

b. 21 March 1960, Sao Paulo

126 Grands Prix; 33 wins; World Champion 1988, 1990 and 1991

Career span: 1984 (Toleman); 1985–7 (Lotus); 1988 to date (McLaren)

Probably the most intensely committed competitor of the current Grand Prix generation, Ayrton Senna realized a major ambition in 1988 when he won his first World Championship by scoring a record eight victories in a single season. Yet this achievement was merely a staging post in a journey which Senna hopes will take him to the very pinnacle of Grand Prix history as the man who wins the most races, pole positions and Championships.

With sixty pole positions by the end of the 1991 season, this was another milestone achieved. But, at the start of 1992, although he still had twelve more Grand Prix victories and three more World Championships to win in order to realize his grand ambition, you would have been hard pressed to find many who would bet against him.

The son of a wealthy Sao Paulo businessman who built him a kart when he was only four years old, Ayrton had been racing such devices very seriously for eight years by the time he exploded on to the national British Formula Ford scene in 1981. Immediately this quiet and shy young Brazilian proved that he had enormous talent. At the wheel of a Van Diemen he took two of the British championships by storm, winning twelve times in twenty outings.

Briefly demoralized by shortage of sponsorship, he returned home to Brazil before graduating into FF2000 in 1982 with similarly spectacular results. In 1983 he won the British F3 title after a season-long battle with Martin Brundle, then catapulted into Grand Prix racing with Toleman.

He scored a Championship point in his second race and it soon became crystal-clear that Senna was a potential winner, even at this early stage of his career. This was dramatically underlined when he forced his Toleman through to second place at Monaco and had closed right on to the tail of Alain Prost's McLaren by the time the race was flagged to a premature halt in torrential rain.

Thereafter it was clear that his talent considerably outstripped the Toleman's potential and, by the time he rounded off the season with a splendid third behind the McLarens of Prost and Lauda at Estoril, he had already decided on a move to Lotus for 1985.

It was a good move, although the manner in which he extricated himself from his Toleman contract was sufficiently controversial for the team to suspend him from the 1984 Italian GP at Monza – a move which stopped Ayrton in his tracks.

His switch to Lotus was absolutely the correct career decision. Senna achieved his first Grand Prix victory on his next return to Estoril, a race held in monsoon conditions which caused even Prost to spin into retirement on the straight. He followed this with a succession of superb performances in the Renault-engined Lotus 97T. In 1986 he started from pole position on no fewer than nine occasions, beating Nigel Mansell's Williams-Honda by one-hundredth of a second to win the inaugural Spanish GP at Jerez, and then adding Detroit to his tally of triumphs, despite being delayed with a puncture.

These successes aside, it was becoming apparent to Senna that as long as Williams had Honda power, the only way to beat them was to join them. So Lotus contracted to use Honda engines for the 1987 season and Ayrton began the year feeling optimistic. Disappointingly, the Lotus 99T simply was not in the same aerodynamic league as the Williams FW11B and, although he applied his customary total commitment to the project, the year yielded only two victories for Senna.

The answer to all this frustration was plain to see. He accepted an offer to join McLaren who were to replace Williams as one of the Honda-supplied teams for 1988. Of course, partnering Alain Prost at McLaren was clearly going to be an enormous challenge which the Brazilian vowed to confront head on. He would, he told his colleagues, out-run Prost by being quicker, fitter, more determined – and faster.

Senna was as good as his word. In this final season of the 1½-litre turbo regulations, he plundered Prost's personal domain and came away with first prize. He won the San Marino, Canadian, Detroit, British, German, Hungarian, Belgian and Japanese Grands Prix – and would have added Monaco and Italy to that tally had it not been for minor driving errors. He also stalled on the grid in Japan, but managed to bump-start the engine and then performed with dazzling verve to climb back from fourteenth place to win, clinching his title. Prost won seven races, giving McLaren an overall tally of fifteen wins from sixteen events, a matchless record in contemporary F1 history.

For 1989, with the new 3.5-litre V10 Honda engine, the rivalry between Senna and Prost reached fever pitch. There was a major row when Prost accused Senna of reneging on a 'no passing' agreement on the first lap at Imola. An uneasy peace was restored, but the trouble exploded again at Suzuka where the two McLarens collided whilst battling for the lead of the Japanese GP.

Prost emerged champion after this débâcle, as although Senna won the race, he was later excluded for avoiding the chicane. It seemed as though FISA, the sport's governing body, had initiated a witch hunt against the brilliant Brazilian. Senna, in turn, levelled some incautious accusations against FISA President, Jean-Marie Balestre. He later

Ayrton Senna (left) shakes
hands with Alain Prost at the
start of their 1988 season
together as McLaren-Honda
running mates. Test driver
Emanuele Pirro (centre)
wishes he had a regular
drive . . .

had to withdraw them before FISA would issue him with his 1990 F1 licence.

Senna won the 1990 World Championship, but yet again the Brazilian was pitchforked headlong into more controversy after his McLaren plunged into the back of Prost's Ferrari in a first corner collision at Suzuka which finally tipped the title battle in Ayrton's favour. A year further on, with Balestre now unseated from the FISA presidency, and having clinched his third Championship, Senna ensured Suzuka was the centre of controversy for the third successive season by launching into an angry attack on the former President's behaviour.

Senna off duty can be a different proposition altogether to the ascetic visage he projects in his role as professional racer. There is a relaxed, gentle side to the man. He loves his family, respecting his father and lionizing his mother. He is at ease with children, treating them as young adults. His efforts behind the wheel of a Grand Prix car have made him a multi-millionaire. Yet few amongst his contemporaries have put in so much single-minded effort and commitment to reach the upper limits of performance perfection which Senna is always seeking.

SERVOZ-GAVIN, 'Johnny' (F)

b. 18 January 1942, Grenoble
12 Grands Prix
Career span: 1967 (Matra); 1968 (Matra and Cooper); 1969
(Matra); 1970 (March)

The handsome and athletic George-Francis Servoz-Gavin was given the nickname 'Johnny', so the story goes, by the legions of adoring young girls who crowded round him on the ski slopes of the French Alps. An erratic early F3 career with a private Brabham brought him to the notice of the French Matra team and he joined Beltoise and Pescarolo on the tidal wave of young talent which surged forward into F1 during the second half of the decade. Yet Servoz-Gavin's addiction to the social high life almost scuppered his career; only a strong fourth place in a ballasted Matra MS5-Cosworth F2 car in the non-championship 1967 Spanish Grand Prix at Jarama saved his bacon.

After Jackie Stewart had damaged his wrist in a practice accident – coincidentally, also in an F2 Matra at Jarama – 'Servoz' was given his big F1 break at Monaco in 1968. He took over Stewart's vacant Tyrrell Matra MS10, qualified second only to Graham Hill's Lotus 49B and stormed off to lead from the start. He led for three laps before glancing a rear wheel against the barrier coming through the waterfront chicane. It was enough to cause a driveshaft breakage and his great moment seemed to be over – but this was not quite so.

At Monza, he drove a second Matra MS10 into a storming second place in the 1968 Italian Grand Prix and stayed aboard the French works team to win the following year's European F2 Championship. He also kept his hand in with some runs in the 4WD Matra MS84, taking the only Championship point ever scored by a 4WD racer with sixth in the Canadian GP at Mosport Park.

For 1970 he was signed as Jackie Stewart's regular teammate in the Tyrrell March squad. Sadly, after knocking off a wheel and failing to qualify at Monaco, Servoz-Gavin announced that he was quitting. The previous winter an outing in an off-road vehicle had seen him struck in the face by a small branch and he was worried that his vision was no longer *au point*.

Others believe he was tricked by the innate uncompetitiveness of the March 701 chassis into concluding he had lost his touch. It would have been an understandable error to have made. Either way, it robbed the sport of a man whose whole demeanour and image cast him in the romantic role of a potential Grand Prix hero.

SETTEMBER, Tony (USA)

6 Grands Prix
Career span: 1962 (Emeryson); 1963 (Scirocco)

A southern Californian of Italian descent, Settember raced Mercedes 300SLs and Chevrolet Corvettes before giving to Europe in the late 1950s and initiating the WRE-Maserati sports car project. He subsequently persuaded wealthy compatriot Hugh Powell to bankroll an F1 project, first with Emerysons and then in 1963 with a home-brewed BRM V8-engined Scirocco. His best Championship result was eleventh in the 1961 British GP with an Emeryson, but he took a Scirocco to a best ever second place in the non-title 1963 Austrian GP behind Jack Brabham.

SHARP, James (USA)

b. 1 January 1928
6 Grands Prix

James R 'Hap' Sharp was a keen amateur racer and Texas oil-man who became a close confederate of Jim Hall in the development of the Chaparral sports cars during the early to mid-1960s. He ran a Cooper-Climax in the 1961 and 1962 US Grands Prix and a Lotus-BRM in the 1963 event. He used a Brabham-BRM in the 1964 event and also at the Mexican race in 1963 and 1964.

SHAWE-TAYLOR, Brian (GB)

b. 29 January 1915, Dublin
1 Grand Prix

This garage proprietor from Gloucestershire finished eighth in the 1951 British Grand Prix at Silverstone in an ERA E-type.

SHELBY, Carroll (USA)

b. 11 January 1923, Leesburg, Texas
8 Grands Prix
Career span: 1958 (Maserati); 1959 (Aston Martin)

A tough Texan who made his name when he shared the winning Aston Martin DBR1 with Roy Salvadori at Le Mans in 1959, Shelby was also a member of the Feltham team's F1 squad. He was later a key driving force behind AC Cobra development and Ford's subsequent onslaught on international sports car racing.

SHELLY, Tony (NZ)

b. 2 February 1937
1 Grand Prix

The son of Wellington's Jaguar dealer, this pleasant New Zealand amateur punctuated a European non-Championship F1 programme with an outing in the 1962 British GP at the wheel of his Lotus 18. He is now based in

Honolulu where he operates the largest US Mazda dealership.

SIFFERT, Jo (CH)

b. 7 July 1936, Fribourg
d. 24 October 1971, Brands Hatch
96 Grands Prix; 2 wins
Career span: 1962–3 (Lotus); 1964–5 (Brabham); 1966–7 (Cooper); 1968–9 (Lotus); 1970 (March); 1971 (BRM)

Siffert was an enormously versatile and substantially underestimated front-rank Swiss driver, the son of a motor trader who became infatuated with cars and motorcycles from an early age. Nicknamed 'Seppi' in his youth, he did anything to make money, from picking and selling flowers to collecting spent Swiss Army shells to sell back to the thrifty services for recycling. All this effort was focused on saving for a motorcycle, and he began racing a 125cc Gilera in 1957, winning the Swiss 350 Championship two years later.

His switch to cars came at the wheel of a F/Junior Stanguellini in 1960, but he soon swapped to a Lotus and found his way into F1 in 1962 with a 4-cylinder Climax-engined Lotus 24, making his Grand Prix début at Soa where he finished tenth. In 1963 he drove a Lotus-BRM initially under the Ecurie Filipinetti banner, but struck out as an independent operator after a few races, having won the non-title Syracuse GP in Sicily. Continuing with new Brabham BT11 chassis into which he installed his BRM V8 engine for 1964, he was taken into the Rob Walker Racing team the following year with the same car. He twice beat Jim Clark to victory in the Mediterranean GP at Enna-Pergusa (1964 and 1965), and was leading the pack at Syracuse when his car jumped out of gear over a bump and over-revved its engine.

With the advent of the 3-litre F1 in 1966, Walker purchased a Cooper-Maserati T81 and slimmed down his team to a single entry, keeping Siffert on as his driver in preference to Bonnier, rather snubbing the bearded Swede who quite clearly believed he would be kept on. Seppi managed to register fourth place finishes in the 1966 and

Jo Siffert's greatest day. The popular Swiss driver (centre) on the Brands Hatch rostrum after winning the 1968 British Grand Prix from the Ferraris of Chris Amon (left) and Jacky Ickx.

1967 US Grands Prix at Watkins Glen, but it was clear that something better in terms of equipment was required.

For 1968 Rob Walker acquired one of the latest Lotus 49s, but the season ended in near-disaster almost before it had started. Testing on a rain-drenched Brands Hatch in preparation for the Race of Champions, Siffert crashed Rob's new jewel quite badly. The wreckage was returned to the team's base at Dorking in Surrey where, during the strip-down, a stray spark ignited a pool of petrol and the premises were gutted. Not only was the damaged 49 destroyed in the conflagration, but also Rob's priceless archives and his ex-Dick Seaman Delage.

It seemed as though that was the end of the Walker team as an F1 force, but thanks to the generosity of Rob's brother-in-law, the industrialist Sir Val Duncan, the team stayed in business. An interim Lotus 49 was borrowed from the factory and a brand new specification 49B was delivered on the eve of the British Grand Prix where Siffert squared his account with Brands Hatch, winning handsomely after a great battle with Chris Amon's Ferrari.

Siffert stayed with Rob Walker through to the end of 1969, but then received an offer from Ferrari. However, Porsche, for whom he was a valued sports car driver, were aghast at the prospect of losing Siffert to their main rival and instead paid for him to drive a works STP March alongside Chris Amon. A disastrous season ensued and Seppi was glad to take a place alongside Pedro Rodriguez at BRM the following year.

The partnership between the 'Mexican Bandit' and the 'Crazy Swiss' was volatile to say the least. They were arch-rivals as well as team-mates within the JW/Gulf Porsche 917 squad, and this rivalry was continued in their F1 operations. Yet although they were not close personally, they had tremendous professional admiration for each other.

After Pedro's sad death on the eve of the British Grand Prix, Siffert lifted the team's spirits with a magnificent victory the following month at Österreichring. Tragically, in the end-of-season Victory Race at Brands Hatch, this great-hearted driver's BRM P160 slewed off the road at Hawthorn Hill, the fastest section of the circuit, following a suspension breakage. The car erupted into flames and Siffert, who had suffered no more than a fractured leg on impact, died of asphyxia. It was the end of a tragic season for BRM, following so closely the death of Pedro Rodriguez.

SIMON, André (F)

b. 5 January 1920, Paris
11 Grands Prix

Another Gordini stalwart from the early days, this garage proprietor from La Varenne was also invited to drive for the Mercedes F1 team at Monaco in 1955 after Hans Hermann injured himself in a practice accident. He finished sixth at Monza in the 1950 Italian GP with a Simca-Gordini T15 and repeated this result two years later with a Ferrari 500.

SOLANA, Moises (MEX)

d. 27 July 1969
8 Grands Prix

This Mexican national racing hot shot competed regularly in his home Grand Prix between 1963 and 1968. He was killed in a Can-Am McLaren at a domestic hillclimb during the summer of 1969.

SOLER-ROIG, Alex (E)

b. 29 October 1932
6 Grands Prix

The semi-professional racer son of a respected Barcelona surgeon who treated Jochen Rindt in the aftermath of his huge 1969 Spanish GP shunt at the city's Montjuich Park circuit, Soler-Roig had the resources to pay handsomely for his F1 racing. March and BRM could not resist his cash, albeit briefly, in 1971 and 1972, but soon got bored with his lack of pace.

SOMMER, Raymond (F)

b. 31 August 1906
d. 10 September 1950, Cadours
5 Grands Prix

The son of a wealthy carpet manufacturer from Pont-à-Mousson in the Ardennes, Sommer was French champion three times in the 1930s, sharing the winning Alfa Romeo at Le Mans in 1932 with Luigi Chinetti. He was fourth at Monaco in 1950 in a Ferrari 125 after consolidating his post-war reputation with Gordini, Talbot and Maserati. This audacious driver, nicknamed 'Coeur de Lion', was killed at Cadours during the non-Championship Haute Garonne GP in an 1,100cc Cooper-JAP borrowed from Harry Schell.

'SPARKEN, Mike' (F)

b. 16 June 1930
1 Grand Prix

A Ferrari sports car amateur who drove a Gordini in the 1955 British Grand Prix. He now has a home in London and owns a restored Alfa Romeo 158 whose rebuild was completed in the late 1980s.

SPENCE, Mike (GB)

b. 30 December 1936, Croydon
d. 7 May 1968, Indianapolis
36 Grands Prix
Career span: 1964–5 (Lotus); 1966 (Lotus-BRM); 1967–8 (BRM)

Following Trevor Taylor and the luckless Peter Arundell into Team Lotus as Jim Clark's number two, Mike Spence took over the role at the 1964 British Grand Prix after Arundell's serious F2 accident at Reims. He had started racing in his father's Turner sports car, switching to an AC Ace-Bristol and then to a Cooper Formula Junior car in 1960.

Spence began to make his name two years later driving his own Lotus 22 F/Junior machine under the yellow and green colours of Ian Walker Racing. In 1963 and 1964 he drove for the works-supported Ron Harris Team Lotus squad, first in F/Junior and latterly in F2. Chapman was sufficiently impressed to offer him a works ride in the 1963 Italian Grand Prix where his Lotus 25 was running seventh when its engine expired.

Inevitably, Spence was overshadowed by Clark – who wouldn't have been? However, close scrutiny of his Lotus F1 performances signalled that he had quite a talent. He ran second early on in the 1964 US Grand Prix at Watkins Glen, finished fourth in Mexico and duplicated that result in the 1965 South African Grand Prix at East London where he followed in Clark's wheel tracks during the early stages. Later that year he was fourth in the British Grand Prix and third at Mexico, his final outing for Team Lotus.

In 1966 he was signed by BRM, but seconded to drive for the semi-works Parnell Racing team using old Lotus 25s fitted with 2-litre BRM V8s. Fifth at Zandvoort and Monza, this could be regarded as something of a holding year, but Mike found himself in the shadow of another Scot when he was promoted to the full works BRM team in 1967 where Jackie Stewart was firmly ensconced as team leader. He still managed a fifth at Spa on the day Jackie finished second, the only occasion that both works H-16s both came home in the points. That year he was also a member of the Chaparral sports car team, partnering Phil Hill to win the BOAC 500 at Brands Hatch.

In 1968 it finally seemed as though Mike was about to make his name as a front ranking F1 driver. With the new V12-engined BRM P126 he was a front running force in both the early season British non-title F1 warm-ups, the Brands Hatch Race of Champions and the Silverstone International Trophy. Now married and running a prosperous garage business at Maidenhead, everything seemed in place for success.

After Jim Clark's death, Colin Chapman invited Spence to join the Lotus Indianapolis challenge and the BRM management obligingly agreed. Testing the Lotus turbine at the Brickyard a week prior to the first qualifying runs, he ran a little too high going through turn one and slammed into the wall. He succumbed to multiple head injuries.

STACEY, Alan (GB)

b. 29 August 1933
d. 19 June 1960, Spa
7 Grands Prix

Stacey was a talented, extrovert driver from an Essex farming family who showed great speed in a works Lotus despite having an artificial lower right leg and needing a motorcycle-type throttle control. He was killed in the Belgian Grand Prix at Spa when he hit a bird on the Masta straight.

STARABBA, Gaeteno (I)

b. 3 December 1932
1 Grand Prix

An amateur from Naples who ran his own Lotus 18, equipped with a Maserati four-cylinder engine, in the packed 1961 Italian GP at Monza.

STEWART, Ian (GB)

b. 15 July 1929
1 Grand Prix

An Ecurie Écosse stalwart, unrelated to the other two Stewarts, Ian Stewart drove at the 1953 British Grand Prix in a Connaught A-type.

STEWART, Jackie

See pages 166–7.

STEWART, Jimmy (GB)

b. 6 March 1931
1 Grand Prix

The Ecurie Écosse Jaguar sports car racing brother of triple World Champion Jackie Stewart, he drove a Cooper-Bristol in the 1952 British Grand Prix. He retired from racing after a big shunt in a works Aston Martin at Le Mans in 1955.

STOHR, Siegfried (I)

b. 10 October 1952, Rimini
9 Grands Prix

An eccentric, bearded gentleman who raised sponsorship to buy a second Arrows drive in 1981. It was not a successful project.

STEWART, Jackie (GB)

b. 11 June 1939, Dumbarton
99 Grands Prix; 27 wins; World Champion 1969, 1971 and 1973
Career span: 1965–7 (BRM); 1968–9 (Tyrrell Matra); 1970
(March and Tyrrell); 1971–3 (Tyrrell)

If anybody was responsible for transforming the image of motor racing from a specialized amateur stance to a level which matches professional golf, tennis and football, then it was this shrewd son of a Dumbarton garage owner.

Written off academically from an early age (it was subsequently identified that he suffered from dyslexia) John Young Stewart proved himself to be a gifted sportsman and came close to earning a position in the British Olympic clay pigeon shooting team well before establishing his prowess behind the wheel of a racing car.

After dominating the British F3 scene in 1964 with a Tyrrell Cooper-BMC, Stewart was offered the chance of joining Team Lotus as number two to his fellow Scot Jim Clark in 1965. Shrewdly, he declined the invitation and signed up with BRM alongside Graham Hill. It was absolutely the right move and before long he was firmly established as the most promising newcomer to the business, a position which was cemented when he won the Italian Grand Prix at Monza, outfumbling Hill in a late-race sprint to the flag.

He kicked off the 1966 season on a promising note by winning the Monaco Grand Prix in a 2-litre V8-engined BRM, but the onset of the 3-litre formula meant that BRM was developing its complicated and unreliable H-16 power unit. Stewart's fortunes were therefore shackled to this unreliable engine through to the end of 1967, but he still managed to produce an epic performance in that year's Belgian Grand Prix when he stormed to second place, holding the bulky machine in gear and steering round Spa with one hand.

In 1968 Jackie joined Ken Tyrrell's new F1 team to drive French Matras powered by the new Cosworth DFV V8 engine, and his career immediately took off. He quickly donned Jim Clark's mantle, clinching the Championship in 1969 for Matra and then again in 1971 and 1973 at the wheel of Tyrrell's purpose-built machines. Early in 1973 he resolved to retire from racing at the end of the season, keeping the decision from his wife Helen right through to

A young Jackie Stewart poses with his son Paul in the cockpit of his 1966 Matra-BRM F2 car.

Jackie raises his arm to signal that his Tyrrell 006 is slowing at the scene of the first-lap accident which brought the 1973 British Grand Prix to a temporary halt. He is alongside Ronnie Peterson's Lotus 72.

the eve of the final race of the season, the US Grand Prix at Watkins Glen, which he failed to start after the tragic death during practice of his dazzling team-mate François Cevert. He exceeded Jim Clark's record of GP wins by two, taking his total to twenty-seven, a record only beaten by Alain Prost fourteen years later.

Stewart debunked the myth that racing drivers should be devil-may-care extroverts to whom the risk of death or injury was a necessary part of their calling. His success brought with it the influence to get things done, so he quickly focused his energies on initiating sweeping improvements in safety standards, both from circuit facility and driver safety viewpoints. He brought about the wide use of guard rails and was responsible for the dropping of

the old Spa-Francorchamps circuit from the F1 schedule – he shunted there badly, during a first lap downpour in 1966.

This attitude did not always find favour with the purists and Jackie was much maligned as a result. But as European motor racing's first dollar millionaire, Stewart continues as one of the sport's most informed observers, influential advisors and highly regarded PR figures to this day.

He has lived in Switzerland since the late 1960s with his wife Helen and sons Mark and Paul, the latter now a professional racer himself with his own team in the F3000 category. The Stewarts are also well connected with the British royal family, Helen being godmother to Zara Phillips, daughter of the Princess Royal.

STOMMELEN, Rolf (D)

b. 11 July 1943, Siegen
d. 24 April 1983, Riverside, California
54 Grands Prix
Career span: 1970 (Brabham); 1971 (Surtees); 1972 (Eifelland);
1973 (Brabham); 1974–5 (Lola); 1976 (Brabham); 1978
(Arrows)

A product of the Porsche sports car team of the late 1960s,
and one of the few capable of taming the flat-12 917 in its
original precarious guise, Stommelen entered F1 as a
member of the Brabham team in 1970 with generous
sponsorship from the German car magazine, *Auto Motor
und Sport*, and some help from Ford who were anxious to
have another German in the sport's most senior category.

A third place in Austria and a fifth in Italy marked out
Rolf as a man with great promise, but a switch to Team
Surtees in 1971 slowed his career's momentum and a de-
tour to drive the Luigi Colani-revamped March 721 for
Heinz Henericci's Eifelland team in 1973 virtually brought
it to a halt.

He made up some ground with Brabham in 1973 and
then got taken aboard Graham Hill's Embassy Lola team
in the middle of the following year. Leading the 1975
Spanish GP at Barcelona, a failure of the rear wing strut
hurled his Hill GH1 wildly out of control, killing four
onlookers and leaving Rolf badly injured. He recovered to
drive for Hill again later that season, but was unable to
reproduce his future form and faded from the Grand Prix
scene at the end of the year.

He was away from F1 until 1978 when he returned
alongside Riccardo Patrese in the Arrows team at the be-
hest of Warsteiner, the German brewery which was sponsoring the team. But the light had gone out and Rolf was
an also-ran, so he switched to sports cars thereafter. He
was killed at the wheel of a Porsche 935 during an IMSA
event in California.

STREIFF, Philippe (F)

b. 26 June 1955
54 Grands Prix
Career span: 1984 (Renault); 1985 (Ligier and Tyrrell); 1986–7
(Tyrrell); 1988 (AGS)

This very tall and serious-minded Frenchman graduated
through Formula 2 to make his F1 début in a third Renault
at the 1984 Portuguese GP at Estoril. But it was not until
1986, when he joined the Tyrrell team, that he contested a
full World Championship programme. He switched to
AGS for 1988 and intended to stay with them for 1989,
but crashed heavily during pre-race testing at Rio prior to
the Brazilian GP, suffering back injuries which have left
him paralysed and a total invalid.

Philippe Streiff's F1 career was cut short by a testing accident
here at Rio in 1989.

STUCK, Hans (CH)

b. 27 December 1900, Warsaw
d. 9 February 1978
3 Grands Prix

This pre-war Auto Union star drove a handful of races at
the wheel of an AFM-BMW F2 car manufactured by Alex
von Falkenhausen, later chief of engine development at
BMW.

STUCK, Hans-Joachim (D)

b. 1 January 1951, Grainau
74 Grands Prix
Career span: 1974–6 (March); 1977 (Brabham); 1978
(Shadow); 1979 (ATS)

This son of the great pre-war Auto Union ace radiated the
unfettered energy and good nature of an out-of-control
golden retriever, bounding around the paddocks with a

Hans-Joachim Stuck displayed an effervescence behind the wheel that mirrored his own personality.

broad grin on his face and applying his hand to the business of driving any racing car with enormous enthusiasm. A great saloon car ace, both for Ford and BMW, he made his F1 début with March in 1974 and drove intermittently for the Bicester team through to 1977 when he switched to the Brabham-Alfa squad after the death of Carlos Pace.

He scored superb third places in Germany and Austria, plus a fifth at Silverstone, and stormed away to lead the opening stages of the rain-soaked US GP at Watkins Glen before sliding into a barrier. In 1978 he drove for Shadow, and slipped further down the pecking order the following year with ATS before finally retiring from F1. He now races Audi touring cars in the USA.

SULLIVAN, Danny (USA)

b. 9 March 1950, Louisville, Kentucky
15 Grands Prix

A charismatic, self-confident, all-American boy who started out in racing when a close family friend, the internationally distinguished paediatrician Dr Frank Falkner – an old racing pal of John Cooper and Ken Tyrrell from the 1950s – gave him a course at Jim Russell's Snetterton school as a twenty-first birthday present. Danny's father was a builder from Louisville and Sullivan Jr worked as a lumberjack, janitor, cab driver and chicken ranch hand as he scraped to keep body and soul together in his youth. With backing from his close friend Garvin Brown, Sullivan drove an F1 season with Tyrrell in 1983, never quite making the grade, but his career burst into flower after returning to the CART scene and winning the 1985 Indy 500 by a couple of seconds from Mario Andretti after a spectacular spin. A true child of his generation, he made his TV début with a part in *Miami Vice* in 1986 and has been very much the jet set socialite over the years, partnering such celebrities as international model Christie Brinkley, while still maintaining his career as a highly formidable and successful racer.

SURER, Marc (CH)

b. 18 September 1952
82 Grands Prix
Career span: 1979 (Ensign); 1980 (ATS); 1981 (Ensign); 1982–4 (Arrows); 1985 (Brabham); 1986 (Arrows)

A talented and popular graduate from the BMW Junior touring car team in the mid-1970s, Surer won the 1979 European F2 title in a March-BMW. His F1 début was with Ensign at end of that season, then a 1980 programme with ATS was thwarted when he broke his ankles in a practice crash at Kyalami. He finished fourth at Rio for Ensign in 1981, and then his 1982 season was thwarted once again with more leg injuries again sustained during testing at Kyalami for Arrows – this meant that his start to the season was delayed until Europe. He stayed with Arrows in 1983 and 1984, had some good Brabham-BMW performances in 1985 and then moved back to Arrows in 1986. His professional career ended when he crashed his Ford RS200 on the Hessen Rally in Germany, a tragedy in which his co-driver was killed. Marc was badly burned and took some time to recover. Since then he has occupied himself as a television commentator, managing his wife Yolande in her F3 career and, more recently, he has taken over as Manager of the BMW racing programme in the German Touring Car Championship.

SURTEES, John

See pages 170–1.

SURTEES, John (GB)

b. 11 February 1934, Tatsfield, Surrey
111 Grands Prix; 6 wins; World Champion 1964
Career span: 1960 (Lotus); 1961 (Cooper); 1962 (Lola); 1963–6
(Ferrari); 1966 (Cooper); 1967–8 (Honda); 1969 (BRM); 1970–2
(Surtees)

A deeply committed and very serious minded competitor, John Surtees came into car racing after a glittering career on two wheels. The son of a well-known pre- and post-war amateur racer and garage owner Jack Surtees, John served an apprenticeship with Vincent-HRD at Stevenage before embarking on an international career which would yield seven motorcycle World Championships for the Gallarate-based MV Agusta team.

Having been invited to test an Aston Martin DBR1 sports car and a Vanwall Grand Prix machine at the end of 1959, Surtees made his car racing début in a Formula Junior Cooper the following year largely because of Agusta's reluctance to make available bikes to run in British domestic races. He showed instant star quality on four wheels to the point that Colin Chapman invited him into the Lotus F1 team for those Grands Prix that did not clash with his motorcycle commitments.

He finished second in the British Grand Prix at Silverstone and qualified on pole position for the Portuguese race at Oporto, losing victory only when he damaged the radiator against straw bales whilst dominating the race. Surtees quit bike racing altogether at the end of 1961, but failed to make the right move when Lotus offered him a deal to run alongside Jim Clark the following year. Chapman had been playing ducks and drakes with his driver contracts, also signing up Innes Ireland, so John opted out of the equation to drive for the significantly less competitive Reg-Parnell-managed Yeoman Credit Cooper team.

One of Surtees's less than successful relationships came in 1969 with BRM. Here he is seen wrestling the P139 round Monza during the Italian Grand Prix.

Opposite: his Ferrari V6 leads Jim Clark's Lotus during the early stages of the 1963 Italian Grand Prix at Monza. *Inset*: on the day he clinched the Championship, John shares the 1964 Mexican Grand Prix rostrum with race winner Dan Gurney.

He turned down an offer from Ferrari for 1962, preferring to drive the Bowmaker team Climax-engined Lolas with which he achieved several good placings, including a win in the non-title Mallory Park 1,000 Guineas race. Finally, in 1963 he did sign for Ferrari and was rewarded with his first F1 Grand Prix victory at Nurburgring, almost two years since Maranello last won a Championship Grand Epreuve.

In 1964 Ferrari introduced the 158 V8 engine which propelled Surtees to further victories in the German and Italian Grands Prix and, when Jim Clark's Lotus expired on the penultimate lap of the Mexican Grand Prix, Surtees moved ahead of team-mate Lorenzo Bandini to clinch the Championship with a second place behind Dan Gurney's Brabham in this final race of the year, thus becoming the only man to win titles on two wheels and four.

The delayed development of the 1½-litre flat-12 Ferrari engine hamstrung Surtees's progress in 1965, the season yielding no further wins, and he sustained multiple injuries when he crashed a Lola T70 sports car while practising for a Can-Am race at Mosport Park, near Toronto, shortly after the Italian Grand Prix in September. For a few days it seemed as though Surtees might not survive, but he fought back to recover from his injuries with a characteristic tenacity which saw him back in a Ferrari – and winning again – early in 1966.

However, a major feud with team manager Eugenio Dragoni saw Surtees storm out of the Ferrari camp after the Le Mans 24-hours race, a move which unquestionably damaged both parties' immediate prospects for success. He joined Cooper, winning the 1966 Mexican Grand Prix

in their Maserati V12-engined car, and then embarked on a tiring two seasons of trying to make competitive sense of the complex Honda V12 project.

This partnership produced a single victory in the 1967 Italian Grand Prix, where John outfumbled Jack Brabham's Brabham-Repco by less than a second, but Honda pulled the rug on the project at the end of the following year. For 1969, Surtees signed for BRM, but it turned out to be a technical fiasco complicated towards the end of the season when John developed medical complications, including viral pneumonia, as a long-term consequence of his Mosport Park accident.

No longer willing to compromise his own technical principles, he embarked on his own F1 project in 1970, producing a succession of promising Cosworth V8-engined cars through to the middle of 1973 when he retired from the cockpit. However, his modestly financed team never recovered from sponsorship problems it encountered in 1974 and, despite a few bright moments, finally ceased competing at the end of 1978 when John was again hospitalized with more medical problems.

On the personal front, there was a bright side to his 1978 misfortune. He struck up a relationship with the ward sister whom he subsequently married and they now live happily in a beautiful Kent country house, surrounded by their three young children, many motorcycles and not a few old Surtees F1 cars.

In middle age, John Surtees mellowed considerably, losing the somewhat dogmatic approach which many of his drivers found made him so difficult to work with during the latter years of Team Surtees's F1 involvement.

171

SUZUKI, Aguri (J)

b. 8 September 1960, Tokyo
28 Grands Prix
Career span: 1988 (Lola); 1989 (Zakspeed); 1990–1 (Larrousse-Lola)

Only the second Japanese driver to race regularly in the World Championship, Suzuki made his F1 début at Suzuka in 1988 standing in for Yannick Dalmas in the Larrousse-Lola team. Encouraged by his father Masashi, who founded the Japanese Kart Racing Association, he competed in this branch of the sport throughout his teens with considerable success. He became the youngest ever Japanese F3 driver when aged eighteen in 1978, and then landed a prestigious contract with Nissan to drive both sports prototypes and touring cars. In 1989 he joined the ill-starred Zakspeed-Yamaha squad and was lucky not to go down with the ship, a fate suffered by his team-mate Bernd Schneider. He found a place with Larrousse for 1991 and his storming third place at Suzuka in the Japanese GP cemented his future in the sport's most senior category.

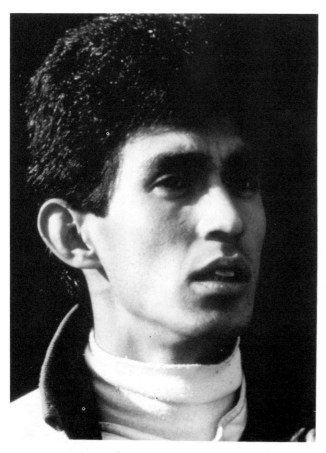

Aguri Suzuki, who took a splendid third place in the 1990 Japanese Grand Prix, is regarded as the best F1 driver yet to be produced by his country.

SWATERS, Jacques (B)

b. 30 October 1926, Woluve St Laubert
7 Grands Prix

A Ferrari-driving privateer who subsequently became the Maranello constructor's importer for Belgium.

TAKAHARA, Noritake (J)

b. 6 June 1951, Tokyo
2 Grands Prix

Takahara started racing in 1969 in a Honda S800 coupé and came to Europe in 1973 for a limited F2 programme. He drove in the non-Championship 1974 Silverstone International Trophy, finishing eleventh, and finished ninth in the 1976 Japanese GP at Fuji in a rented Surtees TS19. He drove a locally brewed Kojima 009 in the following year's Fuji race but crashed on the opening lap. He is now in semi-retirement.

TAKAHASHI, Kunimitsu (J)

b. 29 January 1940, Tokyo
1 Grand Prix

Takahashi started on two wheels and in 1961 became the first Japanese rider to win a motorcycle Grand Prix, on a 250cc Honda at Hockenheim in 1961. He was seriously injured in the following year's Isle of Man TT and switched to car racing in 1965. He drove a Tyrrell to ninth place in the 1977 Japanese GP at Fuji, and more recently has been a regular contender in the Fuji Grand Champion domestic series.

TAMBAY, Patrick (F)

b. 25 June 1949, Paris
114 Grand Prix; 2 wins
Career span: 1977 (Ensign); 1978–9 (McLaren); 1981 (Theodore and Ligier); 1982–3 (Ferrari); 1984–5 (Renault); 1986 (Haas-Lola)

This cosmopolitan gentleman was educated in France and the United States, speaks fluent English and was a talented downhill ski racer before motor racing caught his eye at the end of 1971. Widely acknowledged as one of the most genuinely charming individuals on the F1 stage in the early 1980s, the debonair Tambay never quite reaped the hard results his talent so obviously held in store.

At the Paul Ricard driving school he won the Volant Elf scholarship (the year before Didier Pironi) and, after two seasons in Formula Renault, successfully bypassed F3 to move directly into the European F2 Championship arena. He also sampled Can-Am sports cars in North America before his F2 exploits earned him an F1 chance at the

Above: Patrick Tambay was a debonair and charming gentleman driver. *Below:* he waits patiently in the cockpit of his Ferrari 126C3 while it is refuelled during practice for the 1983 Austrian Grand Prix.

wheel of an Ensign entered by wealthy Hong Kong enthusiast Teddy Yip in the 1977 British Grand Prix. Scoring five championship points in his first six Grands Prix, Patrick earned a place in the McLaren line-up for 1978 as James Hunt's team-mate.

By this stage McLaren was losing its competitive pace as rival teams' ground-effect chassis outclassed their own, so Tambay had two lean seasons before being replaced by Alain Prost at the start of 1980. As something of a consolation prize, he returned to the USA, won the Can-Am and then found a way back to F1 the following year thanks again to the philanthropic Teddy Yip and his tiny Theodore team.

When Jean-Pierre Jabouille retired from the Ligier squad after a handful of races, Tambay took his place only to be dropped again at the end of the season. His next F1 chance came in the tragic aftermath of Gilles Villeneuve's fatal accident when Patrick was recruited by Ferrari. He earned his spurs by winning the German Grand Prix the day after Didier Pironi was so critically injured at Hockenheim, and stirred emotional memories of Villeneuve by winning the San Marino GP at Imola in 1983.

His subsequent stints with Renault and the Haas-Lola teams never offered him machinery capable of producing really decent results and he did not race F1 after the end of

the 1986 season. He is still closely involved with Grand Prix racing as a television commentator.

TARQUINI, Gabriele (I)

b. 2 March 1962
24 Grands Prix
Career span: 1987 (Osella); 1988 (Coloni); 1989 (AGS); 1990 (AGS); 1991 (AGS and Fondmetal)

Capable and pleasant Italian Formula 3000 graduate frustrated by consistently uncompetitive F1 machinery for most of this period.

TARUFFI, Piero (I)

b. 12 October 1906
d. 1989
18 Grands Prix; 1 win
Career span: 1950 (Alfa Romeo); 1952–5 (Ferrari); 1955 (Mercedes); 1956 (Vanwall and Maserati)

Known as the 'silver fox' because of his shock of prematurely silver hair, Taruffi was an all-round sportsman, qualified as Doctor of Industrial Engineering and spent many years dovetailing the task of managing the Gilera motorcycle team with his many car racing commitments.

He started racing on motorbikes in the 1920s before switching to cars, his first four-wheel outings taking place in a Fiat in 1923. He raced in the Mille Miglia for the first time in 1930, finishing third in 1933, but it would take him another twenty-four years to win the famous Italian road race, a success he achieved in its final edition. When the official World Championship began in 1950 he drove an Alfa 158 in the Italian Grand Prix, switching to Ferrari the following year when he finished fifth in the Championship rankings.

In 1952 he won his sole World Championship Grand Epreuve, the Swiss Grand Prix at Berne, in a Formula 2 Ferrari 500. From then on his Formula 1 career dipped as he signed for Lancia to drive sports cars in 1954. He guested in a Ferrari at Monza, an outing he repeated in 1956, but he was fifty-one when he finally bagged that Mille Miglia victory the following year, and thereafter he quit the cockpit.

In retirement he made quite a name for himself as founder of a racing drivers' school and his book, *The Technique of Motor Racing* (published 1966), is regarded as one of the sport's all-time classics.

TAYLOR, Henry (GB)

b. 16 December 1932, Shefford, Bedfordshire
8 Grands Prix

Taylor was a Lotus F1 privateer and farmer who subse-

Piero Taruffi calls for a minute adjustment to his Mercedes-Benz W196 during practice for the 1955 British Grand Prix at Aintree. He finished this race in fourth place, completing a Mercedes grand slam behind team-mates Stirling Moss, Juan Manuel Fangio and Hans Herrmann.

quently became competitions manager for Ford of Britain. He is now retired and lives on the Côte d'Azur.

TAYLOR, John (GB)

b. 23 March 1933
d. 8 September 1966
5 Grands Prix

A popular and mild-mannered Lancashire driver who was badly burned when his 2.0 Brabham-BRM, entered by John Bridges, collided with Jacky Ickx's F2 Matra on the opening lap of the 1966 German Grand Prix at Nurburgring. He died suddenly almost a month later just as it seemed he was on the road to recovery.

TAYLOR, Michael (GB)

b. 24 April 1934
1 Grand Prix

This Wellington-educated amateur had his racing career cut short when his Lotus 18's steering column broke during practice for the 1960 Belgian Grand Prix, with Taylor suffering multiple injuries in the ensuing crash. He later sued Colin Chapman and Lotus, obtaining a substantial out-of-court settlement. The son of a Mercedes car salesman who founded Taylor and Crawley in Mayfair, he married Stirling Moss's former second wife Elaine Barberino in 1980. He founded a private property company which crashed in 1977 with debts of over £8 million. The official receiver later blamed the collapse on 'expensive, ill-judged, speculative ventures'.

TAYLOR, Trevor (GB)

b. 26 December 1936, Rotherham
27 Grands Prix
Career span: 1961–3 (Lotus); 1964 (BRP)

The son of a garage owner from Wickersley, near Rotherham, Taylor was the product of the late 1950s 500cc F3 milieu, initially using a JAP-engined Staride and later an ex-Stuart Lewis-Evans Cooper-Norton. Ten victories in 1958 earned him the British F3 Championship and, after a frustrating year in 1959 spent wrestling with his own F2 Cooper, he received an invitation to run his own newly purchased Lotus 18 as a second works car alongside Jim Clark the following season.

Taylor and Clark shared the 1960 British F/Junior title and Trev retained it solo in 1961 before joining Clark – whom he always refers to as 'that fine man' – in the Lotus Grand Prix line-up the following year. He managed a second place to Hill's BRM at Zandvoort, but that was effectively the sum total of his F1 achievement. Prone to major accidents, many of which were definitely not his fault, and a succession of mechanical disasters, he gradually slipped further into Clark's shadow through to the end of 1963 when Chapman replaced him with Peter Arundell.

In 1964 he joined that other cast-aside Lotus F1 star Innes Ireland in the BRP-BRM team run by Alfred Moss and Ken Gregory, but netted only a sixth place finish at Watkins Glen. Financial pressures caused the team to close its doors at the end of the year and that was the end of Taylor's F1 career, apart from an abortive attempt to

Trevor Taylor heading for the best result of his career – second in the 1962 Dutch Grand Prix at Zandvoort in his Lotus 24.

qualify the tatty Shannon-Climax special for the 1966 British Grand Prix at Brands Hatch.

It is too easy to forget that Trev Taylor, who cut quite a dash in his heyday with his distinctive bright yellow helmet and matching overalls, was a highly talented F1 contender who would probably have shone brilliantly had he not been paired alongside the gifted Clark.

THACKWELL, Mike (NZ)

b. 30 March 1961
2 Grands Prix

Son of the F2 Cooper privateer Ray Thackwell, this young New Zealander earned the distinction of being the youngest driver ever to start a World Championship Grand Prix, in Canada, at the wheel of a Tyrrell in 1980, when only 19.

THIELE, Alfonso (USA)

1 Grand Prix

Thiele drove a Cooper-Maserati in the 1960 Italian Grand Prix at Monza.

THOMPSON, Eric (GB)

b. 4 November 1919
1 Grand Prix

Thompson took fifth place for Connaught in the 1952 British Grand Prix, the sole World Championship F1 outing for this Lloyds broker from Surrey who also gained a reputation as an accomplished sports car performer. In semi-retirement, today he still runs a business specializing in rare motoring books.

THORNE, Leslie (GB)

b. 23 June 1916, Greenock, Renfrewshire
1 Grand Prix

A company director from Troon, Ayrshire, Thorne was also a keen amateur racer. He drove his Connaught A-type to fourteenth place in the 1954 British Grand Prix.

TINGLE, Sam (RSR)

b. 24 August 1921
5 Grands Prix

Like Doug Serrurier, Tingle also drove an LDS-Alfa Special in the 1963 South African GP at East London, after which he was a regular entrant in his home GP, competing regularly in every such race held through to 1969. He still has a transport and earth-moving business in Zimbabwe.

TITTERINGTON, Desmond (GB)

b. 1 May 1928, Cultra, nr Belfast
1 Grand Prix

This prosperous flax and yarn merchant from Ulster became a successful member of the Ecurie Écosse Jaguar sports car racing squad. His one-off GP outing came at Silverstone in 1956 where he retired his Connaught after qualifying very respectably ahead of a host of regulars including de Portago's Lancia-Ferrari, Behra's Maserati and Flockhart's BRM.

In 1972, having sold his businesses, he and his family relocated to Perthshire.

TRINTIGNANT, Maurice (F)

b. 30 October 1917, Ste-Cécile-les-Vignes
82 Grands Prix; 2 wins
Career span: 1950–3 (Gordini); 1954–5 (Ferrari); 1956 (Vanwall and Bugatti); 1957 (Ferrari); 1958 (Cooper, BRM and Maserati); 1959 (Cooper); 1960 (Cooper and Aston Martin); 1961 (Cooper); 1961 (Lotus); 1963 (Lola and BRM); 1964 (BRM)

This dapper little Frenchman was forty-seven years old when a sixth place in the 1964 German Grand Prix earned him the final Championship point in a distinguished racing career. It had started in 1938 at the wheel of a 2.3-litre supercharged Bugatti in which his brother Louis had been killed five years earlier while practising on the Peronne circuit in Picardy.

He used this rugged machine to compete in the first post-war European race, the Coupe de la Libération which was held in the Bois de Boulogne during September 1945. Unfortunately its preparation had been cursory to say the least; whilst stored in a barn during the war a family of rats had made their home in its fuel tank and Maurice retired with rat droppings clogging the fuel lines!

This incident gave him his nickname 'Le Petoulet', the literal translation of which can best be left to the imagination. He suffered severe injuries in the voiturette race held prior to the 1948 Swiss Grand Prix at Berne, but recovered to establish a reputation as a steady, versatile and unspectacular driver over the next decade.

Through his own reliability, and thanks to the misfortune of others, he won the 1955 Monaco Grand Prix in a Ferrari 625 and duplicated this achievement three years later in a Rob Walker team Cooper-Climax. After Stirling Moss's accident he briefly resumed a role as Rob Walker's driver, but eventually faded to the status of distant also-ran with his own private BRM in which he finished his F1 career.

Maurice Trintignant, in helmet and with cigarette dangling.

TUNMER, Guy (ZA)

b. 1 December 1948
1 Grand Prix

A South African amateur who drove a Team Gunston Lotus 72 to eleventh place at Kyalami in 1975.

ULMEN, Toni (D)

b. 25 January 1906
d. 4 November 1976
2 Grands Prix

An outstanding Veritas Meteor special driver, and close rival of Karl Kling, Toni Ulmen drove in the 1952 Swiss and German Grands Prix.

UNSER, Bobby (USA)

b. 20 February 1934, Albequerque, New Mexico
1 Grand Prix

One of the greatest Indianapolis racing stars of all time, Unser was romanced into driving an uncompetitive BRM in the 1968 US Grand Prix at Watkins Glen where he crashed heavily.

URIA, Alberto (U)

2 Grands Prix

The only Uruguayan driver to have competed in the World Championship, Uria contested the Argentine Grands Prix of 1955 and 1956 in an elderly Maserati A6GCM.

VACCARELLA, Nino (I)

b. 4 March 1933, Palermo
4 Grands Prix

This Sicilian lawyer was an accomplished sports car ace in the 1960s, winning the 1964 Le Mans 24-hours in a works

Nino Vaccarella was only an occasional F1 performer, his outings earned largely on the strength of his Targa Florio sports car reputation.

Ferrari 275P shared with Jean Guichet. He also knew the Targa Florio like the back of his hand, winning the classic road race for Maranello on three occasions. He was an occasional F1 Ferrari team member driving on three occasions at Monza. He also drove in the 1962 German GP outing for Porsche.

VAN DER LOF, Dries (NL)

b. 23 August 1919
d. 1991
1 Grand Prix

Van der Lof was a wealthy industrialist from Haaksbergen where he had a factory manufacturing electrical cable. A founder of the Dutch Racing Drivers' Club, he competed in the 1952 Dutch GP at Zandvoort in an HWM. He maintained an extensive old car collection and raced his own Maserati 250F in historic events up to the end of the 1980s.

VAN DE POELE, Eric (B)

b. 30 September 1961, Brussels
1 Grand Prix

This promising newcomer started his career in single-seaters before joining the BMW Junior team in 1987 in the Group A touring car category. An impressive F3000 exponent who won the last Birmingham Super Prix in 1990, van de Poele graduated to F1 with the uncompetitive Lamborghini team in 1991. He was on course for a finish in the points at Imola when his Lambo 291 ran short of fuel on the final lap.

VAN LENNEP, Gijs (NL)

b. 16 March 1942, Bloemendaal
8 Grands Prix

This highly respected Dutch sports car driver shared the victorious Martini Porsche 917 at Le Mans in 1971 with Helmut Marko. He hired a Surtees TS9 for his home Grand Prix at Zandvoort that summer and thereafter enjoyed an intermittent F1 career, briefly with BRM in 1972 and Williams in 1973, scoring his sole Championship point in Frank's car at Zandvoort.

VAN ROOYEN, Basil (ZA)

b. 19 April 1938
2 Grands Prix

A talented South African saloon car racer who had two outings in his home Grands Prix at Kyalami in 1968 and 1969.

VILLENEUVE, Gilles (CDN)

b. 18 January 1950, Berthierville, Quebec
d. 8 May 1982, Zolder
67 Grands Prix; 6 wins
Career span: 1977 (McLaren); 1978–82 (Ferrari)

This tiny French-Canadian was one of those rare personalities who became a legend in their own lifetime. Villeneuve was cast in a heroic mould, his fearless and undaunted approach to motor racing giving rise to more discussion and debate than that of any of his contemporaries. Some thought him wonderful, embodying all those romantically traditional qualities which go to make motor racing such a spectacular sport. Others dismissed his opposite-lock, tyre-smoking antics as a waste of energy.

Either way, he was undoubtedly a great driver who knew no other way but to drive flat-out all the time. Personal risk did not come into the equation at all. He began racing snowmobiles in his native Quebec at the age of eight, displaying from the outset an uninhibited natural flair which was to become the hallmark of his tragically short motor racing career.

Gilles rocketed to international prominence when he won the F/Atlantic race at the demanding Trois Rivières street circuit, on the banks of the St Lawrence River in 1976. James Hunt, then on the verge of winning his World Championship title, finished third in that event and returned to England to advise the McLaren team management that they should keep a firm eye on Villeneuve as possible future F1 material.

In 1977 Gilles was invited to drive a third works McLaren in the British Grand Prix. He qualified an impressive ninth, splitting regular drivers Hunt (in pole position) and Jochen Mass (eleventh on the grid). Delayed by a pit stop, he ran competitively to finish tenth. Despite this superb showing, McLaren opted to sign up Patrick Tambay to replace Jochen Mass at the end of the year. As things turned out, McLaren's loss was Ferrari's gain; the famous Italian team recruited Gilles to replace Niki Lauda at the end of the 1977 season.

Gilles quickly made himself at home in F1. It took him only until the third race of 1978, at Long Beach, to lead commandingly, but he was eliminated after an error of judgement when he tripped over Clay Regazzoni's Shadow DN8 when he came up to lap the slower car. By the end of the season, however, he celebrated his first F1 triumph with an immensely popular win in his home Grand Prix at Montreal at the wheel of the Ferrari 312T3.

In 1979 he was paired with Jody Scheckter and, armed with the new Ferrari 312T4, Gilles added further wins to his tally at Kyalami, Long Beach and Watkins Glen. From the start of that year Gilles fully appreciated that he was cast in a supporting role to his South African colleague.

Gilles Villeneuve *en route* to a great victory for Ferrari at Monaco, 1981. When he died the following year, Grand Prix racing lost one of its greatest exponents.

With that in mind, he displayed his integrity by following scrupulously in Scheckter's wheel tracks to finish second at Monza, knowing that all he had to do was disobey team orders and pass his rival in order to claim the World Championship for himself.

In 1980 the season proved disastrous for Ferrari, their 312T5 eclipsed by far more effective ground-effect opposition from Williams and Ligier. But in 1981 the Italian team followed Renault by adopting a turbo-charged 1½-litre engine and Villeneuve produced another two brilliant victories, at Monaco and in Spain, both achieved in a chassis that was not up to the standard of the opposition.

Throughout 1981 Villeneuve comfortably had the measure of his team-mate Didier Pironi, who stayed on with Ferrari into 1982 when the team's prospects took a distinctive upturn thanks to the arrival of the new Harvey Postlethwaite-designed Ferrari 126C2. Sadly, when Pironi overtook Gilles against team orders to win the San Marino GP in Ferrari's heartland, Villeneuve was incensed and never spoke to him again.

Two weeks later Villeneuve crashed to his death at Zolder, colliding with a slower car that strayed into his path as he attempted to match Pironi's lap times during practice for the Belgian Grand Prix.

Gilles Villeneuve heading for a memorable victory in the 1981 Monaco Grand Prix with the unwieldy Ferrari 126CK – a classic example of his virtuosity and never-say-die spirit.

VILLORESI, Luigi (I)

b. 16 May 1909, Milan
31 Grands Prix
Career span: 1950–3 (Ferrari); 1954 (Maserati and Lancia); 1955 (Lancia); 1956 (Maserati)

This veteran Italian ace started his racing career at the wheel of a Lancia Lambda in 1931. His first important event was the 1933 Mille Miglia, in which he shared a Fiat Balilla with his younger brother Emilio, reaching the big time in 1936 when he was sufficiently accomplished to finish sixth at Monaco at the wheel of a Maserati 4CM.

Both before and after the war Luigi Villoresi achieved considerable success with the Maserati marque, winning his first major race at Brno, Czechoslovakia, at the end of 1937 at the wheel of his 6CM. In 1938 he was recruited to the Maserati works team in an effort to counter the pace of the newly arrived Alfa Romeo 158s, one of which was ironically now driven by his brother Emilio who quickly developed into one of his greatest rivals.

He stayed with the Maserati works team into 1939 and continued racing after his brother Emilio was killed on 20 June testing one of the Alfa 158s at Monza. After the war he resumed racing, winning the Italian championship in 1946 and 1947, while at the same time encouraging the fledgeling career of his close friend Alberto Ascari. He joined him in the Ferrari team for 1949, winning the Dutch Grand Prix at Zandvoort, and accompanied him when he switched to Lancia for 1954. He was deeply affected by Ascari's death in 1955, and he did not race in F1 again until the following year when, after a bad accident in the Rome Grand Prix, he retired for good.

Spry, tanned and healthy, Villoresi was still regularly putting in an appearance at Monza for the Italian Grand Prix as he passed his eightieth birthday.

VOLONTERIO, Ottorino (CH)

b. 7 December 1917, Orselina
3 Grands Prix

A Locarno-based lawyer from the province of Ticino who gained moderate success in a variety of sports car categories, Volonterio demonstrated only a moderate pace when he graduated to F1 in his own privately operated Maserati 250F.

VON OPEL, Rikky (F)

b. 14 October 1947
10 Grands Prix

This Liechtenstein member of the Opel automotive dynasty produced promising form in F3 at the wheel of an Ensign in 1972 which prompted him to bankroll the pro-duction of an F1 challenger from the small Walsall-based constructor the following year. In 1974 he switched briefly to Brabham for three races before quitting the sport altogether.

VON TRIPS, Wolfgang (D)

b. 4 May 1928
d. 10 September 1961, Monza
27 Grands Prix; 2 wins
Career span: 1957–61 (Ferrari)

Nicknamed 'Taffy' by Mike Hawthorn in the mid-1950s ('because I think you look like a taffy!'), Wolfgang Graf Berghe von Trips was a dashing young German count who had been brought up on the family estates near Cologne where his family lived in conditions of genteel, if faded, elegance.

Wolfgang von Trips came so close to taking the 1961 World Championship. Here he celebrates his victory in that year's Dutch Grand Prix in the company of his beaming Ferrari team-mate, Phil Hill (left).

Wolfgang von Trips adjusts his helmet straps prior to testing a Lancia-Ferrari at Modena early in 1956. He was killed at Monza five years later, poised on the verge of the World Championship.

This Robert Redford look-alike was offered his first F1 drive in a perhaps over-generous moment by Enzo Ferrari in the 1956 Italian Grand Prix where he crashed heavily. It was only after the Lancia-Ferrari was stripped down for subsequent examination – and after two of its sister cars had also suffered steering arm breakages during the race – that von Trips was forgiven and offered another chance in Maranello's sports cars. He drove for Porsche in F2 during 1959 and then went back to Ferrari for the 1960 season, finishing third in the Portuguese Grand Prix.

Shrugging aside his reputation as a crasher, he won the 1961 Dutch and British Grands Prix and stood poised to clinch the World Championship as he started the Italian Grand Prix from pole position at Monza. Tragically, he collided with Jim Clark's Lotus as the two cars slowed for the Parabolica right-hander towards the end of the second lap. The Ferrari flipped up into the air, riding along the packed spectator fence, before slamming back on to the circuit. Von Trips and fourteen onlookers were left dead or dying.

VONLANTHEN, Jo (CH)

b. 31 May 1942
1 Grand Prix

A Swiss amateur who got a sponsored ride in an uncompetitive Williams in the 1975 Austrian Grand Prix.

WACKER, Fred (USA)

b. 10 July 1918, Chicago
3 Grands Prix

Founder of the Chicago region of the Sport Car Club of America – of which he was President in 1951 – this enthusiastic amateur driver was a manufacturer of car service tools and liquid metering equipment based in Lake Forest, Illinois. Part of the Cunningham Le Mans assault, he rented a ride with Gordini in a handful of Grands Prix and several non-title events during 1953 and 1954.

WALKER, David (AUS)

b. 10 June 1941
11 Grands Prix

This rugged Australian dominated the 1971 British F3 Championship in a works Lotus 69 before being pro-

Dave Walker dominated in F3, but found the transition to front-line F1 very hard to make.

moted to the Grand Prix team as Emerson Fittipaldi's team-mate the following year. He was, however, totally outclassed by the Brazilian in conditions where parity of equipment between the two men was a matter of some doubt. Thereafter he faded from the racing scene. He now owns and charters out a luxury ocean-going yacht on the eastern coast of Australia.

WALKER, Peter (GB)

b. October 1913, Leeds
d. 1 March 1984
4 Grands Prix

The most heroic single-seater deed from this Herefordshire-based land owner was finishing seventh in the 1951 British Grand Prix with a 1½-litre supercharged V16 BRM, after having half roasted in the stifling cockpit. The same season he won Le Mans for Jaguar, sharing a C-type with Peter Whitehead, the feat for which he is best remembered. He retired from racing after sustaining injuries when he crashed an Aston Martin at Le Mans in 1955.

WALTER, Heini (CH)

b. 28 July 1929
1 Grand Prix

A restaurant owner and used-car dealer from Aesch, near Basle, Heini Walter drove a Porsche 718 F2 car under the Ecurie Filipinetti banner in the 1962 German Grand Prix.

WARD, Rodger (USA)

b. 10 January 1921, Beloit, Kansas
2 Grands Prix

This USAC star won the 1959 Indianapolis 500 and then decided that a Kurtis-Kraft sprint car would be the ideal tool for the 1959 US Grand Prix at Sebring – a misjudgement as things turned out, as he qualified slowest some 43 seconds away from Stirling Moss's pole-winning Cooper. In the aftermath of this event, Ward urged John Cooper to come to Indianapolis, laying the seed of Jack Brabham's 1961 assault on the Brickyard. By the time Ward had his second F1 outing, with a Lotus-BRM at Watkins Glen in 1963, the day of the Indianapolis roadster was all but over.

Mr Nice Guy. Derek Warwick, whose terrific talent never found the right outlet in F1 at the right moment. *Below*: 'Del Boy' heads for his first World Championship points at Zandvoort in 1983 where he took the Toleman TG183B to fourth place.

WARWICK, Derek (GB)

b. 27 August 1954, Alresford, Hampshire
130 Grands Prix
Career span: 1981–3 (Toleman); 1984–5 (Renault); 1986 (Renault); 1987–9 (Arrows); 1990 (Lotus)

Blessed with an enormously gregarious and attractive personality, this son of a Hampshire agricultural trailer manufacturer was regarded as a more certain bet for Grand Prix honours than Nigel Mansell in the early 1980s.

At the start of 1984 he seemed tipped for stardom as he succeeded Alain Prost as Renault team leader. Race wins were regarded as a certainty and some even whispered about the possibility of Warwick winning a World Championship. At last he had the equipment to run consistently at the front of the field – or so everybody thought.

Neither of those eventualities worked out, but since those fleeting halcyon days with Renault in early 1984, when victory seemed just round the corner, Warwick has continued to hammer on the doors of success with a ferocity and determination of Mansell-type proportions. Moreover, Warwick's universally sunny disposition made him enormously popular in a business where ego can be a destructive force.

Encouraged by his father and uncle, who jointly founded the family trailer-building business, Derek was a stock car champion on dirt ovals when little more than a child. Graduating with honours from Formula Ford, he made it into the closely fought world of F3, all the while being financed by his family, and raced competitively

against Nelson Piquet to win the 1978 British National Championship.

His career path progressed through into F2 where he forged a bond with the Toleman team, spearheading their ambitious graduation into Grand Prix racing along with Brian Henton in 1981. He gave Toleman three loyal and determined years before switching to Renault in 1984, only for the French team's fortunes to plunge in 1985 when the company withdrew from F1.

He returned to F1 with Brabham after the death of Elio de Angelis and then switched to Arrows from 1987 to 1989, driving with characteristic determination all the while but seldom scoring any worthwhile results. A switch to Lotus-Lamborghini for 1990 was even more disastrous and F1 abandoned him at the age of thirty-six at the end of that season. He turned to a Sports Car World Championship programme with Jaguar in 1991 and stayed in that category leading the Peugeot squad in 1992.

A devoted family man who lives in Jersey with his wife Rhonda and daughters Marie and Kerry, Warwick was, by common consensus, one of the outstanding F1 protagonists to slip through the net without registering the success his talent so obviously deserved.

WATSON, John

See pages 186–7.

WENDLINGER, Karl (A)

b. 20 December 1968, Kufstein
2 Grands Prix

The second of the 'Mercedes babies' who, together with Michael Schumacher, was 'placed' with an F1 team in late 1991 by the German manufacturer's competitions boss, Jochen Neerpasch. In Wendlinger's case the team was Leyton House (now March), but at the start of 1992 Sauber laid claim to him as second driver for the 1993 season to run alongside Schumacher. He proved his potential by winning the 1989 German F3 Championship in a Ralt-Alfa Romeo, repulsing a strong challenge from Schumacher and Heinz-Harald Frentzen.

WESTBURY, Peter (GB)

b. 26 May 1938
1 Grand Prix

A British hillclimb ace whose 4WD Felday sports cars shone in that category during the mid-1960s, Westbury later became a consistent F2 independent and drove his own Brabham to fifth place in the F2 class of the 1969 German GP. Two years later he tried unsuccessfully to qualify a BRM P153 for the US Grand Prix at Watkins Glen.

WHARTON, Ken (GB)

b. 21 March 1916, Smethwick, Birmingham
d. 12 January 1957, Ardmore, New Zealand
15 Grands Prix
Career span: 1952 (Frazer Nash and Cooper); 1953 (Cooper); 1954 (Maserati); 1955 (Vanwall)

Versatility was the keynote of this steady performer who cut his teeth at the wheel of a supercharged Austin Seven at Donington Park in the immediate pre-war years. Not only was he a reliable F1 performer, but international rallying, hillclimbing and sports car racing were all part of his repertoire. This enormously popular and charismatic personality was killed at the wheel of a Ferrari Monza sports car in New Zealand.

WHITEHEAD, Graham (GB)

b. 15 April 1922, Harrogate
d. 15 January 1981
1 Grand Prix

The sports car racing half-brother of Peter Whitehead, Graham contested the 1952 British Grand Prix in an F2 Alta.

WHITEHEAD, Peter (GB)

b. 12 November 1914, Menston, Yorkshire
d. September 1958
10 Grands Prix
Career span: 1950–1 (Ferrari); 1952 (Alta and Ferrari); 1953–4 (Cooper)

The very first Ferrari F1 privateer, Whitehead nearly won the 1949 French Grand Prix at Reims before gearbox trouble dropped him to third. Remembered as a quiet man with an impish sense of humour, he was killed when the 3.4-litre Jaguar driven by his half-brother Graham plunged into a ravine from an unprotected bridge parapet during the 1958 Tour de France.

WHITEHOUSE, Bill (GB)

b. 1 April 1909
d. 14 July 1957, Reims
1 Grand Prix

A jovial and popular South London off-licence owner and early Cooper 500 F3 competitor, Whitehouse drove a Connaught in the 1954 British GP at Silverstone. He was killed in the 1957 Reims F2 race when his 'Bobtail' Cooper special somersaulted and burnt out approaching the Thillois hairpin after apparently suffering tyre failure.

WATSON, John (GB)

b. 4 May 1946, Belfast
152 Grands Prix; 5 wins
Career span: 1973–4 (Brabham); 1975 (Surtees); 1976 (Penske);
1977–8 (Brabham); 1979–83 (McLaren)

Madly enthusiastic about motor racing from an early age –
his father, Marshall Watson, won the first saloon car race
to be held in Ireland at the wheel of a Citröen Light 15 –
John's rise from club racing to international Grand Prix
stardom proved to be a gruelling, and at times frustrating,
career path.

John's father was a successful Belfast motor trader who
bankrolled his son's racing up to the level of F2, in which
he competed for three years (1969 to 1971) in family-
owned Lotus and Brabham machinery. By 1973 he was
ready for F1, making his Championship début in the British GP at Silverstone where he drove a Brabham BT37. He
drove for the Hexagon Brabham F1 team, backed by prosperous Highgate motor trader, Paul Michaels, throughout
1974 and scoring his first Championship point with a
sixth place at Monaco.

In 1975 he briefly drove for Team Surtees before switching to the new F1 operation established by American millionaire Roger Penske, taking the place of his original
driver Mark Donohue who had died of brain injuries sustained when a tyre failure caused him to crash during the
race morning warm-up prior to the 1975 Austrian GP.
Watson would earn the team a superb victory in the following year's Austrian Grand Prix, forfeiting his beard in a
wager with Penske, the millionaire Ivy League team boss
disapproving of such appendages!

After Penske withdrew from F1 at the end of the 1976
season, Watson switched to the Brabham-Alfa squad for
two seasons during which he was unable to reproduce
that winning form. In 1979 he moved to McLaren as team
leader when the position fell vacant after Ronnie Peterson's death at Monza the previous September, but his
high hopes were dashed when the new McLaren M28 proved disastrously uncompetitive. John's self-confidence
was also somewhat undermined by the not-always sympathetic strictures of team manager, Teddy Mayer.

Only when Ron Dennis and his colleague John Barnard
became involved with McLaren did the team's fortunes

Left: John Watson poses for a publicity shot alongside his 1981 McLaren team-mate Andrea de Cesaris. It was in this carbon-fibre chassis MP4 that 'Wattie' won the 1981 British Grand Prix. *Above:* John could be a tough old boy to deal with as Carlos Reutemann finds out as he rubs wheels with the Ulsterman at Montreal in 1980.

pick up dramatically, and Watson proved to be the initial beneficiary of this upsurge when he won the 1981 British Grand Prix at Silverstone in the Barnard-designed carbon-fibre chassis McLaren MP4.

In 1982 and 1983, Watson found himself psychologically overshadowed by the reappearance of his former Brabham team-mate Niki Lauda as his partner in the McLaren line-up. Nevertheless, John drove outstandingly to win the 1982 Belgian and Detroit GPs and the 1983 Long Beach event before the suddenly available Alain Prost replaced him in the McLaren F1 line-up for 1984.

Apart from a single guest outing for McLaren at Brands Hatch in 1985, that was the end of Watson's F1 career. It was a shame, for although John could be unpredictable in the sense that his form could vary alarmingly, he was a natural driver with great inborn skill.

A perfectionist in the complicated business of 'setting up' a chassis, if he was unhappy about his machinery, then he was frequently less than inspired. But when he hit top form he could display World Championship potential. As an individual, his personality remained unspoiled throughout his F1 career and he remains as congenial company now as he was in the fledgeling days of his single-seater apprenticeship.

Since retiring from Formula 1, Watson has driven for the Jaguar and Toyota sports car teams, and gave Eddie Jordan's new F1 challenger its first track test at the start of 1991. He now concentrates on the Silverstone-based John Watson Performance Driving Centre, as well as commentating on Grands Prix for the Eurosport satellite TV channel.

WIDDOWS, Robin (GB)

b. 27 May 1942
1 Grand Prix

Widdows was an Olympic standard bobsleigher who was amongst the more promising F3 and F2 drivers of the mid-1960s. He was one of many to have a fruitless outing in a Cooper-BRM T81C during 1968, his drive being in the British GP at Brands Hatch.

WIETZES, Eppie (CDN)

b. 28 May 1938
2 Grands Prix

This Canadian semi-professional rented a Lotus 49 for the 1967 Canadian Grand Prix at Mosport Park, and a Brabham BT42 for the same event seven years later.

WILDS, Mike (GB)

b. 7 January 1946
3 Grands Prix

A bearded, popular FF1600 and F3 front runner from the late 1960s and early 1970s, Wilds tried his hand in F1 with an Ensign in the 1974 US GP and then in an uncompetitive BRM P201 at the start of 1975 in the Argentine and Brazilian Grands Prix.

Mike Wilds: cheerful and optimistic, but not for the F1 big time.

WILLIAMS, Jonathan (GB)

b. 26 October 1942
1 Grand Prix

Williams was an ace F3 charger from the same pack that produced Piers Courage and Chris Irwin. He opted for a career in the Italian sun, driving for the Rome-based de Sanctis team, and found his way into the Ferrari works team as the first driver of a F2 Dino 166 in 1967. He drove a second works F1 312 in the 1967 Mexican Grand Prix where he finished eighth. He now lives on the Côte d'Azur where he flew executive jets for some years.

WILLIAMSON, Roger (GB)

b. 2 February 1948, Leicester
d. 29 July 1973, Zandvoort
2 Grands Prix

The rugged, very promising protégé of Donington Park circuit owner, Tom Wheatcroft, Williamson started racing in a Ford Anglia club saloon before making a great name for himself in F3 and F2 during the early 1970s. He was killed when his works March 731 crashed and burned at Zandvoort following a suspension breakage in the 1973 Dutch Grand Prix, despite heroic rescue efforts of fellow March driver David Purley as craven officials stood by helplessly.

WINKELHOCK, Manfred (D)

b. 6 October 1952, Wailblingen
d. 12 August 1985, Mosport Park
47 Grands Prix
Career span: 1982–4 (ATS); 1985 (RAM)

A popular, good-natured German driver who lived life to the full but never had the machinery to produce consistently worthwhile results. He was fatally injured when his Porsche 962 crashed in the Budweiser GT 1,000km at the Canadian circuit.

WISELL, Reine (S)

b. 30 September 1941, Motala
22 Grands Prix
Career span: 1970–1 (Lotus); 1972 (BRM); 1973–4 (March)

This blond contemporary and arch-rival of Ronnie Peterson was another of the great F3 stars of the 1-litre F3 during the late 1960s. Promoted to F1 with Team Lotus after Rindt's death in September 1970, Reine finished third in that year's US GP which was won by fellow novice and team-mate, Fittipaldi. He ran a full season with Lotus in 1971, but was

Reine Wisell: talented and smooth, but overshadowed by his compatriot Ronnie Peterson.

gradually eclipsed by Fittipaldi and moved to BRM for a fruitless 1973 season. A couple of races for March in 1973 and 1974 rounded off his Grand Prix career.

WUNDERINK, Roelof (NL)

b. 12 December 1948
3 Grands Prix

This very enthusiastic and erratic Dutch driver competed during 1975 at the wheel of the works Ensign.

ZANARDI, Alessandro (I)

b. 22 October 1966, Bologna
3 Grands Prix

Zanardi rocketed to prominence in 1991 with some terrific Formula 3000 performances driving a Reynard-Mugen for Giueseppe Cipriani's new Il Barone Rampante organization, only narrowly losing out to Christian Fittipaldi for the International Championship. He was invited to drive for Jordan in the final three Grands Prix of the season after they lost Michael Schumacher to Benetton, and a ninth place in wet conditions on his début at Barcelona marked him out as a man to watch. He says that if motor racing does not work out, he can always work in his father's plumbing business!

ZORZI, Renzo (I)

b. 12 December 1946
7 Grands Prix

A former Pirelli engineer who drove unspectacularly at the wheel of Williams and Shadow F1 machinery in 1976 and 1977. He was inadvertently involved in the tragic accident which claimed his Shadow team-mate, Tom Pryce, at Kyalami in 1977 – it was to his abandoned car, apparently suffering an electrical fire, that the doomed marshal was crossing the track when he was hit by Pryce's sister car.

ZUNINO, Ricardo (RA)

b. 13 April 1949
10 Grands Prix

A cordial and charming Brazilian-resident Argentinian who replaced Niki Lauda in the Brabham team on his sudden retirement mid-way through practice at the 1979 Canadian Grand Prix. He continued with the team until the middle of the following year when he was replaced by Hector Rebaque.

	CHAMPIONSHIP YEAR							CAREER RECORD					
Driver	Year	Car	Points	Races won	2nd	3rd	poles	Starts	Wins	% Wins	2nd	3rd	poles
ANDRETTI, Mario	1978	Lotus	64	6 RA, B, E, F, D, NL	1	–	8	128	12	9%	2	5	18
ASCARI, Alberto	1952	Ferrari	52½	6 B, F, GB, D, NL, I	–	–	5	32	13	41%	4	–	14
	1953	Ferrari	46½	5 RA, NL, B, GB, CH	–	–	6						
BRABHAM, Jack	1959	Cooper	34	2 MC, GB	1	2	1	126	14	11%	10	8	13
	1960	Cooper	43	5 NL, B, F, GB, P	–	–	3						
	1966	Brabham	45	4 F, GB, NL, D	1	–	3						
CLARK, Jim	1963	Lotus	73	7 B, NL, F, GB, I, MEX, ZA	1	1	7	72	25	35%	1	6	33
	1965	Lotus	54	6 ZA, B, F, NL, GB, D	–	–	6						
FANGIO, Juan Manuel	1951	Alfa Romeo	37	3 CH, F, E	2	–	4	51	24	47%	11	1	28
	1954	Maserati/Mercedes	57	6 RA, B, F, D, CH, I	–	1	5						
	1955	Mercedes	41	4 RA, B, NL, I	1	–	3						
	1956	Ferrari	33	3 RA, GB, D	3	2	4						
	1957	Maserati	46	4 RA, MC, F, D	2	–	1						
FARINA, Giuseppe	1950	Alfa Romeo	30	3 GB, CH, I	–	3	2	33	5	15%	9	6	5
FITTIPALDI, Emerson	1972	Lotus	61	5 E, B, GB, A, I	2	1	3	144	14	10%	13	8	6
	1974	McLaren	55	3 BR, B, CDN	2	2	2						
HAWTHORN, Mike	1958	Ferrari	49	1 F	5	1	4	45	3	7%	9	7	4
HILL, Graham	1962	BRM	52	4 NL, D, I, ZA	2	–	1	176	14	8%	15	7	13
	1968	Lotus	48	3 E, MC, MEX	3	–	2						
HILL, Phil	1961	Ferrari	38	2 B, I	2	2	5	48	3	6%	6	7	6
HULME, Denny	1967	Brabham	51	2 MC, D	3	3	–	112	8	7%	9	17	1

Driver		CHAMPIONSHIP YEAR						CAREER RECORD					
	Year	Car	Points	Races won	2nd	3rd	poles	Starts	Wins	% Wins	2nd	3rd	poles
HUNT, James	1976	McLaren	69	6 E, F, D, NL, CDN, USA	1	1	8	92	10	11%	6	7	14
JONES, Alan	1980	Williams	71	5 RA, F, GB, CDN, USA	3	2	3	116	12	10%	8	5	6
LAUDA, Niki	1975	Ferrari	64½	5 MC, B, S, F, USA	1	2	9	171	25	15%	20	9	24
	1977	Ferrari	72	3 ZA, D, NL	6	1	2						
	1984	McLaren	72	5 ZA, F, GB, A, I	4	–	–						
PIQUET, Nelson	1981	Brabham	50	3 RA, RSM, D	1	3	4	204	23	11%	20	17	24
	1983	Brabham	59	3 BR, I, Europe	3	2	1						
	1987	Williams	76	3 D, H, I	7	1	4						
PROST, Alain	1985	McLaren	76	5 BR, MC, GB, A, I	2	4	2	183	44	24%	32	18	20
	1986	McLaren	74	4 RSM, MC, A, AUS	4	3	3						
	1989	McLaren	81	4 USA, F, GB, I	6	3	11						
RINDT, Jochen	1970	Lotus	45	5 MC, NL, F, GB, D	–	–	3	60	6	10%	3	4	10
ROSBERG, Keke	1982	Williams	44	1 CH	3	2	1	114	5	4%	8	4	5
SCHECKTER, Jody	1979	Ferrari	60	3 MC, B, I	3	–	1	112	10	9%	14	9	3
SENNA, Ayrton	1988	McLaren	94	8 RSM, CDN, USA, GB, D, H, B, J	3	–	13	126	33	26%	20	13	60
	1990	McLaren	78	6 USA, MC, CDN, D, B, I	2	3	10						
	1991	McLaren	96	7 USA, BR, RSM, MC, H, B, AUS	3	2	8						
STEWART, Jackie	1969	Matra	63	6 ZA, E, NL, F, GB, I	1	–	2	99	27	27%	11	5	17
	1971	Tyrrell	62	6 E, MC, F, GB, D, CDN	1	–	6						
	1973	Tyrrell	71	5 ZA, B, MC, NL, D	2	1	3						
SURTEES, John	1964	Ferrari	40	2 D, I	3	1	2	111	6	5%	10	8	8

Bibliography

BOOKS

Cancellieri, Gianni and De Agostini, Cesare, *F1: Storia del Mondiale, 1950–1957* (Conti Editore, 1991).

Crombac, Gerard, *Colin Chapman: The Man and His Cars* (Patrick Stephens, 1986).

Dempster, Nigel, *Nigel Dempster's Address Book: The Social Gazetteer* (Weidenfeld and Nicolson, 1990).

Dreyfus, René with Rae Kimes, Beverley, *My Two Lives* (Aztex Corporation, 1983).

Dymock, Eric, *The Guinness Guide to Grand Prix Motor Racing* (Guinness Superlatives, 1980).

Garnier, Peter, *Goodwood: The Sussex Motor Racing Circuit* (Beaulieu Books, 1980).

Hamilton, Maurice, *British Grand Prix* (The Crowood Press, 1989).

Hamilton, Maurice, *Grand Prix British Winners* (Guinness, 1991).

Hawthorn, Mike, *Challenge Me the Race* (William Kimber, 1958).

Henry, Alan, *Ferrari: The Grand Prix Cars* (Hazleton Publishing, 1984).

Huet, Christian, *Gordini: Un Sorcier, Une Équipe* (Editions Christian Huet, 1984).

Jenkinson, Denis, *The Maserati 250F: A Classic Grand Prix Car* (Macmillan, 1975).

Jenkinson, Denis and Posthumus, Cyril, *Vanwall: The Story of Tony Vandervell and His Racing Cars* (Patrick Stephens, 1975).

Kling, Karl, *Pursuit of Victory: The Story of a Racing Driver* (The Bodley Head, 1956).

Lang, Mike, *Grand Prix: Volume 1, 1950–65* (Haynes Publishing, 1981).

Nye, Doug, *Dino: The Little Ferrari* (Osprey, 1979).

Nye, Doug, *Cooper Cars* (Osprey, 1983).

Nye, Doug and Goddard, Geoff, *Classic Racing Cars: The Post-War Front-Engined GP Cars* (Foulis, 1991).

Thompson, John with Rabagliati, Duncan and Sheldon, K. Paul, *The Formula One Record Book* (Leslie Frewin, 1974).

Tremayne, David, *Racers Apart: Memories of Motorsporting Heroes* (Motor Racing Publications, 1991).

Venables, David, *The Racing Fifteen-Hundreds: A History of Voiturette Racing from 1931 to 1949* (Transport Bookman Publications, 1984).

Walton, Jeremy, *Racing Mechanic: Ermanno Cuoghi, Mechanic to a World Champion* (Osprey, 1980).

Wilkinson, W.E. with Jones, Chris, *Wilkie: The Motor Racing Legend* (Nelson and Saunders, 1987).

PERIODICALS

Autosport
Motor Sport
Motoring News
Motor Racing